ALPHABETICAL

Also by Michael Rosen

Selected Poems
Fighters for Life: Selected Poems
William Shakespeare, In His Time For Our Time
Michael Rosen's Sad Book, illustrated by Quentin Blake
The Penguin Book of Childhood

ALPHABETICAL
How Every Letter Tells a Story

Michael Rosen

JOHN MURRAY

First published in Great Britain in 2013 by John Murray (Publishers)
An Hachette UK Company

4

A CIP catalogue record for this title is available from the British Library

Hardback ISBN 978-1-84854-886-2
Ebook ISBN 978-1-84854-887-9

Typeset in Sabon by Palimpsest Book Production Ltd, Falkirk, Stirlingshire

Printed and bound by Clays Ltd, St Ives plc

John Murray policy is to use papers that are natural, renewable and
recyclable products and made from wood grown in sustainable forests. The logging
and manufacturing processes are expected to conform to the environmental
regulations of the country of origin.

John Murray (Publishers)
338 Euston Road
London NW1 3BH

www.johnmurray.co.uk

For the three Es, Emma, Elsie and Emile

CONTENTS

Introduction   xi

The Story of A   1
A is for Alphabet

The Story of B   21
B is for Battledore

The Story of C   41
C is for Ciphers

The Story of D   63
D is for Disappeared Letters

The Story of E   79
E is for e. e. cummings

The Story of F   93
F is for Fonts

The Story of G   107
G is for Greek

The Story of H   121
H is for H-Aspiration

The Story of I   135
I is for Improvisation

The Story of J   149
J is for Jokes

The Story of K   159
K is for Korean

The Story of L   175
L is for LSD

The Story of M   191
M is for Music and Memory

The Story of N   203
N is for Nonsense

The (True) Story of O   217
O is for OK

The Story of P   227
P is for Pitman

The Story of Q   251
Q is for Qwerty

The Story of R
R is for Rhyme
267

The Story of S
S is for Signs and Sign Systems
283

The Story of T
T is for Txtspk
309

The Story of U
U is for Umlauts
323

The Story of V
V is for Vikings
333

The Story of W
W is for Webster
345

The Story of X
X Marks the Spot
363

The Story of Y
Y is for Yellow
375

The Story of Z
Z is for Zipcodes
387

The Oulipo Olympics
403

Acknowledgements
413

Further Reading
415

Index
419

INTRODUCTION

IN FRONT OF me is a line of children and parents who want me to sign their books. As each child comes up to the table I ask their name. For most of the names, I check how it's spelled. Sometimes this is because it's one I haven't heard of, sometimes it's because there are several ways to spell the name, sometimes it's because it's quite possible that the parents have invented a new spelling. So I ask. The child or the parent spells it out for me: 'S-h-e-r-r-i-l-e-e-n.' 'Thank you,' I say. 'Did you come up with that spelling?'

'Yes,' says the mother.

'Great,' I say, enjoying the fact that people feel free to take the alphabet into their own hands and use it for their own purposes, making up names, making up spellings, getting the letters that are given to us to do a job that they want done.

The next child arrives. I write his name: 'Tariq', and have a quiet smile to myself how the rule that the letter 'q' must, must, *must* be accompanied by a 'u' and if it's at the end of a word with a 'u' and an 'e' is quietly but insistently laid to one side by people with Muslim names. Although we talk of 'rules' in language, they are in fact more like treaties between consenting groups. We abide by these until such time as someone or some group thinks that they would like to change things and so a new clause is written into the treaty: people with Muslim names don't have to do that 'u' or 'u' plus 'e' thing.

I write my name in their book: 'Michael Rosen', and I look

at it, trying to be the child or the parent looking at that name for the first time. Will they notice that the 'm' is always asymmetrical; the dot on the 'i' is more like an acute accent, pointing up to the top right-hand corner of the page; the 'r' is flashily curly; the 's' is decidedly uncurly?

Like many people I'm curious about my name, but on occasions when the air in schools is full of talk about 'phonics', I look at 'Michael' and wonder about the history that enabled the 'i' to be 'long' and not short like the 'i' in 'pin'. I wonder why the 'ch' is there when a 'k' would have done the job very well, and indeed some of the children standing in front of me come from places where it is 'Mikel'. And then, what about that 'ae', which I and most English speakers pronounce with the all-pervasive sound which has its own special name – the 'schwa': why is it 'ae'? Were the two letters once stuck together as we used to see in 'encyclopædia' and 'mediæval'? Or was it once an 'ae' which was separated by one of the few dots and slashes that English used to be fairly free with? The double dot that used to sit over the 'i' in 'naïve' – looking like the German 'umlaut' but, because it does a different job, separating out vowels – gets its own special name, the 'dieresis'. And look, here comes a girl to whom, when she tells me her name, I say, 'Is that Zoe with dots, or no dots?'

Then, on to the 'Rosen', which often gives people a moment's bother. Is the 's' like 's' in 'chosen' or the 's' in 'closer'? I tell people it's 'Rose' with an 'n' on the end, a German name. A little flash of German lessons in the late 1950s appears in my thoughts, followed by the memory that the users of English nearly got rid of those 'n' plurals but not quite: 'child' – 'children', 'man' – 'men', 'woman' – 'women'. How interesting that one last refuge for the 'n' plural is to do with our sexes – and the result of those sexual differences. As you follow the development of English, starting out with those cross-Channel migrants, the Frisians from what is now northern Holland, you can see how another wave, the Norman French, put the 'n' to flight. In most circumstances, people change the language they use by choice, not from being compelled to. Over hundreds of years, people swapped Germanic Ns for Romance Ss. I remember being read a Walter de la Mare poem when I was at school that had the word 'shoon' in it. 'It means "shoes",' explained our teacher. 'Rosen, it means "roses",' I think.

In the early years of the nineteenth century, Jews sought equal rights in the German principalities. Part of the deal was that they would take on German names in their daily affairs. This had its price – quite literally; Jews had to buy these new names when some couldn't afford to, and they were sometimes given derogatory, mocking or even obscene names: 'Ochsenschwanz' – 'oxtail' – with the tail being lewdly ambiguous; 'Hinkediger' – 'hunchback'; 'Kaufpisch' – 'sell-piss'. In my family name, though, there is a memory that some forebear had enough money to buy an old German name which was used to record that someone worked in the rose-water trade. What's more, it has been suggested that the Rosen-type names were popular amongst those Jews whose Hebrew name recorded a matronymic, a name that says: 'I am the son of this woman'. So, a man might be Ezra ben Rosa – son of Rosa, and to remember that, some people opted for one of the Rosen-type names. The sound of 'Rosa', transferred across from Hebrew letters, conserved in the Roman letters 'r', 'o', 's' and 'e', was perhaps a piece of cultural self-awareness, resistance even. I take it that people anywhere, any time, can make letters do this kind of work for them. If the situation demands it, they can switch languages, create hybrids, invent new spellings – new identities even. Naming ourselves and others is part of how we and something on how the letter itself is spoken and played with. At the end of the book I have set some alphabetical challenges (see 'The Oulipo Olympics').

The alphabet is not simply a phenomenon or a structure, it's something we each come upon, learn and use in our own idiosyncratic ways. Our personal histories and feelings are wrapped up in what the letters and their means of transmission mean to each of us. The biography of the alphabet is intertwined with one's autobiography of the alphabet. I hope that my inclusion of my personal narrative will alert you to your own stories. It most certainly wasn't included in order to take precedence over yours.

THE STORY OF

• **'A' STARTS ITS** life in around 1800 BCE. Turn our modern 'A' upside down and you can see something of its original shape. Can you see an ox's head with its horns sticking up in the air? If so, you can see the remains of this letter's original name, 'ox', or 'aleph' in the ancient Semitic languages. By the time the Phoenicians are using it in around 1000 BCE it is lying on its side and looks more like a 'K'. Speed-writing seems to have taken the diagonals through the upright, making it more like a horizontal form of our modern 'A' with the point on the left-hand side. The ancient Greeks called it 'alpha' and reversed it, with the point on the right-hand side, probably because, eventually, they decided to write from left to right. Between around 750 BCE and 500 BCE the Greeks rotated it to what we would think of as its upright position. The Romans added the serifs which you can see on inscriptions like Trajan's Column in Rome.

a AND ɑ

Writing the lower-case 'A' by hand seems to have produced first an upside-down 'v' shape, which slowly acquired a connecting loop making it resemble the 'two-storey' 'a' you're looking at now. This belongs to the standardized script known as 'Carolingian minuscule' which Charlemagne's scribes created.

The 'single-storey', lower-case 'a' that persists in children's reading books and a good deal of advertising began its life with Irish scribes.

PRONUNCIATION OF THE LETTER-NAME

The people who preceded the Romans on the Italian peninsula, the Etruscans, were probably the first people to give the name of the letter a monosyllabic sound: 'ah', derived from the Greek word 'alpha'. The Romans followed suit and gave that name to the Romance languages of Europe. Surely, then, with the arrival of the Norman French, we anglophones should be calling it 'ah' as well? However, between the Normans and us lies the 'Great Vowel Shift', a phenomenon that caused people between 1400 and 1600 to change their 'ahs' to 'ays'. (In case you think this is beyond belief and some hokum invented by linguists, you should talk to New Zealanders who are, even as I write, in the throes of turning their 'pins' to 'pens' and their 'pens' to 'pins'. Shifting our vowels is something that groups of us like doing sometimes.)

PRONUNCIATION OF THE LETTER

In English, 'a' – either as a single letter in the middle of a single-syllable word, as the initial letter of a word, or in conjunction with other vowel-letters, 'y', 'w', 'r' and 'h' – can indicate a wide range of sounds: 'cat', 'was', 'all', 'and', 'late', 'father', 'hail', 'haul', 'Michael', 'ray', 'threat', 'beat', 'boat', 'dial', 'ah', 'raw', 'cart' and so on.

On rare occasions we can write 'aa' as in the names 'Aaron' and 'Saab'.

'A' and its partner 'an' does service as our 'indefinite article'. In many cases, this indicates that we are not referring to something that I the speaker or you the listener have referred to just before. 'I was at a football match', 'I was eating an apple'. The plural of 'a' is no article at all or 'some', 'both' or a number. 'I was eating apples.' However, we do say things like, 'That was a day to remember,' where the total construction indicates we are 'referring back' to something that we all know about.

(The 'definite article', 'the', is usually for when you want to indicate that you, the listener, or the world beyond has been talking, writing or referring to the thing spoken about before. 'I was eating the apple,' i.e. the one you mentioned.)

The history of 'an' is a peculiar one. It seems as if there was once a sufficient number of words like 'nuncle' ('uncle') for the 'n' to migrate across from the 'a'. King Lear's Fool calls him 'nuncle'.

'Ah!' is a very useful sound. It can mean many things depending on the notes you hit as you say it. You can indicate that you're surprised, that you knew it all along, that you're satisfied, that you've been hurt, that you're sympathetic, or you're pretending you're sympathetic, that you've caught someone out and so on. It can be linked to 'ha' as in 'Ah-ha' or to four 'hahs' if you're the BeeGees.

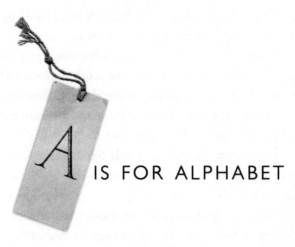

A IS FOR ALPHABET

AN ALPHABET IS a stunningly brilliant invention. We could call it a 'cunning code' or a 'system of signs' whereby we use some symbols (letters) to indicate some of the sounds of a language. By combining two or more letters (as with 'th' or 'sch') we can indicate more of the sounds. Though it is wonderful, there are some snags for users of what I'm calling the 'English alphabet':

- We do not use these letters and combinations to indicate the same sound every time we use them. The letter 'c' can be the soft 'c' in 'ceiling' or the hard 'c' in 'cook'.
- We do not always use the letters to indicate the same sound to different readers over time (i.e. between now and the past), or across space (i.e. from region to region). In Shakespeare's time, 'do' rhymed with 'go'. People with a London accent pronounce the 'u' in 'hut' and the 'a' in 'hat' differently from people with a Yorkshire accent.
- We do not always use the same letter or combination of letters to indicate a given sound. We can make the 'oo'

sound in 'root' by writing 'oo', or 'ou' as in 'you', or 'ough' as in 'through', or 'o–e' as in 'lose', or 'u–e' as in 'rune'.

- We write letters side by side but this shape doesn't always represent the timing of the sounds we make when we speak. Say 'head' and the 'h' carries over into the 'ea'.
- Letters don't represent all the sounds we make when we speak. Think 'due' and 'sue'.

Becoming or being a reader of English involves absorbing all these variations and then forgetting that they exist. We're able to do that mostly because we write and read in order to pass messages or 'texts' between us – messages that we want to be full of meaning, full of stuff that matters to us. As we read and write these messages, we learn the shape and look of words including the ones that grammarians call 'irregular'. We learn that the word 'debt' sounds like 'dett' but is written 'debt'. After all, we see it often enough.

Though it's possible to describe all this as a 'system of symbols and sounds', it's not only that. Our forebears devised alphabets so that they could store and retrieve meaning. 'Meaning' can be the meaning of names, directions, reports, feelings, ideas, dreams, experiments or investigations . . . We store meanings when writing with the alphabet, so that these meanings can survive over time and/or space: a graffito on the side of a train does both, as does an instruction on how to build a flatpack wardrobe. An inscription on a gravestone is usually intended to last over time but we want it to stay put. A tattoo is usually intended to last a lifetime, stay put on a person but move with that person. A birthday card travels from sender to receiver, lasts for the length of the birthday celebration and more often than not is destroyed. Some books have survived long beyond their authors' wildest dreams, sometimes by staying in the same place for hundreds of years.

In the case of the alphabet I'm using, people have used some of the letters in a constant way over thousands of years. Someone in what is now Italy, whose name began with an 's' sound two thousand years ago, may have had someone carve an 'S' on a stone after he died just as someone might do that for 'Sam' in England today. This continuity has enabled us to access meanings going back hundreds or thousands of years.

Some aspects of how we use letters change. Film-makers invented subtitles so that we can hear words in one language, whilst reading it in another; people with impaired hearing can read what people on a screen are saying. When the Norman French took over the ruling class in England from 1066, they brought some sounds (like 'j') that the Germanic peoples living in England did not use. Over time, the 'j' in 'jam' came to be used by everyone in England. Meanwhile, most people in England stopped using the 'ch' sound that most Scots people make today when saying the word 'loch'. These changes show up in the letters of the alphabet. This is part of why and how the alphabet is such a clever invention. We get it to do what we want it to do.

At any given moment, people in a locality or a country speaking the same language do not use the alphabet in the same way. For thousands of years, most people hardly used it at all. The storage of meaning in letters was something that only a very few people knew how to do. The origins of the alphabet lie within those castes of people who had the right to write: priests, the makers and executors of laws and punishments, and accountants, mostly. With TV available on smartphones, voice recognition, automated translation and the digitizing of image and sound, the use of the alphabet is changing rapidly. Another kind of code – based on the serial variations of two numbers – is storing meaning. Though using the technology to store and read meaningful symbols (e.g. pictures, music, speech and writing) is very simple, very few people know how to do the coding. It is quite possible that the use of the alphabet of letters will decline in the next hundred years. We could ask whether a new clerisy has already emerged who have become the tiny minority who know how to write this digital code.

The ultimate reason why the use of the alphabet changes is because we change, whether that's through war, migration, new technology, new kinds of work and leisure, new systems of government or new forms of education. It seems odd to think that the reason why I say a 'j' sound and that there is a letter for that sound is because, nearly a thousand years ago, in the wars between the tribal warlords of northern Europe, a French-speaking group got the upper hand in the part of the world where I happen to live. I can hold an instrument in my hand and tap the letters 'y-i-s-s-s-s' and ten seconds later my son hundreds of miles away knows that we are both celebrating the same goal. The instrument that makes this possible comes after 250 years of scientific industrialization and some dubious exploitation of labour and mineral resources that took place far from where I live. My freedom to write a word in this non-standard way comes as a result of the mass education and artistic revolts of the last 150 years: my son and I have both learned to write but we don't get nervous making up new spellings. We're not scared we might get told off by the invisible teacher, grammarian or priest in our heads.

When I've texted my son, I put the instrument down on the table next to a newspaper and, let's say, my copy of *Emil and the Detectives*, and I go on watching the TV. Though this all seems seamless, the frontiers of different technologies, different languages, different typefaces, and different uses of alphabets, symbols and codes are all nudging up against each other on my table. The names of the footballers I'm watching on the TV are a coming-together of different uses of letters: the commentator tells us that Cazorla would like us to pronounce his name as

'Cathorla' with a soft 'th' as in 'thorn'. Giroud, the commentator explains, has a 'd' on the end of his name but we don't say the 'd', and the 'G' sounds like the 'j' in 'bijou'. The goalkeeper's name is Szczęsny. The commentator explains that the team look like they're 'playing 4, 4, 1, 1' with Cazorla 'playing in the hole'. This too is yet another system of signs created partly in language, partly by the movements of the players.

This running of languages and sign-systems in parallel to each other is not new. In the British Museum sits the basalt slab known as 'the Rosetta Stone'. Though one of its languages – Egyptian hieroglyphs – lay undeciphered for hundreds of years, the stone holds the key to understanding a crucial moment in the history of the alphabet: how human beings invented the idea that squiggles on a surface could indicate the sounds we make to each other in order to express ourselves, to communicate and to make meanings for each other that last as long as the material they are written on. Matching squiggles to sounds is known as the 'phonetic principle'. It's not known for certain who first invented it, and it's not known whether different groups of people invented it separately or influenced each other. Though this kind of behaviour seems obvious to us, it was not how humans first invented writing. The first writing was a form of drawing. Matching signs to speech comes later.

The history of the alphabet is also a history of how we uncovered that history. The Rosetta Stone is inscribed in three languages: Egyptian hieroglyphs and two kinds of Greek. The script gives out the terms of a decree from the 'Manifest God, King Ptolemy' – a decree which included that no rower employed in the task of taking priests to the residence of Alexander should be press-ganged into service – a piece of humane legislation that I always spend a moment of pleasure thinking about, unless it was a neat way to prevent the Emperor from being surrounded by potentially recalcitrant and rebellious strong men. In comparison, the story of how the stone was handled by Europeans is squalid. If ever we were trying to find an example of how language, letters and alphabets can be the subject of rivalries, wars and plunder, the Rosetta Stone does it all.

The British and French invaders of Egypt in the early nineteenth century fought over the stone. Today, people still argue over which of the European scholars who pored over its three languages first cracked the code of the hieroglyphs. The Frenchman Jean-François Champollion is usually given more credit than the Englishman Thomas Young, though Champollion himself gave Young some credit. This overlooks the fact that Ahmad Bakr ibn Wahshiyah, who lived in Egypt in the late ninth and early tenth centuries, wrote a treatise on hieroglyphics, pointing out that the glyphs were both pictorial images and single symbols signifying sounds.

How the international use of letters works across time and place can be seen in the thread of scholarship which links ibn Wahshiyah to Champollion: there was first an Arabic manuscript of the book *Kitab Shawq al-Mustaham* in which ibn Wahshiyah deciphered a number of Egyptian hieroglyphs; there was then a translation of the Arabic manuscript in a book published in English in 1806 by Joseph von Hammer-Purgstall as *Ancient Alphabets and Hieroglyphic Characters Explained, with an Account of the Egyptian Priests, their Classes, Initiation, and Sacrifices in the Arabic Language by Ahmad Bin Abubekr Bin Wahishih*; someone called Silvestre de Sacy – a colleague of Champollion – read this English version of the Arab manuscript; sixteen years later, Champollion's complete decipherment of Egyptian hieroglyphs appeared. There is, then, the strong possibility that an Arab scholar and expert on magic, statues, agriculture, alchemy, physics and medicine, writing at the same time that King Alfred was trying to get people to read English, may have played a significant part in unlocking the crucial fact that hieroglyphs were not only pictures but that some of them also represented specific sounds. To grasp how this works, the Egyptians some four thousand years ago did the equivalent of changing a picture of an apple from representing the word we say as 'apple', to representing the sound 'a', changing our picture of a ball representing the word we say as 'ball', to representing the sound 'b' and so on.

What we don't know for certain is whether the ancient Egyptians were the first to do this, nor whether they passed it on to others. In other words, we cannot be sure that the ancient Egyptian writing is an ancestor of what you're reading now. Around the same time, other peoples living relatively near to the Egyptians were developing scripts that also used phonetic principles – but in different ways. For example, the ancient Sumerians, from what is now present-day Iraq, developed a way of using symbols to represent syllables. An analogy would be if we had a symbol for a bird's beak or 'bill' based on a picture of a bird's bill. This 'bill' symbol could be used again and again in a word like 'building' (where our 'buil-' sounds the same as 'bill'), or in 'possible' (where our '-ble' sounds like 'bill'). Another way to imagine the 'syllabic principle' is to think of the possibility of us using the ampersand, '&', to write 'hand' as 'h&'.

What has just taken me a few minutes to describe would have taken people hundreds of years to evolve. Though these break-throughs lie at the heart of our culture, we can only speculate why people tried to make them. In terms of trade, pictograms are an easier way to translate words because you don't have to use abstract symbols like 'h' or 'y' representing sounds in different languages. The pictogram for 'eye' will work for my word for 'eye' just as well as for your word for 'eye', each of which may well sound completely different.

Alphabets are extraordinarily useful to a group of people

speaking the same language, as they can be compressed and combined to indicate almost any sound – and therefore any word – we might want to say, in any combination of phrases, sentences, verses or passages of any length. Inventing alphabets based on the 'phonetic principle' or the 'syllabic principle' suggests, therefore, some stability on the part of a group of people speaking the same language. But we shouldn't forget that the Chinese have had an incredible stability in terms of language-use but have not felt it necessary to develop an alphabet. And the Chinese are doing just fine.

The Sumerians and ancient Egyptians were clearly crucial players in the history of alphabets. Their invention and the widespread use of their writings can be seen in a place like the British Museum today, where their writing tells stories, shows prayers, gives instructions on how to pass on to the land of the dead and much more. However, we cannot know definitively whether their knowledge was picked up by the first people we know for certain are the key source for the alphabet I'm using. Moreover, in telling the story of deciphering old inscriptions like the Rosetta Stone (rather than that of the evolution of the alphabet), it is important to mention that scholars transfer a principle they've learned from one script across to another.

The archaeologist who applied what I'll call the 'ibn Wahshiyah–Champollion' principle of decoding to ancient scripts was a man by the name of Alan Gardiner and he made the breakthrough in 1916 while studying an inscription of symbols from Sinai which he figured did not say, 'box eye cane cross' but a word made from the initial letter of the Semitic words for 'box', 'eye', 'cane' and 'cross', making, he thought, the word 'baalat' or 'lady'. This piece of writing dates from around 1750 BCE and it was produced by people who are described by scholars as 'Semites'.

By the way, if you ever wonder how excited people get

deciphering ancient scripts, you should remember George Smith. Though this young man with no formal education beyond the age of fourteen wasn't the first person to decipher the cuneiform script of the ancient Sumerians, he was responsible for spotting that they wrote about the Flood before the Old Testament writers did. This eureka moment came in 1872 as he pored over a dusty clay tablet, plucked from the desert sands of Iraq, which constituted all that remained from the library of Nineveh. He was so excited by the discovery that he leaped up, ripped off his clothes and ran round the British Museum.

In the inscriptions of the Semitic people, scholars see the first certain forebears of the alphabet you're looking at. It's possible that they adopted the phonetic principle from the Egyptians, the Sumerians and others, but not certain. It's possible that they incorporated some of the symbols – possible but not certain.

Following the Semites, the next group in the family tree that leads to what you are reading now are the Phoenicians who originated in what is modern Lebanon. They are known to have been a highly inventive, active, trading people, working their way all round the Mediterranean and beyond, speaking a language, it's thought, akin to ancient Hebrew. By about 1000 BCE, they were using a twenty-two-letter alphabet probably inherited from the Semites. Anyone who remembers or knows their Roman history will remember Carthage and the Carthaginians. For some of us, Carthage was an inky word in our Latin exercise books, but it was indeed a real place founded by Phoenicians near to present-day Tunis in Tunisia. We would have hundreds of Phoenician books today if it wasn't for the fact that the Romans sacked Carthage and burned the Phoenicians' library. The history of storing meanings is not always a pretty one.

The Phoenicians used abstract versions of objects to indicate letters: a bifurcated (horned?) sign was an 'ox' (in their language 'aleph'), and on down through the words for 'house', 'stick', 'door' and 'shout' up to 'tooth' and 'mark'. You don't have to be all that fanciful to see that in many of the cases, the sign had evolved from the object and that the corresponding letter came to signify the first sound of the name of that object.

One other point: Phoenicians had no letters for vowels. These days, such an alphabet tends not to be called an alphabet, or even a 'consonantal alphabet'; it's called an 'abjad' – which is a transliteration of the Arabic word corresponding to 'alphabet'. The idea of trying to use an alphabet that has no vowels may seem to some surprising or difficult. If you can read written Arabic this is neither surprising nor difficult as it has no vowels either. Ancient Hebrew, another descendant from Semitic writing, didn't have vowels either, though reforms have added them.

A quick digression (the first of many in this book) on Hebrew vowels: my family were not religious, so I didn't attend Hebrew classes. However, one day I was 'spotted' by a boy at my school who 'claimed me'.

'You are, aren't you?' he said.

'What?' I said.

'Jewish,' he said.

'I think so,' I said, though I wasn't 100 per cent sure. So I went home and asked my parents if I was Jewish.

'Why do you ask?' said my father.

(Remember here, in the kind of Jewish life I was part of, every comment gives rise to a question.)

'Because Peter Kelner says that I am,' I said.

'Oh yes,' said my father. 'And because he said so, you should believe him?'

'He says I should go to Hebrew classes with his mother,' I said.

'Did he? Why's that?'

I don't remember how or why my secular parents, who had spent some time separating themselves off from the religious traditions, enabled me and encouraged me to go to Hebrew classes with Mrs Kelner.

To be honest, I don't remember much of what was taught. Yet, I can distinctly remember Mrs Kelner teaching us some Hebrew vowel sounds.

'Look at that one,' she said, and she pointed at a letter that looked a bit like a 7 with a dot over the top.

'Now look at that one,' she said, and she pointed at another 7 with a dot halfway down the downstroke of the seven.

'How do you tell the difference between those two? I'll tell you. If a football lands on your head, you say, "Oh!" If it lands in your kishkes [your 'guts'] you say, "Ooo".'

'Oh' and 'Ooo'. That's just about the extent of my Hebrew alphabet, and given that one of the things that people know about ancient Hebrew is that it has no vowels, it's ironic that it's vowels I remember.

End of digression.

The Phoenicians didn't have the advantage of Mrs Kelner and her vowel sounds though it is thought that they were just as creative in their teaching of the alphabet. That's why they retained 'ox', 'house', 'wheel' and the rest – as popular memory devices or mnemonics. Though people with my education may well have ended up thinking of the Phoenicians as a people in Latin exercise books, waiting patiently for the Romans to obliterate them and their library, we can look at the Phoenicians' letters and see the objects they derive from; or we can then look at our own letters and trace them back to these objects. Here is the Phoenician alphabet, its name, its sound and the modern letter in the alphabet it corresponds to.

A, 'aleph', 'ox';
sound: a stop in the
breath

B, 'bayt', 'house';
sound: 'b'

C, 'gimel', 'stick';
sound: 'g'

D, 'dalet', 'door';
sound: 'd'

E, 'he', a 'shout';
sound: 'h'

F, U and Y,
waw, 'peg';
sound: 'w'

G and Z, 'zayin',
'axe';
sound: 'z'

H, 'khet', 'fence';
sound: 'ch' as in
Scots 'loch'

For which there is no
equivalent,
'tet', 'wheel';
sound: 'heavy' 't'

I, 'yod', 'arm' and
'hand'; *sound:* 'y' as
in 'you'

K, 'kaph', 'palm of
the hand';
sound: 'k'

L, 'lamed', 'the goad
you prod an ox
with'; *sound:* 'l'

M, 'mem', 'water';
sound: 'm'

N, 'nun', 'water-
based snake or fish';
sound: 'n'

For which there is no
equivalent, 'samek',
'pillar';
sound: 's'

O, 'ayin', 'eye';
sound: a guttural
sound at the back of
the throat

P, 'pe', 'mouth'
sound: 'p'

For which there is no
equivalent,
'tsade', 'papyrus'
plant; *sound*: 'ts'

Q, 'qoph', 'monkey'
or 'ball of wool';
sound: 'q'

R, 'resh', 'head';
sound: 'r'

S, 'shin', 'tooth';
sound: 'sh'

T, 'taw', 'mark';
sound: 't'

This script took some thousand years to evolve from 1300 BCE to 300 BCE.

The next step in the evolution occurs when the ancient Greeks adopt the Phoenician alphabet and use it to express their language. The inscriptions showing this date from 800 BCE so scholars tend to date the first borrowing from two hundred years earlier. Over several hundred years the Greeks were responsible for five major changes:

i)   they used some of the Phoenician symbols to express
       vowel sounds – 'a' (from Phoenician 'aleph'), 'e' (from
       Phoenician 'he'), 'i' (from Phoenician 'yod') and 'o'
       (from Phoenician 'ayin');
ii)   they introduced some new signs for the sounds 'u'

      (pronounced 'oo' or German 'ü') and 'long o' (as in 'phone');

iii)   they created three new signs which they used interchangeably for 'ph', 'kh', 'ks' and 'ps';

iv)   they fixed their writing to run from left to right;

v)   they fixed the Ionian alphabet as standard for use for all Greek dialects.

Because Greek culture and ideas had a major influence on Europe, the alphabet which expressed those ideas had a great chance for survival amongst the European elite and ultimately all Europeans.

It was this alphabet that the Etruscans in what is now Italy adopted for their language – a language that still hasn't been fully deciphered from the 13,000 or so inscriptions discovered so far. The script was written right to left and had twenty-six letters, some of which were separated by dots, indicating perhaps that they worked with syllables.

The Romans started adopting this alphabet from about the seventh and the sixth century BCE onwards. The oldest Roman alphabet had twenty-one letters as the Romans didn't need letters they didn't speak, like 'th', 'kh' and 'ph'. The Romans adapted the letters they adopted from the Greeks, letters we now call 'upper case', to produce them in the form we know them today.

The exceptions are the letters that were added in medieval times, a story you can follow in this book in the sections for each letter.

But I'm jumping ahead of myself. Part of the story of the English alphabet has to include an account of what happened to the writing of those who first spoke Germanic dialects in England. This happened in the time between the end of the Roman occupation and the arrival in 1066 of the Norman French. Frisians, Jutes, Franks, Angles and Saxons settled in Britain, certainly from AD 400 onwards and from possibly earlier. The specialized few who knew how to write could write, either in the old way with the letters of 'runes' (see 'V is for Vikings') or in the new way with the Roman alphabet. What happened to the Roman alphabet in their hands is a good example of people inventing ways of writing letters to suit their needs. The letters they incorporated appear more fully in 'D is for Disappeared Letters'. They include 'thorn', 'ash', 'eth' and 'wynn'. The Roman letters that the Old English speakers hardly ever used were 'k', 'q' and 'z'. (You may be able to find the symbols for 'thorn', 'eth' and 'ash' on your keyboard using 'alt' because they are used in the Icelandic alphabet.) Saying that 'the Anglo-Saxons wrote using Roman letters' obscures something remarkable: people speaking one language adopted letters being used for another. Imagine writing English with Arabic script.

When the Norman French invaded England in 1066, two slightly different alphabets (and two different uses of the alphabet) met up, representing the two languages in contact: Norman French and Old English. The alphabet you're reading was made by the people who amalgamated these two languages. Some Old English letters disappeared – along with another, 'yogh', which was invented and then retired in the 'Middle English' period of the late twelfth to the late fifteenth centuries. These disappearances happened primarily because, to start off with, the Latin-influenced Normans controlled most activities involving writing (see 'D is for Disappeared Letters'). Two Old English letters, not recited as part of 'the alphabet', survived: 'ash' and 'ethel'.

The story of the changes in the English alphabet carried on until as late as the end of the seventeenth century with the letters 'i', 'j', 'u', 'v' and 'w', by which time their present-day use was fixed. Accounts of their individual histories can be found in the chapters for those letters.

A point about Latin. The Romans influenced a good deal of what is now Europe directly or indirectly through conquest, Imperial rule and religion. Their laws, histories and ideas were of course expressed using the Roman alphabet. The ruling, religious and intellectual elites of Europe went on using the Romans' language, Latin, as an international language for several hundred years after the fall of the Roman Empire, a period that secured versions of that alphabet all across western Europe.

One note of caution: because to tell the story as an 'evolution' in a lone chapter called 'A is for Alphabet' might suggest some kind of speedy, easy-flowing passage, with one stage moving inexorably into the next. This would be a gross misrepresentation. All we can say is that at any given moment in time, a writing system is asked, by the people who know how to use it, to perform tasks. If any of these tasks break down because the symbols don't work or are thought to be insufficient or redundant, then it will follow that people will invent new symbols and processes for writing and reading.

There can be no full, unabridged story of the alphabet. That can be found only in the total mass of everything that has ever been written. This book is twenty-six scenes – with digressions – taken from the drama.

THE STORY OF

- **THE FIRST FORM** of 'B' is an Egyptian hieroglyph from 4,000 years ago, meaning a 'shelter' and representing the sound 'h'. If you can't see a shelter in 'B' it will help if you first rotate the 'B' so that the vertical is horizontal and the loops sit below. Break open one of the loops and you have a door, a room and a roof over both.

The Semitic word for 'house' is 'bayt' (beginning with 'b' of course) and this explains the shift from 'h'. The letter itself was rotated to a vertical position by the Phoenicians in around 1000 BCE though at this stage it was facing left or, as we would say, 'backwards'. The Phoenicians wrote from right to left, so when the Greeks switched their own writing from left to right, they flipped the 'B' to face in what we would think of as the 'right' direction. They called it 'beta' and closed the open loop so that it was now one upright and two closed loops.

A further way the word 'bayt' (or 'beth') survives is in Hebrew: Bethlehem is the 'house of bread'.

The Romans added the serifs.

b

The first creators of 'b' were the monks in their scriptoria, speed-writing 'B' in around AD 500. If you can get away with one loop, why bother with two? When the first typeface designers in around 1500 were creating their upper and lower cases (terms referring to the two boxes which held the two different kinds of metal letters for the printing machine), they liked the single-loop 'b' and it's stuck ever since.

PRONUNCIATION OF THE LETTER-NAME

The Etruscans in around 700 BCE adopted the Greek 'beta' and reduced its name to something like 'bah' or 'bay'. 'Bay' was how the Romans and the Norman French pronounced it. The Great Vowel Shift turned it in the mouths of most English speakers to 'bee' though 'bay' survives in, say, Irish speech.

PRONUNCIATION OF THE LETTER

Consonant sounds can be grouped according to how we make the particular sound. 'B' and 'p' are clearly linked because we do virtually the same thing with our lips. What makes the difference is whether we 'voice' the letter or not – in other words, whether we use our vocal cords or not. Then again, the movement of the lips is not all that different from making the 'm' sound, the difference being that with 'b' we 'stop' the sound coming out, but with the 'm' we carry it on.

In the evolution of languages, there seems to be a relation between 'b' and 'v'. People who travel across Europe will be familiar with 'tabernas' and 'taverns'. Down the centuries some peoples have chosen to change this consonant sound by moving their lower lips forwards or backwards.

We are fond of words beginning with 'b' in English; it combines well with vowels and the consonants 'l' and 'r' to make 'blade' and 'brave'. In loan words it combines with 'h' for 'bhaji' and 'y' in 'Byelorussia'.

It doubles in verbs: 'rub, rubbing, rubbed' and in words like 'bubble', but not when it's in '-e words' as with 'tube, tubing'. Putting a consonant sound in front of the 'b' gives us 'asbo', 'albatross', 'amber' and, if you say it quick enough, 'Anne Boleyn'.

Sound-play with 'b' gives us 'babble', 'baby', 'bubby', 'bib', 'Bob', 'bibble', 'B. B. King', 'boo!', 'bah!' (meaning 'you're talking nonsense'), 'blubber', 'to blab', 'a blabber-mouth', an old children's song which began: 'Bee bo babbity . . .' and a group of words including 'bang', 'bish, bash, bosh' and 'biff'.

Some 'b'-heavy expressions include 'the big bad wolf' and 'bye-bye blackbird'. 'By hook or by crook' is a double expression in which the two halves are linked both by the rhyme and the initial 'b' in 'by'.

B-words are not as rude as the F-word but still too rude for me to say on the BBC, or the 'Beeb' as I've ended up saying it.

B IS FOR BATTLEDORE

THE WORLD OF teaching children to read is full of words like 'drilling', 'forcing' and 'whipping', and in the midst of it sits the 'battledore', an object and a word which together imply battling and beating. If you travelled in the French countryside a few decades ago, you would have seen women standing or sitting next to a square pond, with stone or concrete edges sloping down to the water's edge. Women would soap up a piece of washing and then beat it with a wooden object in the shape of a bat or racket, known as 'un battoir'. I have one from the Pyrenees.

In England this was called a washing 'beetle' or, in anticipation of John, Paul, George and Ringo, a 'beatle', a 'beetle-do' or a 'battle-door', eventually being standardized as 'battledore'. Presumably, children, the great improvisers, would borrow these from their mothers in order to play a game which evolved into 'battledore and shuttlecock'. The first toy manufacturers made 'battledores' so that children could play the game and not nick their mothers' beatles.

None of this would have anything whatsoever to do with

the teaching of reading, if it weren't for enterprising folk from at least as early as 1660, who thought of putting letters, syllables and words on these toys. A few decades later they created fold-out cardboard booklets in the shape of battledores, and then from there produced teaching-to-read primers which were in effect plain book-shaped primers. Benjamin Collins, the man credited with inventing this cardboard battledore in 1746, is thought to have sold 100,000 of them between 1770 and 1780.

Battledores were at one point so common that they gave rise to an expression, 'He doesn't know B from a battledore', meaning he doesn't know very much, perhaps along the lines of an expression my father used, 'He doesn't know his arse from his elbow'. The battledore in its 'beatle' form might have little more than the letters of the alphabet on it, but as it evolved, it acquired such texts as how to 'learn Plural and Singular: YOU to Many, and THOU to One' (1660), or woodcuts of Jack the Giant Killer or Old Mother Hubbard, so that by the 1830s you had a complete package: upper- and lower-case alphabet, numbers, lists of syllables, like: 'ab ac ad af ag'; lists of words, like: 'add bad lad mad pad sad'; or rhymes, like:

Go now to bed,
For you are fed.
If Jem can run,
He has a bun.
Now my new pen
Is fit for Ben.

Tim put the fox
In to the box.
We had a cow,

Cat, cur, and sow.
You all may go
To see the doe.

We can see the Victorian ideal at work at the heart of teaching children to read: order in letters, syllables, words, the creation and the universe.

The first concerted and thought-through efforts at teaching the reading of English (as opposed to Latin, Greek and Hebrew) to people outside of the aristocracy had a similar end in mind: devotion. To paraphrase the famous story, we might say, 'What big letters you have!'

'All the better to read the Bible with.'

The first instrument for this purpose – and it was an instrument – was the 'horn-book': a board, usually made of oak, about 9 x 5 inches in size, with a handle at its base, making it look rather like a square table-tennis bat. On one side, was a piece of horn, to protect the piece of paper that the user would slide underneath it, on which was printed the alphabet and the vowels. Below these there was usually a series of syllables (the 'syllabary') in rows 'ab eb ib ob ub', 'ac ec ic oc uc', 'ad ed id od ud', 'ba be bi bo bu', 'ca ce ci co cu', 'da de di do du' and so on. Underneath this was often written: 'In the Name of the Father, & of the Son, & of the Holy Ghost. Amen.' Underneath this was the Lord's Prayer in exactly the same wording that I was taught in school assemblies from the age of four.

It is thought that the simplest form of these began appearing some time in the mid-fifteenth century. There were more luxurious versions made of silver with bas-reliefs on the rear side. The lettering started off by being 'black letter' or gothic style and the syllabary became more complex. An alternative form of the horn-book was the 'criss-cross row' which was shaped more or less like a crucifix. This strand of teaching reading developed into the battledore.

Needless to say, these bats and bat-shaped objects were not the only means of teaching children to read through the period I've described, 1450–1800. From at least as early as 1538, printers started to produce books, calling them 'primers' or 'ABCs', usually including the catechism, the Litany and other religious texts.

Classes in 'Charity' schools could be as large as fifty or sixty, crammed into tiny rooms, with writing done in sandboxes or on slates with chalk or hardly at all. The main method of teaching, according to an account from 1654, seems to have involved the children reading out loud in a group, one syllable at a time, pointing at the syllables with their 'feskews' or pointers. The children had to take turns reading the syllables for seven pages, again and again, until they had learned these off by heart, and so on for twenty-one chapters. The chapters included such lines as: 'Ah! wee see an ox dy by an ax' and 'Let the welch belch in a halch, if they filch' (from *An English Monosyllabary*, 1651). Though I can figure out that the message here is that Welsh people burp and steal things, I'm not sure what a 'halch' is. A hutch?

Another method often used was to teach reading through spelling. First the alphabet was taught and then words were spelled out and learned as spelled. When writing on slates was the order of the day, this was sometimes done to order, in unison, letter by letter or word by word, with children teaching each other down the line with 'the appearance of a machine' as a report from 1815 puts it. Given that this was the precise moment in history when children were being drafted into the factory system, this metaphor seems to serve as evidence that the methods we use to teach reading match the era in which they are employed.

Being debated were such questions as:

i)   whether it was best to learn to spell first in order to read
ii) which syllables were best learned first
iii) what constitutes a syllable and a correct division between syllables in a word
iv) whether it was best to learn the alphabet in chunks or the whole lot in one go
v)   whether to learn the letters in orders other than alphabetical
vi) whether to 'sound' the letters as they were thought to appear in English phonology rather than simply using the letters' names
vii) whether it was a good or a bad idea to spend a deal of time teaching the children to make the shapes of the letters with similes about half-moons or rakes for their configurations
viii) whether the similarity in shape between groups of letters should determine the order in which they were taught
ix) whether pictures should or should not be used in conjunction with letters or words
x)   whether to teach reading through what we would call 'morphology' which includes how words can be changed by doing such things as adding plurals, prefixes, suffixes, verb endings such as '-ing' and '-ed', internal verb changes such as 'drink-drank-drunk'

From the seventeenth century, some guides talked of rules for spelling:

E at the end of words no sound doth make,
Only in these which for Example take . . .

The words 'Chloe', 'Jubilee' and 'Galilee' are cited as the exceptions. Some books list as many as sixty-five rules which had to be learned.

Alongside these varying approaches which try to teach reading from what has been called the 'bottom up', others pondered on whether it could be taught in a top-down way, from learning whole words, titles, phrases or even whole passages. Origins of the 'look-and-say' method of teaching to read can be found as early as 1799, when it was suggested that children could learn to read 'logographically', learning whole words by their appearance. This was sometimes called 'reading without spelling'. Yet another theory believed that dictation was the best method, whereby the teacher (or older pupil) read slowly while the children wrote what was being read. (This was a regular part of my learning French in the 1950s and 60s.) For each of these arguments, there were counter-blasts disproving the worth or efficacy of the method.

Alongside these school-based approaches, many other kinds of initiations into literacy were going on. Some small-time popular printers produced booklets like the phenomenally popular *Reading Made Easy*, a title that originated from at least as early as 1786 and which came to be known in the trade as 'Reading Easies'. The alphabet rhyme begins:

A was an Acorn, that grew on the oak;
B is a Boy, who delights in his book.
C is a Canister, holds mamma's teas;
D is a Drum, you may sound if you please . . .

It finishes:

W is a Wren, that was perch'd on a spray;
X was King Xerxes, well known in his day.

Y is a Yew Tree, both slender and tall;
Z Zachariah, the last of 'em all.

From the mid-sixteenth century a popular street literature put print into the hands of the little or non-educated. We shall never know for certain what kind of contribution this massive, popular and diverse trade made to literacy levels in Britain but I suspect a good deal.

An invention in another part of the print world had an impact too: the invention of the children's book, sold through booksellers as a source of pleasure in itself. Street literature was supplemented with books for children full of wood-cuts and engravings, with rhymes and give-away toys, the most important of which (in my view) is *Tommy Thumb's Pretty Song-Book* from 1744 – a two-volume book of which only Volume 2 survives. Each page carries a picture and a nursery rhyme – long ones carrying over to further pages – some appearing for the first time, some familiar to us today. The tone is set with the first page of the rhymes:

Lady Bird, Lady Bird,
Fly away home,
Your house is on fire
Your Children will burn.

On the last page there is an 'Advertisement' which speaks volumes of what the prevailing methods of teaching children to read involved and what the book stands opposed to:

The Childs Plaything
I recommend for Cheating
Children into Learning
Without any Beating

The author is given as 'N. Lovechild' where 'N' is a joke meaning 'Nurse'. A line stretches from this wild and funny little book through hundreds of thousands of picture books, comics, magazines and annuals for the youngest children, enticing them to read, have fun, ponder and wonder.

As we have seen, across the centuries a theoretical discourse has taken place between experts about order and method. Coming to the present day, a short while ago I was asked to speak at a conference on early reading and was soon engaged in a fiery exchange of opinions with a head teacher about learning to read.

A bit of context: the UK government has stipulated that all 'maintained' schools (those run by local authorities) in England must follow a specific method of teaching its youngest pupils to read. This is what is known as 'phonics', the exact flavour of which in England comes with its full title, 'systematic synthetic phonics'. This is a method which teaches reading according to the 'alphabetic principle', which is that the purpose and history of the alphabet is to provide us with a set of visual symbols ('graphemes') representing the sounds we make ('phonemes') when we speak. It is 'synthetic' because it shows children how we put sounds together to make whole words. For example, the sound of 'b' goes before 'at' to make 'bat'.

The question that has dominated the debate about the teaching of reading for at least thirty years is whether it's best to use phonics as the sole method, the main method, one of several methods or not at all. Of course, before we get stuck into these debates, it's always good to have agreement about what we mean by 'reading'. For hundreds of years, the usual way of testing whether a child can read has been to ask the child to read out loud. One problem with this is that being able to read out loud is no evidence that a child is understanding what they're reading. Most people in education are fully aware of this, which is why the word 'decoding' is useful. It means, in practice, reading a word out loud accurately – and nothing more. It's argued by some that the best way to teach children to read is first to teach 'decoding' – making the right sounds for the right letters and letter combinations; the meanings of the words will flow after that. What's more, say the phonics experts, once children are tooled up with the alphabetic principle they can tackle words they have never seen before.

Some say therefore that the best way to pass on these alphabetic tools is to teach phonics, 'first, fast and only'. This means preventing children from looking at stories and poems that they can't yet read as it will discourage and dishearten them and, they say, one of the main purposes of 'first, fast and only' phonics is that it's comparatively easy and full of confidence-boosting success right from the start.

Several problems hover around all this. I'll pose them as questions:

1. Do we know whether children who learn phonics 'first, fast and only' are better able to read unfamiliar and non-phonically regular words than children who learn to read using 'mixed methods'? After all, it really doesn't matter all that much if a child is brilliant at reading phonically regular words like 'hat' and 'trod', if he or she cannot read words like 'would' or 'laugh'. The evidence suggests that intensive phonics teaching is no better at helping children to read the non-regular words than teaching by using mixed methods.
2. Do we know whether children who learn phonics 'first, fast and only' are better able to understand what they're

reading when they're seven, eight, nine and ten years old? No, there is no evidence to suggest that they are better able to do this than children using mixed methods.

3. Some children find it very difficult to learn to read at the time they are first taught in England which is between four and six. There is evidence to suggest that this applies to as many as one in five children. Do we know if all, most, some or few of these children have these difficulties because they haven't grasped the alphabetic principle or are there other reasons?

What we do know is that most such children have several problems and that these vary between children and vary for any given child over time. This variety and range of differences is surely to be expected, given that the ultimate aim is for the child to be able to read unfamiliar or difficult words and to be able to understand what he or she is reading. Learning to read for meaning and understanding is not a simple matter.

In fact, it is so un-simple, no one is absolutely certain how we do it. What's more, the children who learn to read come from a wide range of emotional and physical backgrounds where there is a massive variance in a number of factors: in attitudes to learning and to the place of print in daily life; in experiences of language; and in rates of maturation and development. In addition, some children have a hearing impairment or no hearing at all, so at least some of them will learn to read using visual methods. Anyone who works with children can 'read' this diversity from the children they teach.

My attitude to language is that it involves making strings of sounds and words in the common ways shared by people in the language community we live in. These strings are the sequences, phrases, sentences, conversations, paragraphs, chapters that we hear, talk, read and write. We do not talk to each other or write to each other isolated letter by isolated letter, or even by isolated word by isolated word. Everything we hear, talk, read and write is in a context of something else heard, spoken, read or written as well as in the context of something else that will be heard, spoken, read or written – immediately after or later on. This happens as part of daily life even when all we seem to be saying to each other is:

'OK?'

'Yep.'

'Mum?'

'Not bad.'

'Uh-huh.'

With nursery rhymes, songs and stories children learn sequences of written English. Part of the problem of 'getting' what reading is about is precisely in learning how these written sequences work: learning that they are similar to the way we speak but not identical to them. One of the best ways to do this is through hearing the sequences and grammar of writing in your head so that when you sit down to read, those structures are familiar rather than strange. An anecdote to illustrate this: one of the ways my two youngest children learned to read – along with all the other input of written and read material – was using a reading scheme which included the word 'would'. This posed problems for both of them, who were being schooled in phonics and had not taken in whatever method the school had used to teach them to read 'would'. Some methods say that they are 'tricky' words, or some such, and teach the children to read such words by a method that the phonics system replaced: looking and saying ('look-and-say'), or learning 'by sight'. Others point out that '-oul-' can, in some words ('could', 'should' and 'would'), be sounded like the 'u' in 'put'. Whatever method the school used, it didn't stick with either child. So in my spell of hearing each of them read – separated by four years – I encouraged both of them to do something else: read on and go back to see if it made sense after that. In both cases this worked. That's because they went beyond the alphabetic principle and moved to a grammatical and semantic one. They could hear in that particular context that it said 'would'; they could make the phrase or sentence make sense if they said 'would'.

A strange situation is emerging in the world of teaching everyone with the same method of systematic synthetic phonics: a fair proportion of children arrive at school who have learned to read a little, quite a lot or very well indeed. These children are treated as if they are in exactly the same place as those who cannot read at all. They are frequently told now that they are 'not really reading' or that they have much more to learn because it is thought they have 'not grasped the alphabetic principle'. Then, in English schools, the children are given a 'phonics screening check' where such children may well find that they 'fail' – partly because the test includes phonically regular nonsense words like 'strom' – a word that a good but very young reader may well try to 'correct' and read as 'storm'.

However, the truth is that many of us for hundreds of years have learned how to read without being taught it exclusively through matching letters to sounds, day after day. There is really no reason to think that such children will not learn to read or will learn to read only using a purely phonic method. We did it by mixed methods: some phonics; some whole-word recognition and memorizing; some learning of rhymes off by heart; some drilling with flash cards; some guessing of words from the context we knew from pictures or repetition; some repeated use of high-frequency words; some repeated use of sounds through alliteration, rhyme and assonance; some through reading back things we said that were scribed for us by parents and teachers; some reading of street signs, adverts, cereal packets, words on TV, product names; some reading of labels on things at school or home; and a little or a lot of being read to by family, friends and teachers.

Meanwhile, the converse is happening: some children are becoming quite fluent readers, passing a 'reading' test – reading out loud – without understanding what they're reading. I can fully understand this: I can do the same with Italian. I've been taught how their alphabetic principles work, and can read quite difficult passages out loud without understanding much beyond the few words I recognize. I am a good bad reader of Italian, fairly useless in fact. My way of reading this language – and indeed the way some young children read out loud without understanding what they're reading – has been nicknamed 'barking at print'.

The way experts, teachers, monks, priests, parents, carers, acquaintances, publishers, booksellers and street pedlars have tried to teach children to read has varied down through the centuries. Evidence consists of the reading materials that survive and a mixture of teachers' and ex-pupils' accounts. Obvious perhaps, except that what people think they're teaching and what people remember being taught may not be the whole story.

Every night, my mother read to me: Beatrix Potter books, *The Little Red Engine*, Babar books, Puffin picture books about farms and planes and trains, Père Castor books translated from French. Each Christmas, I was given a new crop of Puffin picture books which I pored over for hours, inheriting my older brother's pile started four years earlier. At school, we were introduced to the Beacon Readers.

I learned to read.

What I don't know is who out of our class didn't. When I was nine and ten, I was in an unstreamed class. About half of the class were children who had been with me since nursery and I can remember hearing one or two of them trying to read out loud to the teacher but not really managing.

The Beacon Readers and their ilk evolved out of centuries of experiment with method, tone and purpose. In every era, the authors and publishers have proclaimed a certainty in their introductions, prefaces and notes which seems to derive from the fact that the books and schemes are in stages or steps that the teachers and children will take. There is no sense that children might be learning to read in any way other than along a straight line, accumulating skills, whether these be letter by letter, syllable by syllable, sound by sound, half-word by half-word, or whole word by whole word. In my experience, this is not always the case. The children I know haven't moved in a straight line. They have advanced with some aspects of their reading while standing still in others, then ducked back to grab one bit, while forgetting another . . . and so on. Likewise, the primers and 'readers' rarely mention that there is a learning-to-read world beyond this particular, apparently fail-safe, teach-all book or series of books.

No matter what method of teaching reading takes place in the surroundings of school, millions of children have acquired at least some, in some cases all, their reading skills (if 'skills' are what you read with!) from hearing and poring over this kind of printed material in the company of brothers, sisters, cousins, friends, parents, grandparents and carers. In the case of each of the children I've helped bring up, there have been different breakthrough moments, different ways of 'getting' how reading works. With each of them I can point to different ways in which they 'got' one word and figured out that the way they had 'got' it could be applied to other words.

For one, it was the Dr Seuss book, *Hop on Pop*. I can see that boy sitting up in his bed, having looked at it on his own for a while, saying the lines over and over again, laughing and laughing. For another, it was hearing *Where the Wild Things Are* read to him again and again (at his request) so that he reached a point where he knew what word was coming up next, pointing at it, and saying it. The book mattered a great deal to him and on one occasion, as we reached the moment where Max 'wanted to be where he was loved best of all', he blurted out 'Mummy!'

I have often thought of this as a fine example of how the very youngest of children interpret what they hear and start to read. After all, there is no 'Mummy' in the book. 'Mother' is mentioned as someone whom Max would like to eat up and who sends Max to his room. We don't even see her in the pictures. What this three-year-old reader did was fuse his own 'Mummy' (his word, not the author's) with who he imagined was the 'object' of Max's emotions. To do this, he had to interpret a rather odd phrase that he would not have heard outside of the book: 'he wanted to be where he was loved best of all'. He was learning to 'read with understanding' by discovering he could interpret books for himself.

Yet another child became very angry about being taught to read. She decided she couldn't and wouldn't. At the time there was a series of books called 'Jets' which combined cartoons, speech bubbles and a bit of continuous prose; I gave her a pile of them. I said that she didn't have to read them to me, I was quite happy to read them to her if she wanted me to. If not, she could just look at them if and when she wanted to. She opted for a bit of all three: I read a bit, she read bits to me, she looked at a lot on her own. The important thing for the kind of person she is, was that it was all driven by her. She was in control of when, where, how often, and at what pace.

THE STORY OF

• **'C' STARTS OUT LIFE** as 'gimel' in Phoenician. Its shape was something like a walking stick or the number 1 without a serif on the bottom. In fact, it meant a stick as used by a hunter, perhaps something like a boomerang. The Greeks called it 'gamma' and when they switched their writing to run from left to right, they flipped the hunting stick. Some Greek settlers in Italy preferred a crescent-shaped 'gamma'. The Etruscans turned the hard 'g' of 'gamma' into a 'k' sound. The Romans added the serifs and created the elegant thin-thick line.

c

This is of course just a small version of 'C' and it appeared in manuscripts from around AD 500.

PRONUNCIATION OF THE LETTER-NAME
The Normans would have pronounced the letter as 'say', as in modern French, and the Great Vowel Shift turned it to 'see'.

PRONUNCIATION OF THE LETTER
If you've been saying 'Julius Seezer' for 'Julius Caesar' you are both right and wrong: right because that's how we say it, but wrong because the Romans of the time pronounced it 'Kye-' (rhyming with our 'rye') '-sar' or '-zar'. This is yet another indication of how everything in language changes. By the time the Roman Empire was in decline some people were turning the 'k' sound into 'ch' – a sound that persists in English with a loan word like 'cello'.

The Normans arrived in Britain pronouncing the lone 'c' as soft 's' – think 'city' and 'civil'.

If spelling were a matter of a purely rational divvying-out of letters to match sounds, then all soft 's' sounds would be indicated with 's', and all hard 'k' sounds with the 'k'; the 'c' could be buried with Caesar. Instead, we have 'c' which can be the 's' sound of 'ceiling' or the 'k' sound of 'cut' or 'picnic'. You can have a 'tic' or a 'tick'; an 'e' following 'c' in a single-syllable word or the last syllable of a word tells us to use a soft 's' – 'pace', 'police'. To tell us to say 'k', we write 'ache' – double it and we say both 'k' and 's': 'accept'. From at least as early as 1606, scholars were on to this criminal state of affairs. Playwright and poet Ben Jonson – no stranger to crime himself (he avoided execution for a murder he committed) – thought that we should have been 'spared' the 'c' letter but felt that it was already too late to quarrel with those who had laid it down in the first place.

In French, 'c' is soft when it is followed by an 'e' or 'i' and hard when it is followed by an 'a', 'o' or 'u' . . . unless a 'cedilla' has been stuck to its bottom. This little sign (a figure 5 without a hat) tells us that the colloquial 'ça' is pronounced 'sa'. Whether the cedilla outlasts the smartphone keypad epoch is another matter.

'C' combines with all the vowels along with 'r' to make 'crab' 'cress', 'crisis', 'cross' and 'crunch', with 'l' to make 'clam', clench', 'clip', 'close' and 'clunk' and with a 'z' in the loan word 'czar'. It can combine with vowel 'y' in 'Cyprus', 'cynic' and 'Cyril'.

You can find it embedded in the three-letter consonant sound '-tch' as in 'itch' but that sound is of course much more usually written as 'ch' as in 'church'. Putting a consonant sound in front of the 'c' also gives us the very different 'arc', 'alchemy' and 'anchor'.

 IS FOR CIPHERS

An issue of the *Daily Telegraph* during the Second World War included the usual crossword but on one particular occasion was accompanied by a challenge, in which readers were invited to solve the puzzle in under twelve minutes. If they thought they could, they were asked to make contact with the newspaper. Some twenty-five readers were invited to Fleet Street to sit a new crossword test. Five of them completed the crossword in twelve minutes while one other had only one word missing when the time was up. A few weeks later, these six people were interviewed by the intelligence services and recruited as codebreakers at Bletchley Park, where a team of people were deciphering the messages transmitted by the German military through Enigma machines. Some of the clues are straightforward: '16 across: Pretend (5)', for which the answer is 'feign'.

Others are what are known as 'cryptic':

13 across: Much that could be got from a timber merchant (two words – 5, 4), for which the answer is 'Great deal'.

14 down: The right sort of woman to start a dame school (3), for which the answer is 'Ada'.

18 'The War' (anag.) (6), for which the answer is 'Wreath'.

The most cryptic is: '22 across: The little fellow has some beer: it makes me lose colour, I say (6)', with 'impale' being the answer, though the last thing I 'impaled' was a barbecue sausage.

If you tot up the techniques needed to solve these they include: memory of synonyms and definitions; awareness of idioms, homonyms and puns; an ability to see letters on the page divorced from their meaning, usual punctuation and spacing; and the ability to jumble and reassemble letters. At the time it was felt that these capabilities would be useful when faced with the encrypted messages that the centre at Bletchley picked up – pages that looked like this:

FDJKM LDAHH YEOEF PTWYB LENDP
MKOXL DFAMU DWIJD XRJZY DFRIO
MFTEV KTGUY DDZED TPOQX FDRIU
CCBFM MQWYE FIPUL WSXHG YHJZE

. . . and so on across several pages.

I'm not particularly good at crosswords though I did win the *Boy's Own Paper* crossword competition in 1958. I'm pretty sure I was imitating my parents who spent every Sunday afternoon in a huddle over the Sunday *Observer*'s 'Everyman' crossword, an activity that seemed even then to be full of dubious motives: repetitive, compulsive behaviour; enjoyable masochism; rigid, rule-bound process; succumbing to the will of an anonymous tyrant . . . To watch them was an initiation into the inner recesses of the alphabet. The anagram procedure they followed was to write the letters in a ring; words for which they had some letters were written out on the white margins of the *Observer* with the blanks written as dashes; they talked of possible and impossible letter combinations and then roared with laughter when they overlooked the 'cn' in the middle of 'picnic'.

Cryptic crosswords today have become yet more cryptic, using many encoded ways of indicating what procedure you must use whilst embedding the code in a feasible phrase or sentence: the word 'about' will inform you that you must work out an anagram of what comes next, though there is an alternative use telling you that the word preceding 'about' will be split up and positioned around (i.e. 'about') the following word. So, 'Boss about tearfully (4)' is 'sobs' but 'Boss about one trying to be a scary gangsta (7)' is 'booness'. There are at least twenty other procedures like these to make crosswords, some of which involve codes – substituting parts or all of words, and some of which involve ciphers which, like anagrams, involve substituting one letter for another. Together, these methods can be called 'encryption'.

In June 2013, as I've been writing this book, and indeed this particular chapter, an event has had a devastating impact on our ideas about the secrecy of encryption. The first decades of the internet have seen new literacies emerging. These are not simply matters of how we configure letters, words and phrases but are also about the nature of who participates in conversations. Using the instruments of instant messaging, emails and social networks, we've created worldwide interest groups, people who want to write on the internet about things they're interested in. I am an avid 'user' of these. Alongside that, I buy train tickets and secondhand books, and spend hours searching and researching anything from family history to the weather details at our holiday destination. Edward Snowden's revelation was that not one single part, not one tiny jot of it, is secret. It is all available to the security services of one country. It has all been stored and this too is available to the security services.

In other words, our communications can be analysed in two key ways: instantaneously and historically. Put another way, we can be 'spotted' saying or doing something at a given moment, or the pattern of our existence over time can be captured and described. However, this isn't truly public knowledge. I don't have the technological skills to do this myself, nor do I have one of the few jobs which would enable me to get into any of this spotting and storing. The knowledge and the jobs belong to only a tiny number of people, the security services of one country, who choose whether to share what they find with their elected representatives or, indeed, with anyone at all from other countries. Or not.

In one sense, this is no different from Elizabeth I's team of spies collecting knowledge about plots against the Crown, and, for example, deciphering messages between Mary Queen of Scots and her conspiratorial chums. The regime defended itself by finding out what people who endangered that regime were saying to each other. Picture Mary confined in Chartley Hall, Staffordshire. A Catholic supporter called Gilbert Gifford smuggles letters to her by the ruse of arranging with a local brewer for them to be concealed in the bung that plugged a barrel of beer. Mary herself didn't splosh around in the beer, her servants did that for her. In March 1586, in the Plough, near Temple Bar, a dashing young blade of the same religious persuasion, one Anthony Babington, gathered together six conspirators suitable for planning the springing of Mary from her prison, the assassination of Queen Elizabeth, inciting a rebellion and raising support from abroad. All they needed was for Mary to agree to this Shakespearean plot.

Mary heard about this from her French supporters and wrote

to Babington indicating that she looked forward to hearing from him; Gifford was the courier. Surely all that needed to be done now was for Babington and Mary to communicate via the beer-barrel bung. Yes, but Babington made doubly sure of concealment by encrypting his letter, using twenty-three symbols for letters, such as the Greek letter 'theta' for 'g', the infinity sign for 'h', and 'delta' for 's'. He also used thirty-five numbers, letters and signs to substitute for some whole words: '2' for 'and', 'x' for 'in' and so on. There were five other symbols for blanks or spaces and for double letters. Wily Gifford knew his way round the underground and highly endangered Catholic community of Tudor England and he made various detours in order to throw off possible pursuers. A good man to have on your side, was Gifford. One problem: he wasn't on Mary's side. He was acting as a double agent and for at least a year he had been showing Mary's letters to Elizabeth's spymaster-in-chief, Sir Francis Walsingham.

Walsingham had a cipher school going in London with one Thomas Phelippes (Philips) as his main man, who was described at the time as small, short-sighted and 'slender every way, dark yellow haired on the head, and clear yellow bearded, eaten in the face with small pox'. Phelippes worked on the 'frequency principle', matching the frequency of symbols to the frequency of real letters in normal writing, cracked the cipher and the codes, figured out what Babington was up to and told Walsingham. The Tudor regime was extremely well geared up for torturing, disembowelling and executing (in that order) its enemies, in particular Catholics. The point for Walsingham was not simply rounding up a dashing blade like Babington. The real prize was Mary herself. To secure her, they needed Mary's authorization of the Babington plot, otherwise Elizabeth wouldn't authorize Mary's execution. Sure enough, on 17 July 1586, Mary incriminated herself by talking of the 'design'. Phelippes deciphered the letter and marked it with a gallows sign.

But Walsingham was a belt-and-braces spymaster. He wanted names, more names. So he asked Phelippes to forge a postscript (in the cipher) on Mary's letter to Babington, saying: 'I would be glad to know the names and qualities of the six gentlemen which are to accomplish the designment [plot].' Babington and his pals were 'cut down, their privities were cut off, bowelled alive and seeing, and quartered'. (For the record, it was their bodies that were cut into quarters, not their bowels or privities.)

Mary tried it on at her trial: 'Can I be responsible for the criminal projects of a few desperate men which they planned without my knowledge and participation?' It didn't wash and she was beheaded in front of 300 people in the Great Hall of Fotheringhay Castle.

The Snowden story is similar to that of Mary Queen of Scots in that it involves the codes and ciphers that are available to the rulers of a country or countries to defend themselves. In another way, though, it is completely different. No matter how suspicious we have been about the visibility of internet communication, many of us probably believed that our passwords were 'secure' and that most of our internet 'history' got deleted and died. We didn't invent these encryptions. They were given to us. Part of this false sense of security (literally and metaphorically) is intertwined with what we've understood about 'encryption'. If, like me, you are illiterate in relation to the language(s) by which computers turn keyboard taps into words and images, then 'encryption' is a piece of mystical babble. It's like saying: my account is quite secure because it's 'abracadabra-ed'. It turns out that this piece of babble is not only mystical for people like me, it's also nonsense. It's not secure at all. Usually, the reason why encryptions are not secure is because extremely clever people unlock them. In this case, though, something different has happened.

One way of relating the story of global power is to tell the stories of how people in power have tried to make their messages secret whilst trying to read the secret messages of others: it's the history of codes, ciphers and various kinds of encryptions. Novels, films and memoirs have taken us into top-secret rooms and shown us skulduggery in high places, assassinations, lone unhappy geniuses, cranks, saviours and mass murderers. At times, the fate of millions, it's been suggested, has rested on code-setting or code-breaking. The small-room, top-secret-clique image of encryption still holds good with the Edward Snowden revelation – but with some key differences.

Before the age of the internet, the security services used 'intelligence' to locate and observe people. In those days, most people thought that if something was described as 'confidential' this meant that it was kept confidential between the participants, whilst knowing that, under extreme conditions, the police or the security services could get hold of it. What's more, if for any reason you encoded what you said or did, then someone would have to decode it in order to find out what was going on. All this has been wiped away. Now, the 'intelligence' has already been gathered. In effect, it's sitting in the security services' office, in the huge silos of stored electronic data we provide to the security services.

No electronic communication is confidential. The fact that a piece of electronic communication has been encoded is irrelevant. It doesn't even have to be decoded – because we've handed over the keys to the codes even as we thought we had encrypted or encoded something! We are each a double agent cunningly acting undercover against ourselves on behalf of the security services of one country. Snowden's name must go down in the new histories of encryption as the man who revealed this.

This chapter is not called 'C is for Codes' because of a fiddly technical distinction which I'll stick to: if I say my real name is Michael Rosen but my undercover name is 'Alphabetico', that's a code. A whole word is substituted. If I find a way of substituting each of the letters of my name with other letters, numbers or any other kind of sign according to a principle or system, that's a cipher. So, if I write:

A = 1
B = 2
C = 3
D = 4

and so on through the alphabet, I could substitute the 'M', 'I', 'C', 'H', 'A', 'E' and 'L' of my name with numbers and write it as:

13 9 3 8 15 12

Alternatively I could write:

A = B
B = C
C = D

and so on with the two alphabets lined up next to each other as I've begun to do here. If I use that parallel alignment of alphabets, I could choose to write my messages using the letter that comes after the letter I would normally use.

I could write this as a formula. My cipher is N + 1 where

'N' = any letter in the real alphabet and N + 1 takes me to the letter I will use for my ciphered message.

My first name would now be:

Njdibfm

Clearly, you can create ciphers on the principle of N plus any number or N minus any number. You can do this by writing out alphabets on to two strips of paper and sliding one alphabet underneath the other. You'll need to write the alphabet more than once on the strips so that every letter has a counterpart to a letter on the other strip! This is a good game to play with children.

What you would have created here is known as a 'mono-alphabetic cipher'. In *Lives of the Caesars*, Suetonius explains that Julius Caesar used a monoalphabetic code. His formula was N + 3.

If you want to turn this into a game, try this, a party trick I have called 'Cave, Caesar!' (If you want to pronounce it as it's thought the Romans pronounced it, you can say 'Kah-way Ky-sar' with 'Ky' rhyming with 'fly'. It means 'Watch out, Caesar!').

Caesar (probably you) sits with his followers in the room, and Cassius the codebreaker says that whatever cipher ('code') Caesar uses he will be able to crack it. He needs to do this, he says, because Caesar is getting too big for his boots and he's keeping an eye on him. Caesar says that Cassius thinks he's clever but he's not that clever. Cassius leaves the room, ready to take on the challenge. Someone can be chosen to stand guard on him to show that Cassius is not cheating by listening to what's going on from outside the door.

Caesar tells his followers that they are going to choose an

object in the room, and they're going to write it in a 'code'. He suggests to his followers that they use the N + 3 formula which is his favourite and no one has ever cracked it yet. Caesar and his followers choose an object, let's say it's 'table'. Make sure that it's a suggestion from one of the followers and not from Caesar. Vote on it so that it's obviously not been chosen by Caesar. Caesar shows his followers how to make the two strips of the alphabets and apply the formula by sliding the strips. This will deliver 'table' as 'wdeoh'. Hide the strips.

Call Cassius back into the room. Cassius sits down and watches Caesar's hand. When Caesar hands over the ciphered message 'wdeoh', he does so with three fingers on the paper but in a way that the others won't see. Cassius reads that as 'N + 3' and cracks the code, putting on a great show of staring at the letters and doing magic signs and various kinds of hocus-pocus. Cassius then warns Caesar and his followers that he knows everything he's up to and he had better watch out: 'Cave, Caesar!'

Someone in the room may say that Caesar and Cassius obviously worked this out beforehand. So suggest that Cassius goes out again. Choose another object. Change the formula to N + any other number. Call Cassius back, revealing this new number with the same method, leaving your fingers on the page when you hand over the ciphered message.

Now, we can step up the complexity of this, if you have either the mind or the machine to do it. What you can do is change the formula each time you write a letter. So, you could decide to start with N + 1 for the first letter, then N + 2 for the second and so on all through the message you want to send. Or you could make it more complicated by using any sequence of numbers to decide how you make the cipher. You could use your phone number or the repeated use of your flat or house number.

Another way of doing this without using numbers is to make

an alphabet square. Your alphabet square is made up of the twenty-six letters across the top as your 'real' alphabet. Exactly underneath, you write out the alphabet twenty-six times. However, each time you write an alphabet one below the other, you slide it along by one letter. So, now, stretching down below each letter of the 'real' alphabet, you have twenty-six new ways of writing each of the letters from your real alphabet along the top. When you write a word using this square, you could write the first letter of your word using the first line, the second letter using the second line, the third letter the third line and so on. So the word 'table' would be made up of 'u' from the first line, 'c' from the second line, 'e' from the third line, 'p' from the fourth line, 'j' from the fifth line, making 'ucepj' as 'table', using the formula $N + 1$, $N + 2$, $N + 3$, $N + 4$, $N + 5$.

This square is known as a 'Vigenère Square', named after a French 'diplomat' Blaise de Vigenère (1523–96). In 1586, he wrote *Traicté des Chiffres, ou Secrètes Manières d'Escrire (Treatise on Ciphers or Secret Ways of Writing)*. He had been studying the works of previous cryptologists: the Florentine painter, composer, poet, philosopher, zoologist and architect Leon Battista Alberti; a German abbot – Johannes Trithemius; and an Italian scientist – Giovanni Porta. According to Simon Singh, accomplished author of *The Code Book*, the breakthrough in creating these kinds of multiple-letter codes came in around 1460, when Alberti was having a stroll in the gardens of the Vatican with his friend Leonardo Dato. He went on to write a treatise in 1462 on ciphers called *De Cifris* where he revealed the wonders of the Alberti Cipher Disk. A version of Alberti's disc was used by the Confederates during the American Civil War.

If you're ingenious, you could make a version of this. Make two discs out of cardboard, one bigger than the other. For the sake of precision, mark each one of them with lines radiating

ALPHABETICAL

out from the centre, like bicycle-wheel spokes. Make twenty-six segments, so you have spaces for twenty-six letters. Write each of these in turn at the outermost point in each segment and on each disc. Now place the larger disc underneath the smaller disc. You could stick a split pin through the middle to make rotation of this inner disc easier. In one position, all the letters on both discs match exactly, 'A' for 'A', 'B' for 'B', and so on. If you rotate the inner disc by one segment, you will make N + 1. If you rotate the inner disc by three segments, you will make Caesar's 'code', N + 3. These formulae are known as 'keys'.

Cunning old Alberti, who also wrote a treatise on the cunning old housefly, worked like this: before writing to you I will tell you a letter. You own a cipher disc. Before starting to read the ciphered message you must set your discs to the letter I've told you. Alberti set his inner disc with the 'K' on the inner disc matched to the outer 'B'. 'If you want to read my message,' said Alberti, 'you must use the identical formula you have with you, turning the inner movable disc until the letter B corresponds to the index k.' What Alberti called an 'index' we might call the 'key letter'. The inner disc provides the letters for the cipher message, the outer for the 'real' or 'plain' message. He also suggested ways in which you could hide key letters in a message. Very cunning, Alberti.

Of course, with your discs, you can write whatever you want and in any order on the two discs. Provided the people receiving your message have the same letters and signs on their discs, and they know what are the signals to move the inner disc round, you can make your ciphers yet more undecipherable to the uninitiated. However, if you want to behave as we've all done in relation to the internet, you will write a series of messages to people which you think are secret and confidential and then hand your discs and keys to the security services of another country. You will then be surprised that they now know what it is you've been writing.

Between 1938 and 1949, there was an Ovaltine-sponsored radio show in the US called *Captain Midnight* which would end with a secret message. Listeners wrote to Ovaltine for their 'Code-O-Graph' which would enable them to figure it out. In the storyline they were used by agents of the Secret Squadron, a paramilitary organization headed by Captain Midnight. On the outer disc of the 'Code-O-Graph' were letters, on the inner disc numbers. Captain Midnight gave you his secret message and you used your 'Code-O-Graph' to decipher it.

The first Code-O-Graph, called the 'Mystery Dial' unit, was introduced in 1941, as a device to enable Secret Squadron agents in the field to send and receive secure messages. It was in badge form. The front of the badge displayed the number and cipher alphabet scales. The reverse had two windows, one labelled 'Master Code'; the other, 'Super Code'. As an example, if the cipher was designated as 'Master Code 3', it meant that the movable rotor was spun so that the number 3 would appear in the window labelled 'Master Code'. This setting would align the number and cipher alphabet scales correctly to decipher a message.

The 1945 model altered the cipher-key setting scheme. The new method was to align one of the letters on the alphabet scale to a numeral on the number scale. For instance, the 'Master Code X-15' setting meant that the letter X would be moved until it was next to the number 15 on the number scale. The 1946 model was the 'Mirro-Flash' unit; the 1947 was called the 'Whistle Code-O-Graph'; the last Code-O-Graph was the 'Key-O-Matic' unit. Resetting the cipher elements utilized a small key that was inserted into slots over one of the gears, which could be disengaged, using the key and a leaf spring as a clutch.

From Alberti to *Captain Midnight* in 500 years.

An earlier hero of the cipher world was Arthur Scherbius (1878–1929), a German electrical engineer who was born in Frankfurt am Main; his father was a small-businessman. He studied electricity at the Technical College in Munich, and his doctoral dissertation was called 'Proposal for the Construction of an Indirect Water Turbine Governor'. He was a bright chap. In 1918, he founded the firm of Scherbius & Ritter, inventing a number of things, including electric pillows and ceramic heating parts, and in 1918 he patented a machine, initially pitched at the commercial market, which he later sold as the Enigma.

I am not going to pretend to be an expert on Enigma, and unlike Mick Jagger, I don't own one. However, I think we can get a general idea of how the Enigma machines mangle the alphabet if we were to imagine a series of Alberti's cipher discs lined up next to each other. Then by a series of 'trips' whereby a whole 360-degree rotation of one disc can trip off an adjacent disc and along with electrical impulses, we can align and realign these discs in many different ways. Keys or Alberti's index letters can be used to set the machine to 'scramble' letters into a cipher. Scherbius made it even more fiendish with the use of a 'reflector' which entailed sending the scrambling back through the system to scramble it even more. There was also a yet more fiendish element called the 'plugboard' which swapped round some letters from the real message before it even entered the scrambling-reflecting system! There were several commercial models, and one of them was adopted by the German Navy (in a modified version) in 1926. The German Army adopted the same machine (also in a modified version somewhat different from the Navy's) a few years later. Scherbius saw none of this as he was killed in a horse-carriage accident in 1929.

I guess the Enigma machine represents the industrialization of diplomacy and military intelligence. It is the outcome of mathematical knowledge in conjunction with technology applied to the humble old alphabet. Throughout history, the intellectual endeavour involved in all this ciphering has been mostly employed by governments, armies, and spies, as part of their role in gaining and maintaining power or in winning wars. I don't think I'm exaggerating when I say that the pages on which ciphers have been written are stained with blood – always morally justified at the time, of course.

My memory of ciphers from when I was a child, though, is that they are great fun. It's as if the 'real' alphabet is transparent but when you use a cipher it becomes opaque. The truth is on the other side, if only you can get to it. If you're the one using the cipher, you are the owner of this occult knowledge, and it gives you – and those who know the trick – power over those who don't. It is an alphabetic way of whispering behind someone's back: they can hear or see that you're talking but can't make out what you're saying.

Ciphers reveal some important things about the alphabet. Making an alphabetic cipher (substituting one letter for another) drains the letter you are looking at from the purpose for which it was invented, which is to invite you to make a particular sound. The only things that matter in cipher-making, though, are the relationship between one letter and another in the 'real' alphabet and then the relationship between the letters in the 'real' alphabet and the alphabet being used to make the cipher. These relationships are mathematical – to do with sequences. In this sense, this reminds us that the alphabet I'm using now, when viewed as a sequence, is random, more random than counting from one to twenty-six, where the sequence of numbers corresponds to the principle of increasing a quantity by one at a time. Nothing is added when you say the alphabet from 'A' to 'Z' and nothing is taken away when you say it 'Z' to 'A'. It's not even arranged according to any principle of how the letters are used when we speak or write.

There's a reminder here of what the alphabet does beyond the matter of representing sounds. In 'A is for Alphabet' and 'B is for Battledore', I've shown a rather limited and elemental view of the alphabet. When we embed the alphabet in its real and actual use, we can see that it is a necessary part of a chain which goes far further than 'representing sounds'. So, apart from when simply writing out the alphabet or playing with the letters as objects in themselves, we do not use the letters randomly. In use when writing, we group them according to what we want them to do when making words (and, on occasions, exclamations and interjections, and, with onomatopoeia, an imitation of sounds we hear).

Moreover, we don't make words randomly either. We put words into sequences or 'strings', governed by the grammars we invent. And we invent grammars in order to make sense. So while the alphabet is random, and while we say 'letters represent sounds', in fact, the full picture is: 'letters are there for us to make sense'.

To give an obvious example: the letters 'd' and 'e' exist side by side in the alphabet. No one knows why they do. Saying 'side by side' is in its own way a bit of maths or geometry. In fact, all the letters are equidistant from the ones next to them. The 'D' is like 'E' in the way 'A' is like 'B' or the way 'U' is like 'V': they are side by side. As a result, one way in which letters in the alphabet relate is that they are related to each other by similar or different distances. So, we might say, 'B' is like 'L' because they are both five letters away from 'G' (one forwards, one back, but the distance is the same). This kind of thing is what Caesar, Alberti, Scherbius and the rest were able to see and use.

However, back with 'D' and 'E': when we use them in language, we call on them to do a job based on linguistic principles, not mathematical ones. We do this frequently in English when saying – and therefore writing – 'I walked from the bus stop to the station.' This is the '-ed' ending we invented in order to indicate that something happened earlier or 'in the past'. In that sense, no matter what sound or sounds they make, 'E' and 'D' help us position events in relation to where we are now. Letters in context are doing a job in helping us make sense. This way of making sense is through 'morphology' – that is, the making and changing of words; and through 'grammar' or 'syntax' – that is, the stringing together of letters and words in meaningful chunks.

Clearly, not all use of letters is as directly linked to grammar as this. Some of the ways in which we use letters meaningfully are to make distinctions between things, feelings, ideas, sounds, processes and much more. So, 'shut' is different from 'cut' because 'sh' and 'c' are different. We signify or point out differences in meaning through differences in sound, many but not all of which we can then indicate in writing by using different letters. The reasons for choosing 'sh' over 'c' are not only or simply because they are made up of different letters. Our ulterior motive is in order to make a different kind of sense, and that will be governed by what we want to say and who we are saying it to. We could easily think of the different situations in which we might want to write, on the one hand, 'He shut his mouth,' and on the other, 'He cut his mouth.' It's those situations which will be the ultimate reason why we choose between using the letters 'sh' or 'c'.

As I've said, part of the fun of playing around with ciphers is that it involves principles utterly different from these. Cryptographers invent ciphers and use the alphabet by draining it of its purpose. In so doing, they throw into perspective what the rest of us, including cryptographers' masters, use the alphabet for.

THE STORY OF

• **AROUND 800 BCE**, we find the Phoenicians drawing a rough triangle and calling it 'dalet' meaning 'door'. Given that doors to dwellings made of soft materials are often triangular, this seems to be derived from a pictogram. The early ancient Greeks drew it with a downstroke on the right, turned the triangle into a semicircle and called it 'delta'. When they switched their writing to run from left to right in around 500 BCE, they flipped the semicircle over. The Romans added serifs and produced the elegant thick-thin line.

d

Our 'd' emerges in Italian manuscripts around AD 400, perhaps as a result of turning carved letters into one penstroke, albeit with the upstroke bent to the left. The early printers of around 1500 opted for this single-loop and stroke for their lower case but made the upstroke as vertical as the one on the 'D'.

PRONUNCIATION OF THE LETTER-NAME

The Norman French pronounced it 'day' and the Great Vowel Shift turned this to 'dee'.

PRONUNCIATION OF THE LETTER

It's easy to think of letters as having only one 'value' but the moment you listen to someone whose first language is different from your own, you start to hear subtle differences. We make the 'd' sound by hitting the roof of our mouth with the tip of our tongue. The further forward the tongue goes, the nearer it gets to the sound of 'th' in 'them'. Indeed, many speakers of English say words like 'the' and 'them' so that they sound like 'de' and 'dem'. The further back the tongue goes, the nearer it gets to the way many Indian speakers say a word like 'dal'/'dhal'. In a place like London, where speakers of 'dem' and many speakers of the 'd' as in 'dhal' brush shoulders, we should expect some changes to 'd'. What's more, some US speakers of English say 'todally', i.e. 'voicing' the 't'. I can remember being picked up for doing this in the 1950s, perhaps as a result of imitating cowboy movies. Keen-eared phoneticians have spotted aristocratic Brits like Prince Harry, or privately educated politicians like Tony Blair and George Osborne, doing the same.

'D' combines with all the vowels and the vowel 'y', with 'r' for 'drab' and 'drizzle', and with an 'h' in the loan words 'dhoti' and 'dhow'. At the ends of verbs it doubles as in 'rid, ridding' but is single in 'ride, riding'. It also doubles in words with short vowels like 'muddle' and 'piddle' but not with long vowels like 'oodles of noodles'. Putting a consonant sound before a 'd' gives us 'old' (though I'm someone who pronounces this word more like 'oh' with a 'd' on the end), the shop 'Asda', 'abdicate' and 'and'. Django Reinhardt's name has the virtue of including two consonant combinations with 'd' not usually found in English: 'dj' and 'dt'.

D-Day must be just about the most successful use of the name of a letter ever invented. The term 'D-Day' pre-exists the Normandy Landings as it was the phrase used by the military for any opening day of a major manoeuvre, just as 'H-hour' marked the opening hour. 'D' doesn't stand for anything more significant than 'day'.

Sound-play with 'd' gives us 'dad', 'daddy', 'da', 'dadda', 'Dada', 'doodle', 'diddle', 'doddle', 'dud', 'dude', 'DD' and

'Didi', 'doo-doo', 'doh!', 'der!', 'duh!', 'fuddy-duddy', 'doo-be-doo-be-doo', 'Scooby-dooby-doo', 'Hey diddle diddle, the cat and the fiddle' and 'Doo-wah-diddy-diddy-dum-do-ee-day'.

Familiar 'd' expressions include 'every dog has its day' and 'do as you would be done by'. In dull moments, you can try saying, 'Ken Dodd's dad's dog's died'.

O IS FOR DISAPPEARED LETTERS

ONE OF THE strange things about studying Anglo-Saxon, or 'Old English' as we were asked to call it, is that it was quite possible to spend three years working away at it without ever taking a look at the writing itself. When I say 'writing' I mean the actual, material stuff. This was in the 1960s and the texts that we looked at were mostly in printed booklets with light-blue paper covers, with light-red writing on the front. Maybe this was to give us the impression that Anglo-Saxon was a light, fluffy sort of language and if we studied it long and hard enough we would become light and fluffy too. Inside the booklets, the piece we were going to study was in what can only be called a hybrid typeface. Modern printers had modified the Old English handwriting into a font. The real thing looks quite different.

Perhaps I missed the lecture where they urged us all to nip off to the British Museum where for free we could take a look at *Beowulf*, sitting in a glass case in the gallery of specimens of writing right the way up to the Beatles via William Blake, Wilfred Owen and many others. Years later, when I was making a series of radio programmes called *Early Versions*, the manuscripts had all been carefully moved down the road to the British Library, and I was able to get up close and intimate with this extraordinary manuscript. To this day it bears the signs of having been flung out the window of a burning library. Of course it also bears the signs of the person who decided to write down this extraordinary story.

Why would any English people – generally reckoned to be Christian monks – want to spend weeks and weeks of their lives writing down what is mostly a pagan tale of a warrior-superhero from what is now southern Sweden, fighting a 'grim and greedy' monster, then the monster's mother and then a dragon? When you study this at university, you can easily devote all your time to learning very technical things about, say, the rhythms of the epic verse, the alliterative patterns, the grammar of the words, the meaning of the imagery and so on so I wasn't given an answer to that question, and I haven't found one since.

The material the monk has written on is 'vellum', or sheep-skin. And, when this is pointed out to you, you can see how biological that is. As the *Beowulf* scholar, Kevin Kiernan, put it, 'Before Beowulf could slay his monsters, someone had to slay a lot of sheep.' A small flock of sheep was killed in order to make up the pages of the book; a large flock of people got to work preparing the sheep's skins. These had the flesh scraped from them and were then washed, limed, de-haired, scraped, dried, washed again, stretched on frames, scraped again to remove marks and blemishes, smoothed, polished and softened with chalk. The sheets were then folded into 'gatherings' of eight or sixteen pages, and marked up with lines and margins. We do something like this ourselves when we fold up a sheet of paper to make a little booklet.

But wait a minute: do you write your letters and words on what was the hairy side of the sheepskin or the body side?

Or both? The *Beowulf* scribes (or are they poets?) did both. On occasions, in particular the second of the two scribes squashed his writing up to fit it all into the page. Monks wrote with quills, feathers plucked from the tails of geese, swans or crows, that had been boiled and cut. Ancient inks were made from mixtures of wine, soot, blackthorn wood, oak gall and even cuttlefish ink. I'm not sure which recipes were used by the *Beowulf* scribes but we know for certain, as we look at the manuscript, that a thousand years ago, someone breathed on every page, dipped his quill into an inkhorn probably made from a stag's antler and scraped the quill across the sheepskin.

But what lettering did the monks use? Here we have to bring in two terms: Carolingian, and Uncial.

Carolingian was Europe's first agreed standard handwriting, circulating from the the ninth century onwards. It was in what we would call now 'lower case', or more properly when it comes to handwriting, 'minuscule'. It's called Carolingian because it derives from the court of Charlemagne, who, ironically, was not thought to be fully literate himself. He was presumably too busy becoming a soldier-king to worry about learning how to write.

Uncial was an older handwriting, written in capital letters, or 'majuscule', found in manuscripts from as early as the third century. One form of it was imported into England from Ireland as the Anglo-Saxons converted from the Norse religion to the Irish form of Christianity, roughly between AD 500 and 700.

But, of course, nothing in language is as cut and dried as this (apart from vellum), and when it comes to specific manuscripts we see various kinds of blends of these two scripts. So, the modernizers, writing in the Europe-wide Carolingian, often chose to hang on to some of that old-fashioned Uncial stuff – but which letters? 'A', 'D', 'E', 'F', 'G', 'H', 'R', 'S',

'C', 'O' and 'Y'. On reading this you have already undergone a part of the training to become a paleographer, someone who can decipher manuscripts. One tool in the paleographer's toolbox is a mnemonic to remember these Uncial 'retentions': '"Deaf grass" may be "coy",' they mutter to themselves as they pore over an ancient piece of literature. Or, in the letters concerned: 'dheaf ghras' may be 'coy', i.e. an anagram made from those letters 'A', 'D', 'E', 'F', 'G', 'H', 'R', 'S', 'C', 'O' and 'Y'.

So is *Beowulf* a '"deaf grass" may be "coy"' manuscript? No, it's a different blend: it's a manuscript that uses Uncial 'F', 'A', 'D' and 'G'. In paleographers' slang it's a 'FADG' manuscript – with a bit of doing the 's' in both Uncial and Carolingian – even on occasions both in the same word.

At one level, uncovering and describing all this may seem like dusty, scholarly work, conducted in the soft sifty atmosphere of ancient libraries, far removed from reality. Yet, in truth, this is what has revealed the human and material stuff of putting letters on pages, much of which involved what are now lost or rare skills. And if you look at the *Beowulf* manuscript, these are not the only lost things. There are unfamiliar letters sitting there, apparently doing the job that letters do: telling the reader to make a specific shape with his lips, tongue and teeth and a specific effort with his lungs and throat. They are unfamiliar because they have disappeared. So, though this language (according to the way I was taught) was called 'Old English', and though you and I were taught that our alphabet has twenty-six letters, and this 'fact' is a fixed point in our intellectual landscape, over time this matter has been more fluid.

So here are the disappeared letters:

1. THORN

Þþ Þþ

The noise you make when you see this letter could be the first sound of the word 'thorn', or the sound you make for the 'th' in 'this' and 'then'. You'll notice that you make the same movement of the tongue to make the two sounds, but at the outset of 'then' you use your voice-box; at the outset of 'thorn', you don't (in the terminology: this is 'voiced' and 'voiceless'). Incredibly, the letter 'thorn' still hovers, ghostlike, over our high streets, in 'Ye Olde Fishe and Chippe Shoppe'. As ye know, the word 'ye' is a way of writing one of the many different ways people pronounce 'you'. But this 'ye' is not 'You Old Fish and Chip Shop', it's a 'the'. And that's because it's a memory of trying to write one form of the letter 'thorn'. Blame the old 'gothic'-style printers for that, who made the letters 'y' and 'thorn' look almost identical. The French printers didn't have the letter 'thorn' in their box of tricks anyway, and it became common to replace the 'thorn' with a 'y'. Thus 'ye' for 'the'. At some point, when people wanted their signs to look olde, they retained that 'ye' instead of writing 'the'. It's a kind of retro inside retro.

Later, when we get to 'V is for Vikings', we'll read the runes and see that it's even more retro than that.

2. WYNN

The first word in *Beowulf* is one that many translators translate as 'Lo!' but it could be any exclamation to announce that I am about to begin, such as: 'Hey!' or 'Right!' – or even rappers' 'Yo!' Even so, when you hear the sound of it, as deduced by scholars, it sounds like someone with a Geordie accent saying 'What!' rather pedantically by sounding the 'wh' with a blowy sound. Lectures were optional at Oxford in 1966, so I went along to my first lecture on *Beowulf* and, appropriately enough, the first lecture was on the first word in *Beowulf*; a whole hour on the word I might write in modern letters as 'hwaet'. I confess I wasn't gripped. Somehow or another, I just couldn't sustain an interest in 'hwaet' for much longer than about twenty minutes.

I am not going to let this deter me from trying to interest you in two things: the 'w' and 'ae' bits of the word. When you look at the manuscript of *Beowulf* you'll see that these are both disappeared letters or nearly. The 'w' doesn't look anything like a 'w'. It looks more like sawn-off 'p' but difficult though it is to force yourself to say it, the sound we should make when we see it is the 'w' sound at the beginning of 'win', and 'wynn' is what it's called. This is followed by an 'a' and 'e' seemingly stuck together and this is the 'ash', which I'll look at in a moment. The reason why the Old English scribes needed to use a letter for the 'w' sound was because the Roman alphabet that they worked from didn't have a specific letter for that sound, for example the word 'equus', written by the Romans as 'EQVVS'. This was probably pronounced at the time something like 'ekwoose' but, as you can see, the 'w' sound is carried by the first 'V' while the second 'V' is the 'oo' sound. Old English had plenty of 'w' words – the next word in *Beowulf* is a word we still have: 'we' – so the 'wynn' was a useful letter. In the end it became 'double u', but of course should have been, as the French call it, a 'double v'.

3. YOGH

ʒ ʒ

This is the 'yogh' and it asks us to make the sound that most Germans make when they say 'ich', which most Scots people make when they say 'loch', which Welsh people make when they say 'bach', and which some Liverpudlians make when they say 'back'. As the Old English said this kind of sound a good deal, it was very useful to have a letter for it. They had the Roman 'g' which we see in the first line of *Beowulf*. The 'yogh' was used in the 'Middle English' period (late 12th–15th centuries) to represent the 'ch' sound, perhaps as 'g' had other work to do.

Why did it disappear? It seems as if we can blame the French printers again. They weren't very keen on the English people's non-Roman lettering and decided that they would represent that sound with a 'gh'. It reminds me of spelling lessons at school where I wondered why in heaven's name it was 'night', not 'nite'? But what if it was once pronounced 'nichte' with the 'ch' sounding like the 'yogh'? Indeed, it was – in which case, what we should be lamenting is that we lost the 'yogh'. Bring back the 'yogh', I say. Oh no, we don't pronounce it as 'nichte' any more. OK, scrap that suggestion then. As you can see, spelling reform is not easy.

Dumping blame on long-dead French printers is easy and ultimately lazy of me. The truth is that the years between the Norman invasion and, let's say, the 1390s, when Geoffrey Chaucer was writing, are an incredible period of language change for what we call 'English'. In 1066, as William's army defeats Harold's, Old English and Norman French were two different languages almost entirely mutually incomprehensible apart from a cluster of words of Latin origin which had been incorporated into both as part of Christianity. By the 1390s, Chaucer writes his *Canterbury Tales* in what is essentially a 'creole', an elegant amalgamation of aspects of both languages. The core grammar is English with some Scandinavian touches (English acquired 'they', 'their' and 'them' from the Vikings: see 'V is for Vikings'), though some vocabulary ('beauty', 'courage', 'gentle', 'pork'), and some systems of turning one kind of word into another ('morphology'), like adding '-able' on to the end of words, were incorporated from Norman French.

Picturing this is not easy. At the outset, the court and those aristocrats rewarded with land for their endeavours in winning the Battle of Hastings spoke French. However, you can't rule over a people for ever without learning their language. And if you serve masters who speak another language, you start to acquire their language too. After a while, some masters fell on hard times and had to hang out more with servants, and some servants did pretty well and ended up being masters.

Meanwhile, a new class of people emerged, buying and selling to both sides of the class divide ('merchants' – a French word), some working as professionals in the offices of the state or the church: taxmen, customs officials (like Chaucer), spies, clerics, teachers and the like. In this mix of people, the languages also mix. However, it's not an even blend. The most Frenchified ways of speaking and writing English belong in the main to those uses of language which are to do with ruling, making and administering laws, the expression of ideas and religion, and most literature. The least Frenchified ways of speaking and writing belong in the main to those uses of language which are to do with the activities and ideas of the labouring classes and their domestic life, of small-time shopkeepers and lowly officials like sextons. To this day, the language-use of an English building worker and his or her family is likely to contain fewer words of French origin than the language-use of a lawyer and his or her family.

So, my suggestion that French scribes were to 'blame' is unfair. They were not free agents. Ultimately they served their masters, masters who belonged to what I've called the more 'Frenchified' layers of speakers and writers of English. What's more, though scribes in medieval society look as if they're an elite in charge of the language, at most they are guardians of its written form. The evolution of speech is beyond their control. If either by consensus or by decree, when a decision like changing the 'yogh' to 'gh' is made, it is highly unlikely to affect pronunciation. That's being sorted and re-sorted in the jostling encounters of the populace.

4. ASH

Ææ Ææ

So now we're back with the third letter in *Beowulf*, as in 'hwaet'. I'm calling this a 'disappeared' letter but it has disappeared fully only in my lifetime. When I was a child, the books I read usually adopted it for 'mediæval', now usually written as 'medieval'. You might still spot it in the word 'æon' or even 'æther'. However, it was never usually recited as part of the alphabet.

The ash was originally a rune, looking like an 'f' with slanting strokes, but in its Roman form it's a 'ligature', tying together 'a' and 'e'.

5. ETH

Ðð Ðð

This letter, which came into Old English from the Irish scribes, is the voiced or voiceless 'th' as in 'them' and 'thought'. If you want to know how phoneticians describe what you're doing with your tongue to make this sound, it's a 'dental fricative'. (You may find it satisfying to say 'voiceless dental fricative' three times quickly.)

You have to get to line three of the *Beowulf* manuscript to meet 'eth' in what looks like 'huda' which translates as 'how the' – pronounced, it seems, not a million miles off the way some Scots or Geordie people would say 'how the' today: 'hoo tha'. 'Eth' and 'thorn' were interchangeable.

6. INSULAR G

ᵹ ᵹ

This letter crops up twice in consecutive words on the second line of the *Beowulf* manuscript. The words are 'gear dagum' meaning 'former days'. This 'g' is usually called 'insular G' or 'Irish G' because it too came from the Irish scribes. The matter of how it is pronounced is not an easy one, with the experts deciding that, at various times, it can be pronounced as a 'g' as in 'go' or as in 'massage', as a 'ch' as in 'loch', or as a modern 'w', 'x' , or 'y'. In Old English manuscripts you can find it sitting alongside the modern-looking Carolingian 'g' doing the same job but also doing these other jobs. Bit by bit, 'insular G' combined with the 'yogh' and eventually disappeared altogether, though it's used in writing modern Irish.

7. ETHEL

Œ œ

This Latin ligature of 'o' and 'e' survived until the 1960s in words borrowed straight from Latin, like 'fœtus' and 'subpœna'. Originally, it did the job of the double 'ee', the longer form of the short sound made in the word 'kin'. Like 'ash', it didn't make it to recitations of the alphabet. 'Ethel' is the name of the rune that was sounded as 'oe'.

Sometimes, people who talk of lost letters add some symbols devised for syllables and words, the most common of which is the ampersand. I think this is what philosophers would call a category shift. That's to say, though these symbols look like letters being used on the alphabetic principle, they belong in reality to a 'syllabary' – the kind of writing system that the ancient Sumerians used: phonological but with signs representing that language's syllables. So, pedantically and fussily, I'm going to leave the ampersand, the 'that' and the 'eng' to another time, another place.

Also nudging to take part in this parade of letter-ghosts is the famous long 's' of some early print which looks like an 'f' but isn't an 'f' as it has no cross-stroke halfway down its upright, and always indicates an 's' sound, never an 'f' sound, even though the letter 's' was available. (See 'S is for Signs and Sign Systems').

THE STORY OF

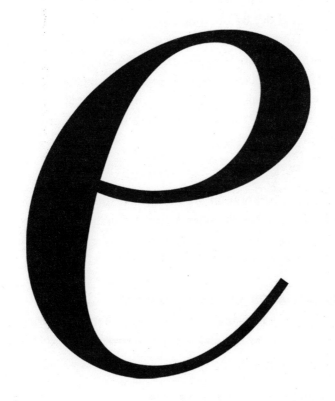

● **'E' STARTS OUT** life 3,800 years ago as a stick man with two arms but only one central leg, a continuation of his body. This is a Semitic letter probably named as 'he' and pronounced 'h'. By the time the Phoenicians get hold of it in 1000 BCE it looks like a reverse form of our 'f' but with two horizontals instead of our one. It's still pronounced 'h'. The first ancient Greeks kept this but later either they or the early Romans flipped it. In around 700 BCE the sign came to indicate the sound 'ee'. The Romans created the serif, thin-thick 'E'.

e

Latin manuscripts from around AD 450 start to show the upright stroke bending into a crescent shape until the top two lines join up. It was this shape that the printers of the 1500s took as the lower-case 'e'.

PRONUNCIATION OF THE LETTER-NAME

The Norman French came to Britain pronouncing it along Etruscan lines as 'ay' and the Great Vowel Shift explains how it became 'ee'.

PRONUNCIATION OF THE LETTER

In almost all counts, 'e' comes out as English's most popular letter and with the rise of emails and e-commerce ('e' for electronic) its future at the top of the charts is assured. It's present in some of the most commonly used words: 'the', 'me', 'he', 'she', 'we', 'they', 'them', 'her', 'hers', 'their', 'theirs', 'here', 'there', 'where', 'some', 'same', 'are', 'be', 'have' and 'were', along with many past tenses (ending in '-ed') and plurals ending in '-es' and '-ies'. As with all English vowels, 'e' is given many jobs to do, very few of which are 100 per cent consistent. We can be sure that in consonant-vowel-consonant formations like 'peg' and 'bet', it will be pronounced with the 'short e' – apart from in New Zealand.

We have several ways of getting it to signify the long 'e' – doubling it in 'feet', adding 'a' in 'seat', putting another kind of 'e' one consonant later as in 'discrete' and 'Pete'. The one-consonant trick used to be called 'the silent e' or even 'the magic e'. This was to 'explain' to children that 'hat' turned to 'hate' by magic. Present-day wisdom tries to show that the 'a' in 'hate' is made by both the 'a' and the 'e' one consonant later.

The history of this represents one of many efforts to make sense of English spelling. Some Old English words had a final 'e' that was sounded as a 'schwa' sound, as with 'name', pronounced as Germans do today 'nah-mer' (but without the 'r' being voiced). However, when 'wif' acquired its 'long i' as we say it today, the spelling reformers of the seventeenth century decided that long vowel sounds, like 'ay', 'ee', 'i' (as in 'I' on its own), 'o' (sounding like 'owe') and 'u' (sounding like 'you'), should have an 'e' on the end of the word to tell readers what to do, thus: 'same', 'Pete', 'wife', 'gnome' and 'plume'. All well and good, but there are some words ending with 'e' where the 'e' doesn't do this kind of work for us: like 'some', 'have', 'shove' or 'gone'. Loan words like 'cafe' (which has mostly dropped its French accent over the 'e') are a rule unto themselves.

Spelling reformers would have us adopting double-vowel letters: one long, one short, then all these complications could be stamped out. It would up the alphabet to thirty-one letters by adding a long 'a', 'e', 'i', 'o' and 'u' but would simplify spelling by miles. If for a moment we imagined that the long vowels were 'aA', 'eE', 'iI', 'oO' and 'uU', we could write, 'MiI wiIf and iI lov eEting a niIc hot meEl at middaA.' NeEt, eh?

The little 'eh?' sound is extremely useful, as it gives us a way of asking questions in different ways depending on the tone of the 'eh?' It can be inviting, contemptuous, rhetorical, all-knowing, wink-winking and so on.

'Eeee' can mean excitement or fear or a mock-version of both. 'Eek' is even more jokey. A Jamaican singer in the 1970s called himself 'Eek-a-mouse'. One girls' skipping song begins: 'Eevy-ivy-over'.

For 'er' see 'R'.

 IS FOR e. e. cummings

In about 1960, my father showed me some poems by e. e. cummings. (Note: not E. E. Cummings.) For a while, I felt dislocated, at a loose end. The point about our conventions of print are that they tell you where you are, without telling you. That simple little duo, the full stop and capital letter, not only tells us of initials, abbreviations and the beginning and end of sentences. Since their invention, they have been part of how we have invented continuous prose. In the history of writing as a whole, they are relative newcomers and their arrival was slow and inconsistent.

Using capital letters to begin things started out as early as the fourth century where they were used at the start of a page. Take a look at the illuminated manuscripts in the great national libraries and you'll see that the scribes must have taken many hours creating these staggeringly ornate openers. By the four-teenth century, many scribes were using capitals to begin sentences, so by the time printing began with Johannes Gutenberg in Germany in the early 1450s, this was the convention that he used too. He seems to have overreached himself a little though.

On his first go, his plan was to typeset everything except the capital letters, leaving a gap for them to be added on the second run-through. Having used black ink first time round, he now fixed the capitals in the frame, changed the ink to red and ran the sheet through for a second time. After a few goes at it, he decided to jack it in and do the capitals by hand. Gutenberg is consistent with this, but it wasn't until the sixteenth century that pretty well all printed material was sticking to the 'sentence must begin with a capital letter' system. Note, it is not grammarians or scholars who are deciding this. It is inky-handed sons of toil.

Gutenberg lived from around 1394 to 1468 and his first work was in Mainz, polishing gems and turning out mass-produced mirrors for pilgrims. His assistant, Peter Schoeffer, a former scribe, is given credit by some for having designed some of the press's letters.

For many years it was thought that Gutenberg created the 'punch matrix' system of printing. Think of a rectangular piece of steel. On one end, the mirror-image of a letter is carved, probably by a highly skilled metal-worker, like a goldsmith. This piece of steel was used as a punch, to make an indentation of the letter in a piece of softer metal, like copper. This is the matrix. To make the 'movable' type (in other words, a metal letter which will be mounted into the printing machine), the printer pours molten metal (an alloy of lead, tin and antimony) into the indentation in the copper matrix.

It was long believed that Gutenberg invented the punch matrix method, but this has been challenged. In 2001, two researchers at Princeton University, Paul Needham and Blaise Agüera y Arcas, studied Gutenberg's type by looking at close-up digital images of individual letters in his Bible, produced around 1455. They found that the letters varied so much in appearance that no two pieces of type could have been cast from the same matrix. In other words, the punch matrix system may not have been what Gutenberg used after all.

Needham and Agüera y Arcas think that Gutenberg may have used an earlier technology to make his type, using moulds of sand. Because these moulds had to be broken to remove the finished piece of type, a new mould had to be used for each individual letter or punctuation sign. This technology had been used in Asia long before Gutenberg's time.

If this is right, then Gutenberg must have had to create thousands of pieces of type. About 300 different sorts were needed for his two-volume, 1,282-page, mechanically printed Bible (which was in Latin), of which he produced 180 copies, including upper-case and lower-case letters, punctuation marks, special characters, and common abbreviations. Each page required approximately 2,600 individual pieces of type.

To digress for a moment: an interesting question to pose here is whether the invention of the practice of using capital letters at the start of sentences helped construct formal prose or whether it's the other way round: that formal prose in its popular printed form adopted capital letters to mark what was already there. Just to be clear, we don't talk to each other in formal prose. A transcript of you in conversation will show you interrupting yourself, tailing off, interrupting others, completing what others say, repeating last words, using many exclamations and single words, far more pronouns, far more colloquial and local dialect forms, and slang connected with your locality, work or leisure activity. This would suggest that we don't think in formal prose either – or at least not for much of the time.

Meanwhile, we call on formal prose to do many things: tell fictional stories, give accounts of events, present arguments, summarize views, pass on news, inform friends of arrangements, make pleas and complaints, give reports of people's behaviour, outline the characters of others, make conclusions for future action and so on. In all these cases and more, the capital letter, in tandem with the full stop, does its work as the marker, separator, segregator, announcer, and initiator of the next thought. The reason why it's hard to learn when we're children, and hard to do when we have to write in a way that is not familiar to us, is that our thoughts really don't flow in sentences. We hold several ideas or several feelings in our heads at the same time, often not similar in length or even in order of importance. Continuous prose – with its capital letters and full stops for sentences – is a way of putting this into a particular kind of order and it's apparent in the very first page of Gutenberg's Bible: Genesis 1.

People around Europe were quickly on to Gutenberg's invention. In 1458, Charles VII of France sent Nicolas Jenson to Mainz to spy on Gutenberg's 'invention of printing with punches and curious characters'. By 1470, Jenson was producing stunningly beautiful printed books in Venice, including some of the first to use 'roman' type in imitation of the kind of lettering you can see today on the Romans' arches and tombstones. His innovation was to create lower-case roman-style letters to match the majuscule letters from the Romans' own time. In his texts, full stops and capital letters reign. Making type and using it to print is highly skilled, laborious and extremely heavy work. Clearly, it got the better of one or two printers in these early days. The great Dutch printer Gheraert Leeu, who produced a book of fables in 1480, ended up being killed by his punch-cutter. It seems to have been a 'labour dispute'.

We know almost nothing about how Gutenberg set his type or printed his Bible (apart from how many pieces he needed to do it), but we do know quite a bit about traditional printing techniques in later years.

Early printers set type by arranging individual pieces of type in a line on a tool known as a composing stick. Think of the 'Scrabble' rack where the letters of type are put into a groove. The person who did this work was known as the 'compositor' and he worked from a manuscript. Letters were sorted into box-shaped divisions in two 'cases', an upper case for the capital letters ('majuscule') and a lower case (placed below the upper one!) for the small ones ('minuscule'). Once each line of type was completed, it was moved off the composing stick onto a board known as a 'galley'. When enough lines of type were stacked above one another to make a page or a column, they were tied together and locked into a frame called a 'chase'.

The chase was placed in a construction called a 'form' which was in turn placed in the bottom portion, or 'bed', of the press. Printers spread ink on the form using tools known as ink-balls. These, balls of wool covered in leather and attached to wooden handles, were first coated in a sticky oil-based ink and were then beaten against the form.

Finally, dampened paper was placed over the inked chase, and, with a hard pull on the press, a heavy plate, or 'platen' was brought down onto the other side of the paper. This pressure caused the raised surfaces of the type to leave behind on the paper their impressions in ink.

Probably picking up from the layout of the Bible into verses, each headed by a capital letter, poetry took the convention of starting each line with capital letters. In 1476, the English printer William Caxton did just this with his edition of Chaucer's *The Canterbury Tales*. By the time I sat face to face for the first time with e. e. cummings' poems I was thoroughly and overwhelmingly tutored in the convention that the sentence is a capital letter plus full stop, and a poem includes that convention but adds on the poetry capital letter. Though this looks neat, it pretty well defies any purpose of logic, other than to help the printer and poet announce that what you are reading is a poem. *Gawain and the Green Knight*, from a hundred years or so earlier, uses a capital only for the beginning of each verse or stanza.

Cummings used letters to represent the accent, dialect, tempo, pulse, compressions, self-interruptions and volume of a speaker. In ways that are now commonplace in poetry, comics, drama and advertising, he played with our upper–lower-case expectations about letters. Cummings got his fair share of scorn, as when the critic Colin Wilson wrote: 'the really serious case against Mr. Cummings's punctuation is that the results which it yields are ugly. His poems on the page are hideous.'

In my late teens, I carried my Penguin *Selected Poems* edition of his poetry around with me in my pocket, hoping that some of its modernity would end up stuck to me. Cummings acquired some of that avant-garde-ish position by hanging out in Paris in the 1920s and 30s. He got the taste of Paris from a spell there in the US Army Ambulance Corps during the First World War, though some letters in which he expressed anti-war sentiments resulted in him being held in a military detention camp for more than three months. At this point in his life, it's fair to say he was an oppositionist in deed, word, page layout and orthography.

When he chose to use the alphabet to represent in poetry non-standard ways of speaking, he was drawing on long-standing traditions of making letters respond to non-standard forms of speech.

He also tried to do something more than simply spell things in different and new ways. He tried to create a pattern on the page with the look of the letters. This business of drawing attention to the shapes of letters, the shapes they can make, the shapes you can pour them into, are all part of the repertoire of what came to be called in the 1950s 'concrete poetry'.

There are many starting points for this way of treating letters, most giving credit to the ancient Greeks who played with the idea of writing poems that fit into the shape of the subject of the poem – wineglasses and the like. The metaphysical Welsh poet George Herbert wrote a religious poem called 'Easter Wings' in the shape of wings (first published in 1633). In the Islamic tradition of the Bismala or Bismilla, for centuries Muslims have been using the visual qualities of the Arabic alphabet, versions of which you can sometimes see hanging from the mirrors of Muslim cab drivers. In Lewis Carroll's *Alice's Adventures in Wonderland* there is the 'long and sad tale' of the mouse, which expresses visually what is being said in the poem. Apollinaire dubbed them 'Calligrammes'.

Concrete poetry has now burgeoned into a worldwide game, with people swapping these visual word and letter plays online, while teachers find that children can quickly adopt and adapt the many different visual tricks. People who like classifying things slot these into categories. I show children that you can write the word 'play' with a loopy 'y' and turn that 'y' into a swing; you can write the word 'look' and put eyes into the 'o's; you can write the word 'zoo' so that the letters are very long and tall, forming bars, then put a speech bubble coming out from between the bars that says, 'Let me out'; you can make the letters of 'bed' make a bed, the letters of 'bridge' make a bridge, and so on.

In the 1960s, concrete poets did something different: they used the visual quality of words and letters being repeated across a page. I remember a German poem which repeated the word for 'apple' in an apple shape, and erasers that erased letters. The Scots poet Edwin Morgan imitated print-outs in order to convey the imagined mechanical speech of a computer with his famous 'Computer's Christmas Carol'. Some poets went even more abstract and used the letters as a painter might use a repeated motif. Sometimes this produces new words, so in German the word 'luz', meaning 'light', when repeated with no spaces starts to look like 'zulu'. This is the visual equivalent of that oral game that children play where they get you to push your fingers through your hair repeating the word 'leaf' – it starts to sound like 'flea'. Just as repetition produces both sound and visual rhythms, you can also create gaps and surprises in anything regular. A gap in a repeated pattern of the word 'silence' becomes a silence.

One continuous line of visual play with letters is the monogram, a miniature concrete poem. My brother's initials are B. R. R. He discovered that he could lay the three letters over each other in a neat fit. All the minor accoutrements of his schooling were covered in this natty monogram: exercise books, rulers, school bag, sports kit . . . One pleasure in monograms is the element of disguise coming from the fact that the letters so intertwine and mingle as to conceal the true identity. Mine are M. W. R. Laying the 'W' over the 'M' gives you an 'M' with a 'V' stuck on the side but there's nowhere pleasing for the 'R' to go. The monogram ends up looking like a box waving for help.

The alphabet developed so that when we write we can represent most of the sounds we make in the order we say them. Monograms can often defy this by not revealing the order in which the letters appear in our names. Old London schools display a monogram using the letters S, B and L. Is it the London School Board or the School Board for London? Either way, it's a memory of a great democratic institution I enjoy being reminded of. (It was the School Board for London.)

It's thought that monograms were invented by the authorities of the cities in ancient Greece, one being found in the city of Archaea combining the letters 'alpha' and 'chi' from as early as 350 BCE. It is Greek letters which provided one of the world's most famous monograms, the so-called 'chi-ro' sign. This is a fine example of how most forms of language we see and hear are a consequence of evolution – a mixture of continuation and variation, arising out of adaptation to the needs of its users. So, the letter 'chi' is the first letter of the Greek word for Christ and 'ro' is the second. Superimpose the one over the other and you get the 'chi-ro' symbol. But all is not quite as it seems, as the symbol pre-dates Christ. That's because the Greek word for 'good' also begins with the letters 'chi' and 'ro', and Greek scribes used to use the 'chi-ro' symbol to indicate that a passage of writing was good or useful or worthy in some way.

The 'chi-ro' symbol was also taken up by King Ptolemy III, who ruled over Egypt from 246 to 222 BCE. It seems as if his press office cunningly arranged for the symbol to be put on coins, so that every time you bought yourself a papyrus you were reminded of how good the king was. Nearly 500 years later, it was the act of the Roman Emperor Constantine taking on the symbol which married 'chi-ro' to Christianity, though its first probable purpose was to help Constantine win wars.

In this long history, declaring yourself with a monogram has been especially popular with the aristocracy and with painters. So we can define ourselves not only with our names. A monogram on your exercise book, embroidered on to your sheets, or tucked away in the corner of your painting is about a kind of self-actualization – making yourself real, making yourself known to the world. What's strange, though, is that we can do this with the letters of a monogram, as these letters aren't doing the usual alphabetic job – suggesting the sounds and

THE STORY OF

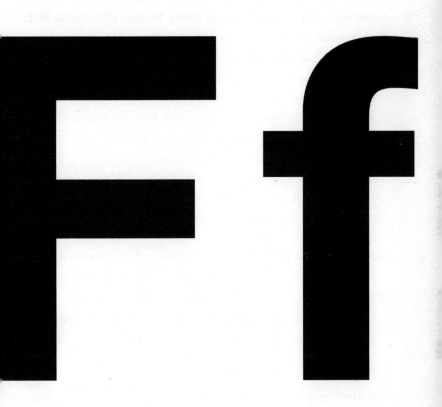

● **THE HISTORY OF** 'F' may seem rather tenuous. It starts out looking like our 'Y', with the name 'waw', indicating a 'w' sound. That's how the Phoenicians had it. The first ancient Greeks had it first as 'wau' then as 'digamma' and tipped the 'Y' over to look like a backward-looking version of our 'F', still indicating the 'w' sound. The Etruscans kept more or less to the same shape and sound but it was flipped to face the other way when the writing ran from left to right (by about 650 BCE). The Romans regularized this way of writing it, making the cross-lines at a firm geometric right angles to the vertical.

The Romans were also responsible for turning the 'w' sound to an 'f' sound. People who write about this change tend to describe this process as an act of great rationality along the lines of saying that the Romans suddenly became aware that (a) they didn't need a 'w' and could give that job to 'u', and (b) they needed a letter to indicate the 'f' sound, so (c) they did. Given that the Romans built Hadrian's Wall in a straight line across hills, this is indeed a possible scenario.

f

As with the letters preceding 'f', the early medieval scribes were responsible for bending the right angles and the early modern printers took that shape for their lower-case 'f'.

PRONUNCIATION OF THE LETTER-NAME

As we know, the name for 'F' doesn't rhyme with the letter-names for 'B', 'C', 'D', 'E', 'G', 'P', 'T', 'V' and the US-pronounced 'Z'. Instead it chimes with 'L', 'M', 'N', 'S'

and 'X', along with 'R' if you're calling these letter-names
vowel sounds plus the letter's value. Lovers of regularity
would have us say 'fee', 'lee', 'mee', 'nee', 'ree' and 'see',
and, for 'X', they'd want something like 'ksee'.
Interestingly, there is something that unites 'F', 'L', 'M', 'N'
and 'S'. They are consonants that can all be pronounced
continuously, though they aren't alone in this (see 'V'). At
one point in Roman times they appear to have had double-
syllable names like 'effay' and 'emmay' and perhaps they
kept their first syllables to make it easy to distinguish when
spelling out words: we say, 'Emmm, not ennnn,' to make
things clear. That's one theory, anyway.

PRONUNCIATION OF THE LETTER

'F' is one of the more consistent letters, telling us to put
our teeth over the top of our lower lip and breathe out.
Some Londoners have found this so pleasing that the sound
that most other speakers of English deliver as the 'th' in
'thorn', they pronounce as 'f'. 'Free' and 'three' are
pronounced identically. I once wrote a silly poem joke that
plays on the names of English football clubs: 'Manchester
United 1 Manchester City lost; Everton nil Arsenal not very
well either . . .' In some schools where I've read it, this has
immediately set off a bout of punning on football club
names and numbers: 'Aldershot 2 Birmingham shot 1'. In
London, one boy said, 'Hang on, sir, I've got an international result here: "Finland 3 Fatland 2".' More intrigu-
ingly, a girl once handed me a story in which she wanted to
represent the speech of her friends. One of them in her
story said, 'Thuck off, Diane!' She was trying to compen-
sate for the fact that she had been told over and over again
to say and write 'three' for when she said 'free'.

We write the voiced form of 'F' as 'V' except in the word 'of'. On the other hand, in German the letter 'V' is pronounced as we pronounce the letter 'F' and the sound we make with 'V' is represented by the letter 'W'. This gives German and British comedians a good deal of stereo-typic scope in their imitations of Brits and Germans respec-tively. English spelling once made no distinction between the 'F' and 'V' sounds, representing them both as 'F'. It was only when the Romance 'V' became sufficiently popular that it pushed the 'F' for voiced 'F' out of the way. 'Love', once spelled with an 'f' but never pronounced 'luff', became 'love'.

'F' combines with all the vowels along with 'r' and 'l' as in 'fry' and 'fly'. 'Ffiona' exists as a Welsh spelling form. Placing a consonant sound in front of the 'f' gives us the great slang word 'bumf' (supposedly short for 'bum fodder'), the un-transliterable acronym 'MILF', the name 'Wilfred', the word 'infant', and the film company 'Agfa'.

'F' gives us the 'F-word' which can't really be a eu-phemism because the moment someone says it, we know the word they're referring to.

Sound-play with 'f' gives us 'fluff', and the word my father used for 'don't fuss' – 'don't faff'. 'Fee-fi-fo-fum . . .' has lasted several centuries. There is also a noise of disbe-lief doing the rounds which sounds something like 'fwof'. Unhelpfully enough, sometimes the 'f' sound can also be written with a 'ph': when we say 'phew' to tell people we're tired or relieved. 'Phwoar' – as the noise to mean, 'You're sexy'.

'For better or for worse' is a double phrase in which each half is linked by the initial 'f' in 'for'.

And there's a far, far better thing . . .

Ff IS FOR FONTS

ONE OF THE pecularities of writing is that you don't usually arrive at thinking about the design of letters until long after you have learned the letters themselves. Most of us learn the letters at school when we are shown a letter as if it is a part of nature: this is a dog, this is a tree, this is the letter 'B'. But of course, the letter 'B' comes in many shapes, sizes and colours and, whether it is handwritten, printed or produced electronically, it shows the mind of its creator. It has been designed. We discover this in stages.

My first encounter with the idea that there was a person hiding behind and in any letters came when we were taught to write according to someone called Marion Richardson. In fact, we were told when I was about seven that we were 'doing Marion Richardson writing'. I'd always been under the impression that my mother met Marion Richardson but since I found that she died two years before my mother started training to be a teacher, I've started to doubt it. Marion Richardson was 'joined-up writing' and it was taught to me as strictly 'no loops'. As with so much of schooling, this was taught as if that's the way the world is and will always be, though I think we were aware that our parents didn't write this way. But then they belonged to a strange and foreign place called 'before the war'.

One of the early doyennes of school handwriting was Margaret Bridges, wife of the poet Robert Bridges. Her letters were tall, thin, curly and loopy, much influenced by William Morris and the Arts and Crafts movement. Competing with this in the world of teacher training was the italic style popularized by 'Dryad Writing Cards'. The third competitor in this was 'print' or not-joined-up writing, first developed in 1919 by the Director of Education for Camarthenshire, David Thomas, in a book called *Handwriting Reform*. From then on, the nation learned how to write according to which side your teacher had taken in these handwriting wars.

Marion Richardson kicked off by weighing in against the 'print' style, which, I have to say, I often use, particularly if I want to do that extreme thing of wanting to read my own writing. She was also against those who made a fetish out of not lifting the pen off the page when doing joined-up writing. She said that a 'pen-lift' wasn't a loss of time – an observation which reveals what really lay at the root of all this agitation about handwriting. For most people, learning to write clearly and quickly would enable them to join the huge army of clerks keeping British industry and the British Empire going. Time is money, speed saves both.

'Very quick writers,' wrote Marion Richardson, 'nearly always write in a series of short spurts, and such writing is usually crisper and stronger than the more flowing hand. There is no point in trailing your pen to the end of a word just for the sake of doing so.'

Her first teaching aids, the Dudley Writing Cards of 1928, look pretty italic to me, and when the *Evening News* wrote about them, they thought the same: 'Zig-Zag Writing, woman invents New System – no Rounded Letters'. They all liked and believed in the idea that a zigzag was the easiest and quickest way to write.

By 1935, Marion Richardson had created the script that I learned in her *Writing and Writing Pattern*s books: no loops, no zigzags, nothing looking like 'print' apart from the letters with tails: 'g', 'p', 'q' and 'y'. She had turned from being doctrinaire about zigzags to being doctrinaire about no zigzags. What turned her? Observation of very young children. She discovered that they found it very hard to master the zigzag, broad-nib, italic approach to writing. To learn how to do Marion Richardson-style writing, teachers took us on a journey of drawing the letters one by one, joined to each other, and on what turned out to be an exotic expedition of drawing patterns. You can see these in her writing guides. At school, if you finished these patterns 'early', you were allowed to colour them in with different-coloured crayons. Is it mean to say that Marion Richardson's own writing wasn't Marion Richardson writing? Well, it wasn't but then she wasn't taught to write according to Marion Richardson principles. Neither were my parents.

My father's writing was small, neat and illegible. I was ten before I could read it. Meanwhile, at teacher training college in the late 1940s my mother had learned Marion Richardson Mark I – the italic. She had several pens, all of which were broad, and if you asked her, she would show us how she could write 'thickthin', varying the up and down strokes, one way thick, the other way thin. This was the style of writing that she taught and even proselytized. I got to feel that italic writing was like tomatoes. It was good for you. And another thing: because she and my father were very ideological people, always doing things from the body of principle and dogma of the Communist Party, there was a time when I thought that italic writing was Communist. It's not.

At the age of seven, I changed schools where they said that we wouldn't do Marion Richardson, we would do 'cursive', and they said wherever we did 'straight up and down' we would do loops. Loops were now OK. Clearly, they fought for the other side in the writing wars and were harking back to Margaret Bridges. This was a brand-new school, and I think the teachers had brand-new-school anxiety which expressed itself in a distressed way of making sure that we got everything right, over and over again. We did handwriting lessons, drawing the letters time after time on a mysterious paper where the lines were doubled up so that you got the tails of your gs, ps, qs and ys exactly right.

This was before the days of smooth-flowing ballpoint pens. The biro was making headway but it was blobby and banned from schools anyway. I've forgotten exactly why biros were banned other than that schools start off banning any new technology to do with writing. So, we had to use what we called 'dip pens' with a wooden shaft, a replaceable metal nib which took on board the ink which sat in an inkwell in the corner of our desks. I was an utterly hopeless dip-pen technician, always taking on too much ink and holding my pen at the wrong angle. Far from being liberated by the arrival of loopy letters, what happened was that the loops nearly all turned out as solid crescents and ellipses.

My parents tried to be helpful and bought me a brown-green mottled fountain pen called a Conway Stuart. In fact, I was so proud of it that I didn't call it a pen, I always called it 'my Conway Stuart'. Fountain pens at that time had a narrow rubber balloon inside, which you filled with ink by first pulling out a little lever on the side, sticking the nib into the ink, then pushing the lever slowly back. This was a help and I found writing easier.

Much more interesting than writing was the fact that both kinds of pens were good for other things. The dip pens were excellent for throwing at the floor in the brand-new school where they stuck in the lino like arrows. The fountain pens were ideal for squirting. The same lever you used for filling the pen could be used to squirt a jet of ink over someone. We were issued with rectangles of blotting paper, highly absorbent pink paper. Instead of writing, you could tear off bits of blotting paper, put them in your mouth, roll up the paper into a blobby ball and then, using your ruler, you could flick it at the wall. Writing on blotting paper, instead of using it for blotting, was also a good way to spend valuable school time, as it was extremely hard to form your letters or look coherent.

I tell this because the making of letters always involves a technology, a set of tools, and these become in one's mind inseparable from the writing itself. When a teacher said, 'Write a story' or your parents said, 'Write a thank-you letter,' you, as a child, would not only be thinking of the language of writing and the shape of the letters, you would also be thinking of this elaborate, fiddly technology of pens and ink and blotting paper. From the time of my Conway Stuart, until the end of university, almost every teacher complained about my handwriting. Looking back at it, I would say that it's not illegible, just very irregular. I couldn't make the writing even, I couldn't make any given letter the same size and the same shape each time I used it.

I had objections too. The cursive capital 'T' we were taught was, I thought, wrong. My moral standpoint on the matter was that the whole point about a real capital 'T' is that the upstroke hits the cross-stroke right bang in the middle. Our cursive 'T' started off with a tiny upstroke, went horizontal and then turned down on the right-hand end-point of the horizontal. That wasn't a 'T', that was a 7. Ridiculous. And the 'Q'. Even More Ridiculous. It was a 2. They said it was a swan. I didn't like what seemed to me an unduly frilly 'r' and I could never stick to the same way of doing an 's' and, nearly sixty years later, still don't. As I have an 's' in my surname, this means that halfway through 'Rosen', my signature varies. My favourite letter was the cursive 'E'. I loved the double curl of it, and the fact that it ended up looking like a mirror of 3.

(A word on the word 'cursive': it sounds like a description of sweary language: 'We enjoyed Billy Connolly but he was a bit cursive . . .' In fact, it means runny. It's an eighteenth-century import from the French 'cursif', which ultimately goes back to the Latin 'currere', meaning to run or to hurry. (When we say that something has 'run its course', we are saying it has 'run its run'.) So cursive writing flows and runs. Technically and pedantically, Marion Richardson writing was also cursive.)

Though I have portrayed my mother as a Script Stalinist, she didn't ever criticize my writing, she didn't ever try to convert me to her Communist italic. My brother, on the other hand, apprenticed himself to her, bought the pens (which were dark green) and became a superb writer of flowing italic, which he drew in indelible deep black ink. Ooooh, it looked so professional.

This is all part of a personal psychology of letters. How you make the letters yourself is part of how you read and write, how you prefer one typeface over another, and ultimately part of who you are. In a classically Freudian way, my writing resembles – some would say, competes – with my father's. Do the letters say to my mother, 'Look at me, I write like your husband'?

Typefaces have their own psychology too. The first one I was asked to 'decode', as some modern literacy experts say, was the writing of the Beacon Readers. 'Here is Old Lob. Here is Farmer Giles. Here is Mrs Cuddy the Cow. Here is Rover the dog.' I promise you that comes from memory. And I can remember the typeface: a thick serif lettering, fairly large on the page. Of course, children will try to make meaning out of writing and symbols all around them, so for me this also meant trying to read the curly red lettering of Kellogg's; the old classic lettering of Golden Syrup; the titles of books and authors' names on my parents' shelves. There were letters on toys, on government-issue ration books, on train stations – even on trains; there were names on cars, on houses, on shops, on roads. All different, all needing 'decoding'. Thirteen years of schooling immersed us in the typefaces of textbooks.

Then they invented Letraset.

Into the world of school magazines, university papers, political leaflets, and underground rags, came sheets of letters which could be lifted off and on to a page by rubbing the backs of the sheets with the corner of a ruler or your nail. The font broke out of centuries-old print shops and into students' flats. As you wrote a heading, you designed it. Everyone knew Helvetica and Gill Sans. What had been a grumpy interview at a print shop with a man in overalls was now a matter of kneeling on the floor of your room, getting into heated arguments about what a particular typeface 'says about us'. The choice was overwhelming. We could fill a single page with five different typefaces in five different point sizes. For the first time, we could choose what kind of print was us. Am I a Times person? Or a Playbill? Are we Cooper Black people? Are these ideas Futura?

I think this changed how most of us thought of the alphabet. Up till then, it was only printers and designers who could move fluidly over the world's print-making judgements and decisions about what letters could or should look like. Now it was within the reach of almost everyone. Only occasionally had we got near to the idea that professional letters could be made. On Baker Street station, just up from the men's toilets near the trains to King's Cross, stood the great lettering machine. On a clock-like dial, you chose a letter, pulled a lever, chose another, pulled again, till you had spelled out your name, or a label. Then you pulled another lever and a thin alloy strip appeared with 'Michael Wayne Rosen' or 'My Room' pressed into it. And there was nothing to stop you writing 'Bum' and bringing it into school. But with Letraset, you could do all this and more. You could now own the alphabet itself. No machine, no man in overalls, no teacher, no book told you what the alphabet looked like.

And that's how it's been ever since. Though now, those hours of thumbnail rubbing seem like the Stone Age. At the top of the screen, as I'm typing this, there is, as you almost certainly know, a small panel with a couple of arrows. I click on it and there are over a hundred fonts. Click on the panel next to it, and it can be regular, oblique, italic, bold. Click on the next panel and it can be tiny or huge. Yet, when I write in Twitter or Facebook or any other chatroom, the design of my alphabet is chosen for me. But when writing a poem, a diary, a blog, a powerpoint presentation, a report – I choose. I could, if I knew how, even design my own.

Before print, those who could write the letters could also appear as if they owned the law and religion. They could turn pages and, by looking at the signs, they could reveal the difference between good and bad, or what could guide you, entertain you, fine you, terrify you, lock you up, or even take your life. If you couldn't read and write, you couldn't own any of this. When print was invented, new kinds of people elbowed their way into taking possession of it: merchants, tradesmen, teachers, artisans. Lords, masters and leaders could create laws; writers could compose stories, plays and poems; master printers alone owned the secret skills to get the writing from hand-drawn script to printed page. Only they, really, knew the letteriness of each letter. That's how it stayed for 500 years, from Gutenberg to Letraset. Of course, there were writers, painters, designers and masons who could design letters but, without a printer, they couldn't distribute what they did.

Now, with our digitized, non-sticky Letraset, up on our computer screens, whiteboards, tablets and phones, the alphabet is a much more mutable, flexible tool. Even as teachers are asked to teach the correct way to write, the designers of machines are allowing people to choose what is the correct way to write. For a lot of the time, this may seem as if it's about layout or design, but behind it all lies the fact that the choice of letter (albeit from a fixed range) doesn't have to be made by someone other than you. The smallest building blocks of the shared written language (i.e. print) are more in your hands now than they have ever been. I suspect that this shift in the materials of how the written language reaches us is at the heart of why the language of writing is changing so fast. I explore this further in 'T is for Txtspk'.

THE STORY OF

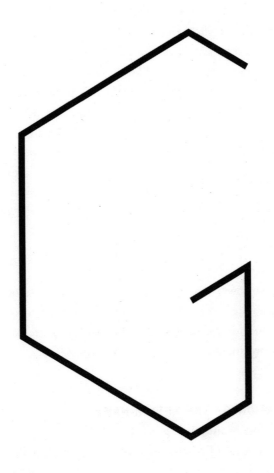

● **THE LETTER-SHAPE** of 'G' derives from the Greek letter 'zeta' – a letter looking like our capital 'I'. It was pronounced 'z' which is how the Romans picked it up from the Etruscans. However, they didn't need a continuous 'zzz' sound in Latin. Around 250 BCE the Romans altered its shape to look more like an 'E' without the middle horizontal stroke and it was at this point that they decided it wasn't a 'zzz' but a 'hard g' as in our word 'gap' or in the Latin word 'agricola' (one of the first words that I learned in Latin which I have put in here for old times' sake). The letter shape then curved to a crescent so that by the time it appears in classic Roman carved inscriptions in the second century AD it has the shape of our serif 'G'.

g AND g

There are two lower-case Gs: two storey and single storey. The two-storey 'g' comes from the French typeface of the 1500s, Garamond; the sans-serif, single-storey 'g' derives from the 'Carolingian minuscule' drawn up by Charlemagne's scribes.

PRONUNCIATION OF THE LETTER-NAME

Because we can pronounce 'g' in three different ways – the 'g' of 'gap', the 'g' of 'courage', and the 'g' that some represent as 'zh', which is one of the pronunciations of the last 'g' of 'garage' – we have to speculate why we say the 'g' of the letter-name as 'jee'. In Latin it was 'gay', early French made it 'jay'. The Great Vowel Shift turned it into 'jee' – which is just as well given that 'j' is pronounced 'jay'! (See 'J' for why 'G' and 'J' didn't kill each other in a fratricidal quarrel.)

PRONUNCIATION OF THE LETTER

The three pronunciations depend on when and how any given word appears in the language and then what changes people work upon it. When I studied Chaucer, we were alerted to the cool way in which he slots into his English a stream of words of French origin. The experts seem to know that words like 'courage' were pronounced at that time as 'coor-ah-zh-er', rather than modern-day 'curridge'. However, as you will have noticed, we don't write it as 'curridge'.

That '-dge' ending is one of the 'trigraphs' we have in English – meaning three letters indicating one sound.

'G' combines at the beginning of words with all the vowels and vowel 'y' as in 'gyre', along with 'r' as in 'grip', and 'l' as in 'glad'. It's the closing letter of one of our most popular word endings, '-ing', which is pronounced as 'hard g' in some parts of Britain, as a soft nasal combined sound in other parts, and not at all in London or in 'old posh' as in 'huntin', shootin' and fishin''. Other ways of putting consonant sounds before 'g' give us 'bulge' and 'sponge'.

We also have several kinds of silent 'g': 'gnat', 'sign', 'fight', 'delight' and even Gs that look as if they should be silent but don't have to be, as in 'gnu'.

'gnat':   owes its 'g' to Old English 'gnaett'.
'sign':   owes its 'g' to Old French 'signe' and before that, Latin 'signum'.
'fight':   owes its 'g' to French scribes rendering the guttural 'ch' sound as 'gh'.

'delight': owes its 'g' to wise but foolish lexicographers
demanding that 'delite' from Old French should
look like 'fight'.

'gnu':   owes its 'g' to German traveller Georg Forster
(1754–1794) giving us 'gnoo' from Dutch 'gnoe',
representing a native southern African word for a
'wildebeast', 'i-gnu'.

However, the main reason for all this is to make children
(and people for whom English is an additional language)
cross, unhappy or both.

We play with the 'g' sounds by saying someone is
'ga-ga'; people used to play with 'gew-gaws'; Gigi was
famous; you can bet on the 'gee-gees' and say 'Golly, gee'
which is probably to do with 'Jesus'. We talk of 'go-getters'
who may or may not have 'get-up-and-go'. Something can
'get my goat' and you can 'give it a go'. Some people used
to sing: 'Ging-gang-goolie-goolie-goolie, ging gang goo . . .'
The best way to offend a ventriloquist is to say, 'Gottle a
geer'. Some people have 'the gift of the gab'.

IS FOR GREEK

As is often said, we owe the Greeks big-time.

First – vowels.

The words 'facetious' and 'abstemious' have something in common: they contain all the vowels in the order in which they appear in the alphabet.

We are taught to say, 'a, e, i, o, u are the vowels' as if this was something correct and significant. However, there are three problems:

1. If there really is something called a vowel sound, then the letter 'y' is an invitation to say at least two: the 'y' in 'lovely' and the 'y' in 'fly'. 'Y' should get an invite to the party.
2. By far the most common vowel sound in spoken English is the 'schwa'. Think how you say the 'a' in the word 'about' in the phrase, 'I'm about six feet tall.' It's time we had a 'schwa' letter. On the basis of the rule that writing changes according to need, one day we will. The phonetic alphabet symbol for it is an upside-down 'e'.
3. We make many more vowel sounds than there are 'vowels'.

We represent vowel sounds by using the 'vowels' singly, in twos, threes and using consonants as well.

The 'schwa' was given its name by one of the Brothers Grimm – Jacob. It's everywhere. Most of the times we say the words 'the' and 'a' we do the 'schwa'. We like the 'schwa'. The 'schwa' is like a giant octopus that spreads over the whole of speech, sucking up thousands of words, replacing 'ay' and 'ee' and 'eye' sounds with the same short noise. It is also one of the reasons why trying to teach reading purely and only according to the sounds that children make is not easy and, some would say, wrong: the 'schwa' does uniformity where the letters do difference. To make the letters sound different, you end up 'stressing' the unstressed words like 'to', 'the' and 'a', enunciating them as 'too', 'thee' and 'ay'. You start to sound stressed.

Vowel sounds are 'open mouth' sounds, where we open the mouth, often leaving the tongue sitting on the floor of the mouth. As we rattle along in speech, we alternate between 'open' sounds and ones where we 'close' the sound, using the back of the throat, tongue, lips or teeth or any of the three in combination with each other. We try to signify these closed sounds with consonant letters, used in ones, twos and threes (e.g. 'f', 'sh', and 'str') and occasionally with a vowel letter to guide us, as with 'occasionally' where the 'si' invites us to make a 'zh' sound.

Similarly (to illustrate point 3 from above), a single vowel letter is not the only way we signify a vowel sound. We can do it with two vowel letters, as with 'ee', 'ou' and 'oa'; with 'split' vowel letters as with the 'i' and 'e' of 'site'; when guided by 'silent' consonant letters as with 'fight'. We also put three vowel letters together in 'beauty' to make a sound very similar to 'you'. If you come from London, as I do, we also make vowel sounds when we see 'ar' in 'bar'. We don't 'stop' the vowel with the consonant letter 'r'. For me, the three letters in 'oar' signify a vowel sound. Again, the way I pronounce the word 'deal' could be represented as something like 'dee-oo' where the 'al' indicates to me when I'm reading out loud that I should say 'oo'.

Vowel letters have quite a lot to do with the Greeks.

One story goes that the Phoenician alphabet was consonants only. Then came the Greeks. They invented vowel letters.

The problems with this story are:

a) the late Phoenicians had already started to invent vowel letters;

b) the Greeks adapted four already existing Phoenician consonant letters to signify the equivalents of 'a', 'e', 'i' and 'o': 'aleph' became 'alpha', 'heth' became 'heta' ('epsilon' was added later), 'yodh' became 'iota', 'ayin' became 'o' (later called 'omicron' and 'omega' – or 'o little' and 'o big'); and

c) they invented one vowel letter, the 'u' ('upsilon').

The ancient Greeks get the credit for inventing everything from democracy to houmous, so maybe they can take this small downgrade in inventiveness.

Now to the Greeks, their letters and the other world of the scientific alphabet. Here's the Greek one:

Αα Alpha	**Ββ** Beta	**Γγ** Gamma
Δδ Delta	**Εε** Epsilon	**Ζζ** Zeta
Ηη Eta	**Θθ** Theta	**Ιι** Iota
Κκ Kappa	**Λλ** Lambda	**Μμ** Mu

Nν Nu	**Ξξ** Xi	**Oo** Omicron
Ππ Pi	**Pρ** Rho	**Σσς** Sigma
Tτ Tau	**Υυ** Upsilon	**Φφ** Phi
Xχ Chi	**Ψψ** Psi	**Ωω** Omega

For hundreds of years, non-Greeks have used the individual letters. At university, my essays were marked with the first four, just as people themselves are categorized in Aldous Huxley's *Brave New World*. The Phi Beta Kappa Society has been celebrating excellence in liberal arts and sciences in the US since 1779. You can't talk about the volume of circles without 'pi', we have 'alpha males', 'gamma rays', 'river deltas', 'not one iota', 'omega-3 fatty acid' and Omega watches. I learned that Jesus was 'alpha and omega'.

Here are the uses of just one of the letters, 'lambda' (both forms). Please recite this at high speed:

a) the von Mangoldt function in number theory
b) the set of logical axioms in the axiomatic method of logical deduction in first-order logic
c) the cosmological constant
d) a type of baryon
e) a diagonal matrix of eigenvalues in linear algebra
f) the permeance of a material in electromagnetism
g) one wavelength of electromagnetic radiation
h) the decay constant in radioactivity
i) function expressions in the lambda calculus
j) a general eigenvalue in linear algebra
k) the expected number of occurrences in a Poisson distribution in probability
l) the arrival rate in queueing theory

m) the average lifetime or rate parameter in an exponential distribution (commonly used across statistics, physics, and engineering)

n) the failure rate in reliability engineering

o) the mean or average value (probability and statistics)

p) the latent heat of fusion

q) the Lagrange multiplier in the mathematical optimization method, known as the shadow price in economics

r) the Lebesgue measure denoting the volume or measure of a Lebesgue measurable set

s) longitude in geodesy

t) linear density

u) ecliptic longitude in astrometry

v) the Liouville function in number theory

w) the Carmichael function in number theory

x) a unit of measure of volume equal to one microlitre (1 μL) or one cubic millimetre (1 mm³)

y) the empty string in formal grammar

To get an idea of how mathematicians, physicists and engineers handle the Greek alphabet in their abstract thinking, here's a line from Goldstone's boson:

$$L = -\frac{1}{2}(\delta^\mu \varnothing^*)\delta_\mu \varnothing + m^2\varnothing^*\varnothing = -\frac{1}{2}(-ive^{-i\theta}\delta^\mu\Theta)(ive^{i\theta}\delta_\mu\Theta) + m^2v^2$$

In 1964, I went to Middlesex Hospital Medical School. This came about as a consequence of a notion that had crossed my mind two years previously which went something like this: 'I enjoyed doing Biology. What a shame I am now going into the sixth form to study English, French and History without doing any Biology.' I shared this notion with my parents who fell on it like an eagle on a lamb. 'We know what you would like to do. You would like to be a doctor. Come and talk to our old doctor friend.' Any resemblance that this story has to stereotypes of Jewish parents longing for their offspring to be doctors, lawyers or accountants is purely coincidental. Or not.

The doctor friend explained that at the Middlesex Medical School, they welcomed people with little or no science background on a course called 'First MB' where they would take you from 0 to 60 mph in Biology, Physics and Chemistry in a year. I could carry on with my English, French and History and then embark on years of science and medical study. So it was, two years later, I came off A-level courses in such things as Chaucer, Conrad, the unification of Italy and Voltaire to be hit by hours of rat dissection, photons and mitochondria. In the Physics lab I met the Greeks. It seemed to me at the time that the Greeks had named or labelled anything of any importance. I don't think I was fully aware at the time that it wasn't the Greeks who did this but the pioneers of scientific discovery. Like Young. And his modulus. Incredibly, we have already met Young in 'A for Alphabet'. It was his work that helped Champollion decipher the Rosetta Stone.

Thomas Young was born into a Quaker family in Somerset in 1773. He learned French, Italian, Hebrew, German, Chaldean, Syriac, Samaritan, Arabic, Persian, Turkish and Amharic. He studied medicine, then moved on to studying Physics in Germany. With the help of an inheritance, he set himself up as a physician in London and became a professor of natural philosophy at the Royal Institution. He established the wave theory of light; he gave his name to 'Young's modulus' which enabled engineers to predict strain. He founded the study of the physiology of the eye and described the change of the curvature of the human lens, astigmatism and the eye's reception of colour. He deduced capillary action (water rising up a capillary), and was the first to define 'energy' in its modern sense. He developed a system for determining children's dosage of medicines and derived a formula for the wave speed of the pulse of blood through arteries. He proposed a universal phonetic language, and introduced the term 'Indo-European languages' by comparing the vocabulary of 400 languages. Shockingly, he wasn't entirely successful in cracking the hieroglyphic code on the Rosetta Stone, though Champollion, as we've seen, credited him with having made great progress by correctly finding the sound value of six of the hieroglyphs. Oh yes, and he also developed 'Young temperament' – a method of tuning musical instruments.

Young was clearly tiresomely brilliant at everything. I discovered while I was studying science, including his modulus, that I wasn't brilliant at science.

What I'm about to say is entirely from memory, so excuse me if I've got it wrong. I'm doing it as a way of testing to see if these important features of the known world have survived for fifty years in my head. We were given some springs. We attached one end to a hook and the other to a weight. The weight pulled on the spring so that it stretched. We measured how far. We attached heavier weights to springs. We drew a graph showing how the springs got longer if the weight was heavier.

Now the next bit gets hazy. Something was 'sigma'. I think it was the relationship between the weight and the length of the spring. I think we were introduced to another variable: the thickness of the spring's wire. As I write this I am desperately hoping that I've got this right and that feeling is reminding me of how I felt doing First MB. It's a sense that there is a world of precision which reveals characteristics of the real world, but I live in a parallel world that is constantly beset with vagueness and indeterminacy. In an entirely illogical way, I have a sense that the precision world is precise because it uses Greek letters. Greek letters name precisely observed features. Calculations can be made using these Greek letters which, in the case of that experiment, will enable engineers to calculate how thick the hawsers need to be on a suspension bridge. The Greekness of the letters is an essential part of how I feel about all this. I can hear my scientific brother talking about 'sigma', 'mu', 'theta' and 'lambda' as entities. When he does Maths he can manipulate them in the precision world.

There's an irony here. Non-Greeks have used Greek letters to be scientifically precise and specific, yet the reason why Greek was chosen – and is still being chosen – is cultural. In Roman times, Greek was the language of teachers, and in art the Romans looked to the Greeks as their progenitors. In the medieval period, the two foundation languages were seen to be Latin and Greek, with Greek being the older. Early scientists were assumed to have a level of education which would include knowing the Greek letters. For the writers of fiction and the namers of new substances or new products, the key issue is connotation – that cloud of associations that runs through and around every word we say and write. Using a Greek letter lends the object, being or character a scientific identity. Because so much modern science is beyond the uninitiated, the association is not only with science but also with mystery, something that only true boffin-heads really know and understand. This is ideal for sci-fi, which likes to bundle up science, mysterious power and uniqueness into a single entity.

'Beta' has been enlisted as an acronym for 'beings of extra-terrestrial origin that are an adversary of the human race', in a video game, an organization in the TV series *The Adventures of the Galaxy Rangers*, and as the 'Beta Quadrant' (part of the universe in *Star Trek*).

Another form of science fiction is written by the people who invent the names and write the blurbs for products like the Sigma make of camera. The manufacturers boast that their product can help you to take 'the perfect image', using standards 'above and beyond industry norms', with lenses analysed by 'ultra-high definition sensors', built with 'premium materials'

So, what you're buying has a founding myth (from 'day one', the puff says, referring to a point in time way back in 1961) and it involves 'perfect' technology, that is beyond the normal, as it is 'ultra' and 'premium'. This manages to invoke both science and mystery. A Greek letter is ideal for this kind of sales push. And the results of a successful sales push could be expressed, I'm sure, with some kind of coefficient of expansion which would beg to be expressed with another Greek letter too.

THE STORY OF

"I BEG YOUR PARDON, MA'AM, BUT I THINK YOU DROPPED THIS?"

- **SEE 'H IS** for H-Aspiration'.

Sound-play with 'h' includes 'high hopes', 'have a happy holiday', 'ho ho ho', 'hooray Henry', the 'whole hog', 'come hell or high water', 'higher and higher', donkeys go 'hee-haw' and rap's precursor was 'hip-hop'. At the beginning of the word 'huge', many speakers make a sound that is different from the sound they make at the beginning of 'hoop'.

 IS FOR H-ASPIRATION

NO OTHER LETTER has such power in dividing people into opposing camps, whether in terms of how the letter is named or in how people pronounce words with the single letter 'h' in them. The way to avoid civil war over these is to accept that what's on offer are 'variants', not rights and wrongs – but then saying this in itself can start wars too. My position is this: we don't have to take instructions or directions on either 'aitch' or 'haitch', we can say 'aitch' *and* 'haitch' and the sun won't fall out of the sky. Saying either or both doesn't harm anyone, doesn't destroy civilization, doesn't cause damage to property. Just as we can write 'judgement' or 'judgment' and the world goes on turning, so we can say 'aitch' or 'haitch'. Even more dangerously and subversively, I'm happy to say that we can 'aspirate' our Hs, or not aspirate them, or indeed pronounce them with or without a 'glottal stop'.

Glossary: 'aspirate' = making a breathing-out sound at the beginning of a word like 'happy'; 'glottal stop' = a speedy little constriction in the throat accompanied by an exhalation – a noise that can be the way some people pronounce 't' or 'h' and is sometimes represented in writing with an apostrophe, as in 'bu'er' (butter), say.

Some people disapprove of glottals and non-aspirated Hs and call them 'lazy'. Clearly, there is nothing lazy about constricting the back of your throat and producing a short, sharp exhalation. Because that particular way of producing sounds has been connected to people deemed to be of low status in society, the attitude that it's undesirable or lazy is nothing more or less than prejudice disguised as judgement.

Concerning the name of the letter itself: several observations are made about who says one rather than the other. More and more young people are saying 'haitch'. The two variants used to follow the religious divide in Northern Ireland – 'aitch' amongst Protestants, 'haitch' amongst Catholics, mostly because that's how it was taught in the separate schools. Most schools in the Republic teach 'haitch'.

The letter-name doesn't have a clear etymology. To fit in regularly with the other letters, we might expect it to be 'hay' or 'hee', but it needs saying: nothing in language is 100 per cent regular. 'H' owes its name to the Normans who came in saying that it was 'hache' or 'ache' – perhaps because they too couldn't decide whether to aspirate the word or not. (If you can pronounce French, you'll know it as 'ush'.) 'Hache' is the origin of the English word 'hatchet' and one theory is that this tool is described by the appearance of the lower-case 'h'. The only other theory knocking around is that 'hache' is derived from a Latin name that was never written down.

(The reason why etymologists can have theories like that is because not everything that the Romans said was written down and of course we have only written Roman, not spoken Roman, to go on. The Latin word for 'horse' is 'equus' but all over Europe where Romance languages are spoken, people have versions of a word for 'horse' that begins with a 'c', has a 'b' or 'v' sound in the middle and an 'l' sound at or towards the end. This suggests that there was a low-status word doing the rounds in Roman times – possibly 'caballus' – but it was so low status it never made it into any piece of writing that has survived.)

Back with 'h': given that the sound we associate with 'h' is so slight (a little out-breath), it'll be no surprise to know that there has been some debate since at least AD 500 whether it was a true letter or not. Letters and sounds are so imprinted into the heads of fluent readers, it's always hard to think round a question like this. We have to remember that when we write we do not indicate all the sounds or variations in sounds that we make. What's more: though we write letters one after the other, the sounds we make blend into each other. Think of 'skew' or 'trial'.

One consequence of using letters is that by themselves letters and combinations of letters cannot indicate variations in stress, rhythm and pitch. We leave it to musical notation to do that. If I were writing dialogue in a novel, and wanted to represent the end-of-phrase down-pitch of a Russian speaking English, or the end-of-phrase up-pitch of a young Australian, American or English person, I have no graphic way of representing that. 'Loan words' sometimes survive in English with a trace of their origins: 'lingerie' is now an English word and the 'in' is usually given some kind of the nasalization that French people use though we have no way of indicating that. In other words, though there is an apparent precision about what sounds letters signify, on close examination it's all much more fluid than that. Most people do not say 'linn-jer-ree'. They say something like 'longzh-er-ee'. Our alphabet can't be that precise, particularly when it comes to loan words like 'lingerie'.

So 1,500 years ago, Latin scholars noticed that what is peculiar about the breathy little sound of 'h' is that it doesn't seem to be very distinct and that it overlaps with the next sound or even 'colours' it. (We might ask ourselves why the 'h' in 'hoot' is pronounced differently from the 'h' in 'hew'?). As Latin evolved in France, people decided to drop saying the 'h' altogether, just as we say 'our' when we mean or read 'hour'. Formal French demands that distinctions are made between the two types of non-pronounced 'h'. Getting it wrong was something that lost us marks in our French conversation exam in 1964. I can't look at a green bean in a French supermarket without pondering on how to say 'les haricots'. In French, this is not a matter of whether or not to make the out-breath sound of 'h'. It's a matter of how you make the sound in front of the 'h'. Is it 'lay urry-co' or 'laze urry-co'? Say the wrong one and you're doomed to ignominy. It's 'lay urry-co'. Say 'laze urry-co' and they'll think you're over-correcting and trying to sound better than you are. Like I said, doomed to ignominy and you won't deserve the beans.

In Britain, there have been centuries of dispute about it. The most up-to-date research suggests that some of the dialects in thirteenth-century England were h-dropping but by the time elocution experts came along in the eighteenth century, they were pointing out what a crime it is. Pause for one particular absurdity in this: when words such as 'horrible', 'habit' and 'harmony' first came into English from French, they weren't pronounced with the 'h' sound. Nor were they originally spelled with an 'h'! Yet, for some, saying ''orrible' is an error. Second absurdity: some 'dropped aitches' are more of a crime than others. ''Appy birthday' is seen as more distinctively cockney, lower class and undesirable than 'could've' which almost all speakers say at some time or another. Of course, when people object to the way other people speak, it rarely has any linguistic logic to it. It is nearly always because of the way that particular linguistic feature is seen to belong to a cluster of social features that are disliked. At times, this can get quite nasty. Over a hundred years ago, an adjective, 'h-less', was in circulation and *The Times* and other polite newspapers used it to refer to such undesirables as 'h-less Socialists' or the nouveau riche who made stacks of money but were still 'h-less'.

If you want to imitate cockney or Jamaican speech, then one way to do it is to leave off the 'h' in some words which are spelled with an 'h', and to add an 'h' to some words that have no initial 'h'. Ted Johns, the tenants' leader on the Isle of Dogs in the East End of London, told me that when he was a boy in the 1930s, the class used to have to do elocution exercises in order to stamp out the 'dropping of Hs'. 'Be honest, humble and humane, hate not even your enemies,' they would chant. 'Even now,' he told me in his fifties, 'I get them muddled and say, "Be honest, 'umble and 'umane, 'ate not heven your hene-mies".' Sticking 'honest' in that exercise was a cruel move, because that's where English has retained the French 'h', as with 'heir' and 'honour', and in US English 'herb' and 'homage' with not a breathy sound within hearshot, I mean earshot. Why couldn't all these French 'h' words have been lumped in with 'ostler' (meaning the man who works in a hostel) and 'arbour' (once 'herbier', the place where they grow grassy stuff)? Answer: because a lot of spelling – especially when it comes to the letter 'h' – does not follow logic.

So 'h' is not only rather a slight sound, but it wobbles about both in print and as it is spoken across different communities. *Poor Letter H, its uses and abuses* was the title of a little book jokily authored by 'the Hon. Henry H', published in 1859. 'You can't pass from Kensington to Mile End Gate,' writes the Hon. Henry, 'without hearing thousands of well-dressed and ill-dressed people, all alike, inflicting the greatest injuries upon these little letters, whose wrongs I have stepped forward to redress.' Henry travels about incognito and tells us that he has spotted people saying ''ock' and ''ouses' when they should be saying 'hock' and 'houses' and others talking of the 'haims' and 'hends' of their projected plans. Henry is pleased to report, however, that things are better in Northumberland, where people get it right.

In the book, the letter 'H' sends a letter to the vowels (to their home in Alphabet Lodge from his home in Holly House, Hertfordshire) and tells them that he has the most 'honourable aspirations'. (That's my favourite gag in the book.) 'I have heard,' says H, 'the little prattling child tell his mamma that he had "'*urt* his '*and*", and to my surprise, his mother did not ask him what he meant.'

Are you picking up an ironic tone here? Was the Hon. Henry H someone having his cake and eating it – pretending to be censorious whilst pointing out some of the absurdities of the objectors?

H goes on to say that he's heard high-class and educated people talk about the 'Hottoman Hempire', and 'hadvocate' causes when they had no right to mention him (i.e. to use the letter 'h' in that context). H has heard a 'shopman' offer a lady a ''andsome hopera dress', and a politician talk of 'hagitate, hagitate, hagitate'. Someone, H claims, once suggested to Rowland Hill, the inventor of the postage stamp, that the letter 'H' be abolished, to which Hill replied: if that happened, it would make him 'ill for the rest of his life'.

In his next letter to the vowels, H lays out a chart of correct pronunciation and there we see that he says the following words should not be aspirated: 'heir', 'honest', 'honour', and 'hour' (as indeed are unaspirated in our speech today), but also 'herb', 'hospital' and 'humble'. All other 'h' words, he says, should be aspirated.

Put plainly then, if I had wanted to talk 'correctly' in 1858, I should have said 'erb', 'ospital' and 'umble'. The 'incorrect' aspiration of those three words somehow became 'correct' aspiration by the time I was being corrected at school in the 1950s. By what strange processes did these transformations take place?

Much less contentiously, 'h' is put to work in a lot of other ways too: think 'ch' and 'sh'. When it combines with 't' to be 'th', it runs into problems with some elocutionists who try to stamp out Londoners and 'Estuary' speakers saying 'free' for 'three' and 'fevver' for 'feather'. My youngest son got so confused by these attempts to match up the 'f' sound to the letter 'f' and only the letter 'f' that he started pronouncing 'f' words with a 'th' sound: 'first' became 'thirst' and 'difficult' became 'dithi-cult'. These 'digraphs' (two-letter combinations of letters) do the same job as many of our single letters: they indicate one clear sound. It used to do similar work in 'wh' as in 'what', making it all breathy, and it used to do work in 'gh' as in 'fight' but the Germanic 'ch' sound slipped away.

The exclamation 'ugh' uses 'gh' to indicate the in-the-throat 'ch' at the end of 'loch'. 'H' appears in 'rh' as in 'rhino' and in 'ph' as in 'phone' to remind knowledgeable people of their Greek origins and to make life hard for children trying to spell correctly. You can spot 'h' digraphs in loan words: 'bh' as in 'bhindi' (okra or ladies' fingers), 'dh' as in 'dhow', 'kh' as in the name 'Khan', 'nh' as in Viet-Minh, and 'zh' as in 'muzhik' (a humble Russian peasant), which my mother used to call me in moments of affection. My favourite, though, is 'yacht' where it pretends to be doing something very useful by doubling up with the 'c' but ends up not doing very much at all. Modern phonics teaching would say that 'ach' in 'yacht' is a way of saying the same sound as 'o' in 'hot'.

You could say that 'H' is not doing a lot when we write 'oh', because 'o' sounds just the same as 'oh'. The other way of looking at that is to say 'oh' as a digraph does the same kind of work as 'o' and 'e' in the 'split digraph' of 'hope' but not the same as the 'oh' in 'John'. If you think this is complicated, don't blame me. You could say that 'H' is doing a lot more than the 'h' in 'oh' when we write 'ah', 'eh' and 'uh' or even 'uh-uh', as, some would say, it indicates how we should pronounce the vowel letter. To the new school of teaching, though, they are all digraphs which indicate vowel sounds in themselves. These are sounds not necessarily indicated by the five vowel letters on their own. Using 'h' to create the digraph 'ah' tells us how to make this particular vowel sound. Ah, the phonetic philosophy of 'h'.

The shape of 'H' has aroused interest because there seems to be a direct lineage from a hieroglyph for a fence, to an old Semitic letter, to Phoenician 'heth', to Greek 'heta', to Etruscan and then to Latin.

Egyptian hieroglyph fence

Old Semitic h

Phoenician heth

Greek heta

Etruscan H

Latin H

Because I played rugby, 'H' is connected in my mind to being unable to kick a ball over it but ultimately the rugby posts too can be traced back to some kind of fence that blokes with nothing else to do would practise kicking inflated pigs' bladders over. It all fits together.

And so to hotels and historians.

The world is full of people laying down the law about the 'correct' choice between linguistic alternatives: is it 'a hotel' or 'an 'otel'; is it 'a historian' or 'an historian'? People try to derive rules from stressed and unstressed syllables, whether 'hotel' is a French loan word, and so should be pronounced 'otel' and so on. If the unstressed syllables rule applied, then we should say 'an hostility' and 'an hysterectomy'. If the loan-word rule applied then we should say, an 'oop-la' at the fair. Once again, I will pull out my logic-of-the-variants argument: all the above are fine. There is no single correct version out of the above. You choose. And once you've chosen, please don't tell someone else that they've got it wrong. We have no academy to rule on these matters and, even if we did, it would have only marginal effect, and wouldn't apply across all English-speaking communities in the world. Just think, if people didn't choose how to pronounce things on the basis of wanting to be understood, then the whole of France, Spain, Portugal, Italy and Romania would be speaking Latin. The people living in those territories made choices on how to speak and ended up speaking languages that are no longer Latin. Pronunciation changes because people make choices to change it.

Talking of Latin, I would like to bring in Catullus here. Gaius Valerius Catullus (84–54 BCE) lived in pre-Imperial times, in the Roman Republic. He came from the 'equestrian' class, which meant high status, high prestige – so high in fact that his parents knew Julius Caesar. Catullus spent most of his adult life in Rome and prominent contemporary Romans appear in his poetry including Cicero, Caesar and Pompey.

One hundred and sixteen of Catullus' poems survive to the present day, thanks to the Italian copyists of the medieval period, the printers of the early modern period and an amazing find in 1896 by William Gardner Hale, the American scholar and expert on the anticipatory subjunctive in Greek and Latin. He found a Latin manuscript from around 1390 of Catullus' poems lying in a 'dusty corner' of the Vatican Library where it had been 'lost' for several hundred years. The manuscript happened to have been catalogued wrongly. There is a good reason why this was done: many of Catullus' poems are highly insulting; some are about love and sex; some are about love and sex between men; and the word 'obscene' has been attached to a good few of them.

Here are the first two lines of Catullus' poem to Arrius:

Chommoda dicebat, si quando commoda vellet
dicere, et insidias Arrius hinsidias.

Without necessarily knowing what this means, you can see in the first line there are the words 'chommoda' and 'commoda' and in the second 'insidias' and 'hinsidias'. Catullus is remarking on the use of our friend 'h'. The lines translate roughly as: 'Arrius says "hopportunity" when he wants to say "opportunity" and "hambush" for "ambush".'

The last two lines of the poem read in Latin as:

Ionios fluctus, postquam illuc Arrius isset,
iam non Ionios esse sed Hionios.

They translate roughly as:

 After Arrius has been with the Ionian waves,
 it's no longer Ionia but Hionia.

Catullus has picked on this feature of Arrius' speech in order
to mock him for a very particular reason: he thinks that Arrius
is trying to sound more Greek than he is. With Greeks hired in
Rome as teachers and scholars, with their ideas and literature
given great esteem by the Romans and being recycled by Roman
scholars, 'trying to sound Greek' was an act of pretension. From
the evidence of Catullus' poem, it seems as if the little out-breath
of 'h' could carry all that significance. In different ways, whether
from its presence, absence or with an alternative sound being
used, it can still bear burdens just as heavy.

 Poor letter 'H'.

THE STORY OF

- **AROUND 1000 BCE**, 'I' was the letter 'yod', meaning the whole of the upper limb, i.e. the arm and the hand as one item or unit. The ancient Semitic, pre-Phoenician form of the letter looked like a backwards 'F' with a tail on the bottom. Perhaps this derives from an arm held aloft with a stylized hand on the end? The sound designated by the letter was the 'y' sound we make at the beginning of 'yod' or, in modern English, at the beginning of, say, 'yes'. The Greeks adopted this letter as 'iota' and it became not much more than a vertical two-jointed squiggle. By 700 BCE it became the vertical straight line we know today. The Romans added the serifs.

i

Charlemagne's scribes gave us the 'minuscule' version around AD 900, a tiny head plus a small downstroke with an upward tail on the bottom – almost a shadow of the early Greek 'iota'. The Italian printers of the 1500s added an accent above the stroke which slowly evolved into the dot. This leaves us with a cluster of words about dots, jots and iotas, all signifying next to nothing and the proverbially pernickety necessity of dotting your i's. Crossing t's can wait till we get to 'T'.

PRONUNCIATION OF THE LETTER-NAME

The Normans pronounced this letter as 'ee' which evolved in the late medieval period into the present-day 'eye' sound. It has occurred to me that the old rhyme, 'Fee-fi-fo-fum . . .', with the first 'Fee' usually pronounced 'fee', holds a memory of this vowel change.

PRONUNCIATION OF THE LETTER

'I' in consonant-vowel-consonant words like 'pin' is 'short', and in combination with an 'e' after the last consonant becomes 'long' as in 'pine'. We use 'i' to combine with the other vowels to give us quite an array of single and double sounds (diphthongs) as in, say, 'daisy', 'dial', 'view', 'pie', 'sleigh', 'sleight', 'quoit', 'riot', 'ruin', 'suit' and 'suite'; and it combines with the letter 'r' to give us 'first', 'fire', 'iron', 'fair', 'coir', 'choir' and 'liar'. We also manage to keep it as a separate sound in words like 'lying' or in loan words like 'naive' and names like 'Eloise'.

In the Roman alphabet there was no 'J'. Many words that we start with a 'j' derive from Latin words that began with an 'i': 'iustitia' (justice), 'Iunius' and 'Iuno' (giving us the month of June). However, we have to remember that at this stage in Roman Italy these words were pronounced with the 'y' sound of the opening sound of 'yes'. This continues in modern Italian. When Latin evolved in the mouths of the Norman French, the 'y' sound became the way we pronounce the 'j' in 'judge' today. So, the Normans arrived making a 'j' sound at the opening of some words (and some syllables) that were written with an initial 'i' (like 'iustice' and 'majestie'). The speakers of Old English had no 'j' sound in their speech.

So, we have to say that amongst the words spoken in Britain, there was a time when the letter 'i' also signified in some circumstances the 'j' sound. When I was ten or eleven, I remember being taken by my parents to a little tower opposite the Houses of Parliament. The Beefeater-like guard pointed at the initials 'I. R.' carved on a door or wall and said, 'I bet you don't know what that "I" stands for,' and I said, 'James? John?' And in that moment my path towards a particular kind of irritating know-all way of life lay clearly ahead of me.

One of the most famous sound-plays with 'i' was in the song about the 'itsy-bitsy, teeny-weeny, yellow polka-dot bikini'. The phrase 'In the beginning' from John 1: 1 is 'i'-heavy and may well help to capture our attention.

In the 1950s, we were told that the plural of 'radius' is 'radii'. If we failed to write this, the skies would open and a large hand would grab hold of us, remove us from the classroom and fling us into a raging furnace.

IS FOR IMPROVISATION

THE ALPHABET OFFERS improvisers two overlapping playgrounds: a place to represent sounds beyond what we think of as words – or indeed any sounds around us, of cars, animals, wind, avalanches; and a place to invent new things you can do with letters. Here's the problem: you want to show someone blowing a raspberry. You don't want to write: 'And then she blew a raspberry at him.' You want to be more immediate, following the timing and chronology of the dialogue. He says, 'I'm too tired to do the washing-up.' And the raspberry is her response. How to do it? Unlike 'moo' or 'burp' or 'crash', there is no consensus on what to do about raspberries. Is it 'thpbpthpt'? Or 'ffpbttphhhftt'? Or 'thhhbbt'? Or 'pppphhffttt'?

This comes together in the world of cartoons where the writers and artists enlarge, shrink, twist, and squeeze letters to do all these things at the same time: represent animal noises, snoring, farting, grunting, cars revving, aliens being threatening and so on. Because the letters are often drawn, not typeset, the letters themselves express the sound. This is obvious to us now, but of course it had to be invented.

Perhaps Aristophanes ought to get some credit here. At the Festival of Dionysius in Athens in 405 BCE, he put on his play *The Frogs*. His frogs have the power of speech but they also make frog noises, which the god finds very annoying. Aristophanes had to use Greek letters to represent frog noises: Βρεκεκεκὲξ κοὰξ κοάξ, which when translated into English comes out something like this: 'Brekekekèx-koàx-koáx'. This is sufficiently on the button for zoologists to have identified them as marsh frogs.

Animal noises become standardized in two ways: in the noise itself and in the official naming of what they do. In British English (because that's what the animals in Britain speak), dogs go 'Woof!' and they bark. Cats say 'Miaow' and they mew. Pigs say 'Oink!' and they grunt. Many British Aristophaneses are responsible for these inventions and of course there are thousands more across the world: in France, ducks are nasal and say 'Coin, coin' (pronounced 'kwang-kwang'); in Turkey, horses' hooves go 'deg-a-dek'; in Italy cockerels say 'Chicchirichí'. When I was a boy, frogs said 'Croak'. Under American influence, they now say 'Ribbit, ribbit', adapted for this joke: 'Why are frogs the most educated animals?' 'Because when you say, "This is a good book," they say, "Read it, read it."'

This is not only about trying to make letters fit animal sounds. It's about trying to fit the sounds in your language to the noise you hear the animals make. The alphabet is not a scientific representation of sounds, it's a cultural one. Take 'ain't'. Following the rule that the apostrophe indicates a missing letter or letters of the alphabet, the longer form should, by analogy, be 'ai not', just as the longer form of 'haven't' is 'have not'. But where people say 'ain't', there isn't an 'ai not' expression hanging about that's been shortened to 'ain't'. It doesn't seem to be a version of any one thing, as it conjugates: 'I ain't, you ain't, she ain't, we ain't, you ain't, they ain't' and it can mean: 'am not', 'is not', 'are not', 'have not' or 'has not'. There is no missing letter: 'ain't' is really a 'negative particle' that could be written 'aint' or 'aynt'. Today's Aristophaneses have decided that the new 'colloquial negative interrogative particle' that has come into everyday speech should be written as 'innit', rather than 'i'n'it'. Representation of sounds has beaten typographical consistency.

Talking of apostrophes marking missing, or so-called missing, letters, George Bernard Shaw was having none of it, calling all apostrophes 'uncouth bacilli'. When I read his play *Candida* for my A-level English exam, it was a shock to see 'dont', and 'cant'. So far, Shaw hasn't won the battle for the abolition of the apostrophe for missing letters, though the apostrophe for possessives is fast losing ground with people's names: e.g. St Johns Road and the like, which brings it more in line with German.

One story of the alphabet is, in a tiny way, a story of how to represent what are thought of as letters (or is it sounds?) that are believed to have gone AWOL. Lewis Carroll (Charles Lutwidge Dodgson) tended to write 'sha'n't' because he felt that the 'll' of 'shall not' was missing. Again, I have to say, these letters are not missing. People make a choice about how to say things and saying 'nt' is not 'leaving out something', it's choosing to say 'nt' because 'nt' does a job for the speaker and for whoever that speaker thinks he or she is speaking to. Since we have admitted into formal prose the writing of 'it's', 'haven't' and the like, we can also say that this choice is also made by a writer choosing a form to do a job for him or her and for whoever that writer thinks he or she is writing for. Lewis Carroll exposed an inconsistency in the rule: an apostrophe marks the missing letter(s) but, interestingly, he wasn't able to get the rest of us to do the same.

So, who decides? Aristophanes had won himself a position of such prestige that he was entitled to invent a transliteration of frog noises and no one could stop him. In 'D is for Disappeared Letters', we saw that the people called 'French scribes' hacked away at the Old English alphabet, replacing letters with 'gh' and the like. The history of spelling could fill a book, but in brief we can say that up until Samuel Johnson's dictionary in 1755, these things were mostly decided by London printers. They owned the presses in the commercial, legal and executive centre of England; they did the printing, they had the power. Dictionaries, in particular the *Oxford Dictionary*, ruled for many years after Johnson, but from the twentieth century onwards, other powers have forced their way in. People who own businesses and those they hire to create their logos, letterheads, product design and advertising copy have made up their own rules.

I spent many hours being taught (and forgetting) how to lay out an address at the top of a letter and on an envelope. Some of this was about punctuation and layout but some of it was also alphabetical. Here is the rule: on an envelope, when writing to a man, you must write after his name, 'Esq.' Millions of young people were taught this for seventy years or so. It was the rule. We were examined on it. Some children were beaten for getting it wrong. Others were rewarded for doing it beautifully. Then it stopped. It wasn't modified. No one said that perhaps it didn't need to be a capital 'E', or that perhaps it would be more logical to use the whole word, 'Esquire'. It just stopped. A piece of alphabetical work just ground to a sudden halt. What was a rule one day stopped being a rule the next. There was now no rule.

This happened because of the stuff going on above the radar. This was due partly to the slow but steady decrease in the use of formal methods of address, and partly to the rise in functionalist minimalism in the business world's typography. Where addresses once slanted to the right, they were now justified to the left margin; where there were commas after numbers and at the end of lines, now there were none; where there were full stops after Mr and Mrs, now there were none. Perhaps there is a document somewhere explaining how much printer's ink and secretaries' time this saved. In truth a justification wouldn't matter much, because this was also about effect: we are a clean, new, efficient outfit; we don't mess about with commas and esquires. When those with the power break the rules, they may get told off by sticklers, but the rule changes anyway.

The capital-letter–full stop/exclamation mark/question-mark rule for sentences and questions doesn't apply to posters. They're mostly present in the Victorian era but by the time of the First World War, the picture is mixed: 'Fling the Kaiser's insult back in his teeth by making the "little" Army BIGGER – you can't make it BRAVER' came out at the same time as: '78 Women and Children were killed and 228 Women and Children were wounded by the German Raiders ENLIST NOW.' By the Second World War these conventions were virtually all gone: 'your BRITAIN fight for it now'. No need for full stops or capital letters on posters had become a new rule.

For centuries, there have been other traditions, acting for a lot of the time below the radar, away from the academy – popular, subversive or avant-garde – and they have experimented with the alphabet too. Sometimes these strands are taken up by the authorities – which is what happened with Second World War posters, which incorporated surrealism, the Arts and Crafts movement and many others.

Once sufficient numbers of people could read, then the poster became a pleasure park for the alphabet, appealing, coaxing, commanding, seducing and cajoling audiences to look, follow, act, laugh, cry as required. The French Revolution was announced on the street in red, white and blue, roman serif print, 'Liberté, Egalité, Fraternité ou la Mort' ('Liberty, equality, fraternity or death'). Political movements and calls to fight in wars more often than not seemed to want their letters to shout and match the muscularity of their images of upright, marching figures.

One way in which the alphabet broke away from its conventions was with the speech bubble. In Europe, the first representations of some kind of speech attached to the speaker's mouth appear on illuminated manuscripts as early as the tenth century. These are usually lines from the Bible in Latin, written on banners ('banderoles') or on scrolls.

It's as if the scribes could not believe that writing could appear on anything other than places where writing was found in real life! The secular world got hold of the technique and started to produce cheap satirical prints, with vernacular speech graphically attached to the speaker. In the sixteenth century, there is an explosion of cheap prints full of asses, monkeys, pigs and owls representing popes, Jews, fools and the rest, most of them with speech scrolls and banners, with mocking and self-mocking words. This was the moment that the alphabet was launched on the people as a whole. Though at home and at church it served to teach the Bible, liturgy and prayers, in the streets it was at work satirizing and telling stories in the cheap 'penny' literature, a tradition that ran from the early 1500s through to the early 1800s. In Britain, in the eighteenth century, the cartoonists and engravers Gilray, Rowlandson and Hogarth filled their pages for a largely middle-class readership, with caricatures of real or imagined contemporary types, and around them huge speech bubbles, jam-packed with seemingly handwritten letters, spewed forth great speeches revealing the characters' stupidity.

Print and image combined has been a fruitful playground for many other alphabet improvisers. We are so familiar with 'kapow', 'vroom', 'blam' and the rest that it's easy to forget that people had to invent the idea that you could accompany actions with the letters of a supposedly related noise next to the image itself. These are the cousins of the many exclamations that people make in comics too: 'Gasp!', 'Blerg!', 'Sigh!', 'Erk!' and, as I remember from my childhood, the noise that the Mekon, ruler of the evil Treens, made when Dan Dare punched his enormous green head: 'Grunkle!'

The person who made it a regular feature was Roy Crane (1901–77), who started a strip called 'Washington Tubbs II', later shortened to 'Wash Tubbs' when he enlarged the strip into a full-page comic adventure series. It was in this format that he invented the new language and lettering we associate with comics: 'bam', 'pow', 'wham', 'ker-splash' and 'lickety-wop' amongst them.

Lettering could be used as a parody. One of the most successful was George Cruikshank's mock banknote, which imitated the curly script of the current banknote. In 1818, Cruikshank had passed by a public hanging and was appalled to see that a woman was being executed for 'passing' a counterfeit banknote. Cruikshank's note displays a row of hanged men and is 'signed' by J. Ketch, the hangman. The popularity of this squib is said to have contributed to the abolition of the death penalty for the passing on of forged notes.

In 'F is for Fonts', I mentioned the effect of Letraset on those of us involved in writing and producing magazines and newspapers in the 1960s, which meant that the alphabet as a tool could be drawn, clipped, mocked, enlarged, shrunk, or reversed in a hundred different ways. Some preferred to use other methods: silkscreen, woodcut, linocut. On the one hand new kinds of Gilray art appeared, the paper seeming to crawl with grotesque images of enlarged bits of the body, guns, bombs, dogs, or army helmets, while, intermingled with it, vast amounts of text, handwritten in capital letters, seemed to typify an era of thousands of new words and new forms of speech which were needed to change the world. On the other hand, another kind of stark, highly economic script appeared, sometimes laid over Matisse-like images of a hand, a factory, a fist, a tank. Matching this, graffiti moved out of toilets on to walls, written at first in chalk or slapped on with white paint. The wittiest plucked the words from one source and adapted them to the new one. 'Beanz Meanz Heinz' was turned by students raging at arbitrary university justice into 'Deanz meanz finez'.

As if that wasn't a big enough bull in the china shop, along came Punk: 'anarChy in The Uk!' was written with real or mocked-up cut-out letters, most of which (apart from the 'U' of 'Uk') looked as if they had been cut out of the posh source, *The Times* newspaper. Cheap fanzines were produced which were made to look as if they were created at the back of a classroom. Some were. When typewriter typefaces had 'dropped' letters, these were hand-drawn back on and printed like that. Photographs of official figures or the singers themselves were drawn on or labelled. Lou Reed's photo appeared as if he had written on his own face. What had been started by Marcel Duchamp and the *Mona Lisa* in the rarefied environment of Parisian art galleries was now being carried forward by anyone who felt like doing it. The alphabet itself was desecrated. No form in which it appeared was safe. There were virtually no places it could not now crop up.

The present era's experimentalists inherit the possibilities created by all these forerunners. Graffiti lettering has turned into a worldwide art form, with the entry of every city, by road or rail, informing us of the presence of 'This Guy', 'LBJay' and a million gangs. The letters sometimes look like squashed fruit – it's the effect of the spray-can technique. When my son died, the day after, a graffito appeared on the concrete wall by the motorway near his home, saying his name. The huge yellow letters folded into each other and the name as a whole looked as if it had been splatted into a syrup. Occasionally, someone has decided to break the pattern and use gigantic stencils, just as I remember a student doing when he sprayed a perfectly matching 'I' in the middle of a giant 'TO LET' sign on the side of a new tower block development.

For the time being, some of the most unusual and experimental work with the alphabet is being done in the 'straight' world of magazines, book covers, children's books and commercial ads. The internet tends to constrain the informal interchange between people to the unchangeable typefaces of Twitter, Facebook, blogs and forums. In children's books, Sara Fanelli and Lauren Child have used the computer to wind words round and through the pictures so that the letters look as if they are part of the action. Oliver Jeffers draws his text as if he's writing as he's thinking it. As you read it, you get the impression that he doesn't know what to do next, which is the state of mind of some of his characters.

Strangely, the world of cartoons, posters, badges and T-shirts has, if anything, got a lot more sober since the explosions of the 1960s and Punk. In 1807, you could get a silver badge with 'WILBERFORCE FOR EVER' engraved on it. The letters of 'FOR EVER' fit snugly into the open arms of a laurel wreath, promising victory to the named person. Now, you can make up your own slogans and gags for badges and T-shirts as much as you like. You can put on cheeky, obscene, subversive, drunken, lascivious messages to your heart's content. You're likely to get them made up in a store that will do it for you from a fixed set of typefaces, in the right order, very neatly and professionally. No matter what they say or mean, they will still look more like 'WILBERFORCE FOR EVER' than Lou Reed's graffiti'd face.

THE STORY OF

● **IN CONTINENTAL EUROPE**, the old Latin 'i' sound was also being pronounced in a variety of other ways, the main three being: hard 'j', soft 'j' ('zh') and the back-of-the-throat 'ch' sound that is used in Spanish. In the 1500s when printing started to standardize spelling, the letter 'j' began to be used. The Spanish were first off as early as the 1470s; French printers adopted it about a hundred years later. In Britain, where speakers retained the Old Norman pronunciation of initial 'i' as 'j', the letter 'j' appeared consistently in print from about 1640.

'J' is the Johnny-come-lately of the alphabet. Indeed, Samuel Johnson, as late as 1755, regarded 'J' as some kind of lower order of letter, referring to it as a variant of 'I'. In the 1950s, in my grammar school, where doodling was an important way to pass the time when lessons got tedious, there was much silent debate (secret passing of notes) as to whether the upper-case 'J' should have a 'hat' on or not.

The shape of the letter derives from scribes putting fancy tails on their 'I's as early as AD 400. The Carolingian scribes of Charlemagne adopted the tail for their upper-case 'I' so by the time the Spanish printers were looking around for a symbol to represent their 'ch' to distinguish it from the 'i' in the middle of words, the old decorated 'i' was waiting for them.

j

The lower-case 'j' seems to have first appeared in the work of French printers in the early 1600s, who adopted the dot as part of its familial relationship to 'i'.

PRONUNCIATION OF THE LETTER-NAME

At the outset, 'J' maintained its bloodline to 'I' and was pronounced 'Jye' to rhyme with 'I'. This poses a small mystery: most of the changes in letter-names are a consequence of the late medieval Great Vowel Shift, but the letter 'J' was created in England after the vowel shift. Perhaps 'jye' and 'jay' were both in usage and reciters of the alphabet preferred to rhyme 'j' with the letter after it, rather than the letter before it.

PRONUNCIATION OF THE LETTER

Thanks to the Normans, this is a consistent consonant in English – 'jam jar', 'jetski', 'jilt', 'joust' and 'January' – nearly always appearing as a first letter. We don't usually combine it with other letters, though one of the spellings of 'genie' used to be 'djinn' and you can spell Norwegian sea-inlets as 'fjord' rather than 'fiord'. The most common sighting of a 'j' on the end of words is in the word and name 'Raj' and I wouldn't have got through university if it wasn't for regular visits to 'The Taj'. We do have other ways of making the 'j' sound – as in 'gorge' and 'bridge' – but these haven't as yet evolved into 'gorj' or 'brij'. I confess there are times when I've texted words like 'frij'.

The words 'jelly', 'gel' and 'jello' mean nearly the same things but not quite. 'Jo-jo' and 'J. J.' crop up a lot and 'J.' or 'Jay' are going through a popular phase for singers' names.

The word 'judge' with its two 'j' sounds has a weighty air about it, so when we say someone is acting as 'judge and jury' we can sound even heavier.

IS FOR JOKES

THESE ARE FOR sharing. It's disastrous to put any kind of commentary on jokes, but I'll make the observation that the alphabet is a source for humour because it is a seemingly obvious bit of knowledge. Alphabetical jokes are really different ways of pointing out that there is an aspect of this that you hadn't thought of. For children, there is an extra twist in that the alphabet remains mysterious until it is so embedded that they've forgotten about it. To release these hidden meanings is comedy magic – like conjuring. Talking of which, how do you turn a rabbi into a furry animal? Give him tea.

The most alphabetical kind of a joke is the 'letter rebus' where some way of saying letters will give you a word or part of a word.

You could write, 'Are you ready?' as 'RUE?' (that is, if the 'E' were coloured red).

2Ys UR, 2Ys UB, ICUR 2Ys 4ME
is: 'Too wise you are, too wise you be, I see you are too wise for me,' though purists write it: 'YYUR YYUB ICUR YY4ME.'

You can also write things to add up like arithmetic:

```
 UR
2  GOOD
2  ME
2  BE
4  GOT
──
10
```

Or: 'You are too good to me to be forgotten.'

Try this in a South African accent:

F.U.N.E.X.? ('Have you any eggs?')
S.I.F.X. ('Yes, I have eggs.')
F.U.N.E.M.? ('Have you any ham?')
S.I.F.M. ('Yes, I have ham.')
I.L.F.M.N.X. ('I'll have ham and eggs.')

A comment on our common biology:

```
IP
UP
we all P,
don't we?
```

People use these letter rebuses as a kind of abbreviation. In the film industry people will write 'sound effects' as 'sound FX' and there are shops in Essex and on the Essex Road called 'SX stores'). Marcel Duchamp's moustached *Mona Lisa* of 1919 has the title: 'L.H.O.O.Q.' Sound that out (in French) and it sounds like 'elle a chaud au cul', meaning 'she has a hot bum', or, in animal terms, 'she is on heat'.

Which US state is this? EEEEEEEEEEC. ('Tennessee'.)

LOV
is 'endless love'.

N N N N N N N
A A A A A A A
C C C C C C C
is '7-up cans'.

R. P. I.
would be a grave error.

UAMAAME
'You amaze me.'

NOPPPLEE
No peas please.

BAYBGGUS
Baby Jesus.

UFOFOL
'You effin' fool' (or '"f" is in the word "fool"').

I met Tiger Woods once and said,
'In your line of work,
UUUAT, don't you?'
And he said, 'Yes.'
('You use a tee.')

These circulate in the playground:

Which 3 letters of the alphabet make everything in the world move?
NRG.

> Old Mother Hubbard
> Went to the cupboard
> To fetch her poor dog a bone
> When she got there
> The cupboard was bare
> so she said:
> O-I-C-U-R-M-T

Which two letters are always jealous?
N-V.

What begins with T, ends with T, and is filled with T?
A teapot.

I'm only close friends with twenty-five letters of the alphabet because I hate U.

Why has the alphabet got only twenty-five letters at Christmas?
[sing] No-el, no-el, no-el, no-e-e-el . . .

Teacher: Millie, give me a sentence starting with 'I'.
Millie: I is . . .
Teacher: No, Millie . . . Always say, 'I am.'
Millie: All right . . . 'I am the ninth letter of the alphabet.'

What do you call a deer with no eyes?
No idea.

What do you call a dead deer with no eyes?
Still no idea.

If you leave alphabet soup on the stove and go out, it could spell disaster.

Why can't pirates learn the alphabet?
They get lost at C.

I can never remember how to get to the end of the alphabet.
I don't know Y.

But I can say the alphabet backwards.
Go on then.
T, E, B, A, H, P, L, A, E, H, T.

But my favourite alphabetical joke of all is a joke alphabet. The cockney alphabet has to be said aloud to get the jokes but it's a good grounding in how to sound like an East Ender of old. There are many versions but these are my favourites, which I offer you now – explanations in brackets.

A for 'orses (hay for horses)
B for mutton (beef or mutton)
C for miles (see for miles)
D for ential (deferential)
E for brick (heave a brick)
F for vessence (effervescence)
G for police (chief o' police)
H for consent (age for consent)
I for lootin' (highfalluting)
J for orange (Jaffa orange)

K for teria (cafeteria)

L for leather (hell for leather)

M for sis (emphasis)

N for a penny in for a pound (in for a penny etc)

O for the wings of a dove

P for relief

Q for a song (cue for a song)

R for mo (half a mo)

S for Williams (Esther Williams – pre-war Hollywood star)

T for 2 ('Tea for Two')

U for mism (euphemism)

V for la France (Vive la France)

W for a quid (double you for a quid)

X for breakfast (eggs for breakfast)

Y for mistress (wife or mistress)

Z for 'is 'at. (his head for his hat)

THE STORY OF

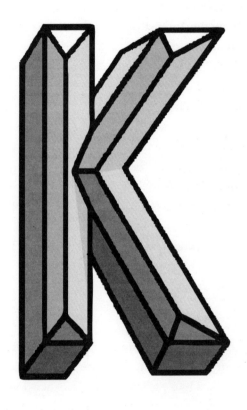

• **'K' STARTS OUT** life as an Egyptian hieroglyph in around 2000 BCE. It looks like an outstretched hand, as seen from the side, with only one finger visible and the thumb laid on top. The ancient Semites took the notion of the hand, showed the palm (minus the thumb) and called it 'kaph', meaning 'palm of the hand' and signifying the sound 'k'. It's a wide 'U' with two unattached strokes within the frame of the 'U'. This sign appears on inscriptions dating from around 1750 BCE.

The Phoenicians turned this into a three-stroke sign, three lines converging on an apex at the base. This was around in 1000 BCE. Two hundred years later, it has rotated to look like the reverse of our 'K' with the downstroke as a diagonal. The ancient Greeks took this as their 'kappa', with the downstroke now in a vertical position, and when their writing moved to be consistently left to right, 'kappa' flipped to resemble our 'k'. The classic Roman inscriptions added the serifs and the thin-thick strokes.

k

The small 'k' derives directly from Charlemagne's scribes in 'Carolingian minuscule' in the ninth century and the typographers of the 1500s picked that up for their lower case. The key difference between lower- and upper-case formations of the letter are that the lower case's upper diagonal stroke doesn't reach the height of the top of the vertical stroke.

PRONUNCIATION OF THE LETTER-NAME

Down through the centuries, the sound 'k', whether attached to a 'c', a 'q' or a 'k', has had the option of being called 'kah', 'koo' or 'kay'. The Etruscans probably called their 'c' 'kah', their 'q' 'koo'. The Normans would have called it 'kah' and this evolved into 'kay'.

PRONUNCIATION OF THE LETTER

Apart from its silences in 'knock', 'know', 'knuckle' and the like, 'k' is a consistent consonant: 'king', 'kind' and 'keen'. The typographers and lexicographers seemed to think it needed bolstering with a 'c' when it ends syllables or words: 'lack', 'pluck', etc, though it can stand alone when it 'makes cakes'. The silent 'k' wasn't always silent and that first sound was more like 'ken' or 'kan'. The Yiddish word for a know-all or clever-dick is a 'knakke' (pronounced 'ken-ucker'), a word that has the double distinction of doing two things we don't usually do in English: pronounce a 'k' in front of the 'n' and double the 'k'. As the word came my way, far too often for comfort, it seems only too familiar. In a Yiddish word sometimes used in the entertainment industry, 'k' combines (in a rare combination for speakers of English) with 'v' to give 'kvetsh', a word that can mean 'whinge' or 'be sick'.

In the 1950s 'k' got a boost from advertisers and brand-namers who decided that we would be more likely to buy something that was 'kumfy', 'kwik' or 'kleen' and cartoon-ists created 'kats' and 'karts'.

For several centuries, any loan words from the rest of the world – especially from the British Empire – carrying a 'k' sound seemed to be transliterated with a 'k', perhaps to avoid the ambiguity of the letter 'c' and the cumbersome deal with 'q' requiring its 'u'. So we have acquired 'kiosks', 'skunks', 'kiwis', 'kung-fu fighters', 'kepis', 'kayaks' and 'polkas'. 'K' does very well in names of Russian and Polish origin – my mother's maiden name was Isakofsky – and the Old Norse 'sk' sound is a 'k' in 'sky', 'skin' and 'skip' but not in 'scum', 'scoot' or 'scar'. Other ways to put consonant sounds before 'k' give us 'silk', 'stink' and 'disk'.

It now exists as a stand-alone initial-word meaning a thousand metrical somethings. People can earn, run or weigh '100k'.

In some parts of the English-speaking world, the 'k sound' gives people an alternative to the 'sh-word' with 'cack', 'cag' and 'cuck', or my mother's version, 'cuckle-berry'. Some people's trousers are 'kecks', and 'kick' is probably onomatopoeic, as is 'click', 'clack', 'cluck' and 'crack'. The 'cuckoo' says 'cuckoo' but who knows why 'cook' is so percussive in sound? In Britain people do the 'hokey-cokey' but in the US they do the 'cokey-cokey'.

IS FOR KOREAN

IN 2004, EIGHT years or so before 'Gangnam Style' became the world's first YouTube video to reach a billion hits, the singer 'Psy' or 'PSY' (real name: Park Jae-Sang) was the subject of linguistic scrutiny. The question winging around the US press was whether Psy had been singing: 'Kill those fucking Yankees who have been torturing Iraqi captives' or did the words say nothing about killing but talked instead of 'foreign barbarian Americans'? Now that he is, by some counts, the world's most popular pop video star, millions more people have got stuck into deciphering the meaning of Psy's lyrics.

Perhaps the Korean language has never aroused as much worldwide interest. All it took was a joker to pretend to be a horse while singing of a district in Seoul. Linguists had been interested in Korean for many years before all this, partly because it is the earliest known successful example of a sudden, conscious, total transformation of a country's writing. This is what's meant by a 'constructed script'. Of course all scripts are constructed by human beings, but the commonest way for that to happen is through incremental evolution, as with the script you're reading now. Throughout the world, though, there are examples of one person or a small group of people devising a script for the local language and for this to become that community's written language. This is what seems to have happened with Korean. The names of the two very similar alphabets of the two Koreas are 'Hangul' – South Korea; 'Choson'gul' – North Korea. What follows concerns Hangul.

For centuries, it wasn't known for certain how the Korean alphabet was created but then in 1940 a crucial document turned up. It was the *Hunmin Jeongong-Eum* (literally *The Correct Sounds for the Instruction of the People*) published first in 1446. It told how an entirely new way of writing the Korean language was invented two or three years earlier by, or under the auspices of, King Sejong. The key passage from this document, roughly translated, goes:

As the speech of this country is different from that of China, this spoken language does not match the Chinese letters. So, even if illiterate people want to communicate in writing, many of them in the end cannot state their concerns. Saddened by this, I have had 28 letters newly made. It is my wish that all the people may easily learn these letters and that this will turn out to be convenient for daily use.

This is a remarkable statement: it expresses a wish that everyone should be literate; that for this to happen, a simplified script is necessary, following which everyone can express what concerns them; and that it saddens the ruler that illiterate people cannot make their condition known. I cannot think of anything in the world of alphabets more humane than that.

What the king and his scribes had invented was more than an alphabet of letters: it was an alphabetic system where what we would regard as letters are combined to fit the sounds of the Korean language. So where we put one letter after another to show sounds that aren't represented by a single letter ('cl' or 'oy', say), in Hangul the letters are amalgamated on the page, forming what we might call syllabic monograms.

Then again, in English we make 't' and 'd' with the same part of the mouth. What differs between the two is what we do with our voice-box. So we might imagine, in a new Korean-style alphabet for English, the unvoiced letter 't' could be voiced by putting, say, another stroke across the 't' to make it sound like 'd'. Now imagine that this is exactly what you do to turn the letter 'f' to 'v', 'p' to 'b', or 's' to 'z'.

The same goes for other pairings, let's say, when elongating vowel sounds: turning the 'i' of 'pin' to the 'ee' of 'sheet', the 'schwa' sound in the middle of 'look' to the longer (and narrower) sound of 'oo' in 'food', or – particularly important for Korean – the addition of a 'y' sound at the beginning of a vowel-sound as we do without an extra letter in 'refuse' and 'huge', but which we mark with the letter 'y' with 'yellow' or with 'i' in 'palliative'. One stroke across a vowel could indicate the addition of the 'y' sound, let's say. The Korean way of running an alphabet, it's said, makes it very simple and easy for new learners. Admirers of Hangul have other reasons to praise it.

Our letters can be traced back eventually to the initial letters of words for images and from there back to pictograms (see 'H is for H-Aspiration' where it's suggested that the letter 'H' owes its shape to a picture of a fence). The only problem with this is that 'fence' doesn't begin with 'h' (though I suppose we could cheat and call it a 'hedge').

How about another system of letter design? You analyse which part of your mouth and throat makes a sound, you create a symbol (a stylized pictogram, if you like) to represent that action, and then you create groups of letters which use that core symbol for the different parts of the mouth and throat. I've already mentioned 't' and 'd' as linked but you could also add 'n' which we make in almost the same place of the mouth with very similar tongue movements. It's just that we 'explode' 't' and 'd' but create a continuous sound with 'n'. So let's have one core symbol for all three – and make it so that it looks something like a tongue meeting the very front of the roof of the mouth just above your front teeth. How about a semicircle to represent the roof of the mouth, a short line down to represent the teeth and, where those two lines meet, draw in a line to represent the tongue: a 'c' balanced on the stroke of an 'i' with a line into where they meet? That'll do for the 't'.

Now, put a stroke somewhere to indicate you've 'voiced' it to make it into a 'd'. You'll need another symbol (a curvy line?) to indicate a continuous sound to turn it into an 'n'. You could repeat the process to create 'p', 'b' and 'm', indicating closed lips, or the sounds of 'k', 'g' and 'ch', indicating the back of the mouth or the entrance to the throat.

In effect, this is what the amazing Hangul letters do.

Because it is all so consciously designed for purpose, people have tried to figure out where it all came from. All the Korean consonants, it's claimed, derive from imitations of the mouth movements needed to make the sound. For vowels, the traditional answer is that they derive from and build on three symbols: •, – and |. Here, • symbolically stands for the (sun in) heaven, – stands for the (flat) earth, and | stands for an (upright) human.

What also remains remarkable with the Korean example is that there was an already existing system of writing which was, to all intents and purposes, overthrown in its entirety – not adapted. This wasn't done because a new power invaded and demanded that the people switch to the new rulers' writing system – as has happened in world history – but because one part of the ruling elite decided that a total change was the only way in which everyone could read and write easily.

Another reason to create an alphabet is because one doesn't exist for that language. Up until the early nineteenth century the Cherokee nation didn't have a writing system. A man who wrote his name as Ssiquoya (English speakers tended to call him George Giss, or George Guess, though nowadays he is called Se-quo-ya) is the only known example of someone from a non-literate people independently creating a working system of writing. Se-quo-ya, who lived from around 1770 to 1840, worked as a silversmith. What's truly remarkable is that he was himself non-literate prior to devising his writing, which is called a 'syllabary' rather than an alphabet because the symbols represent what we would think of as syllables, though Se-quo-ya experimented first with a one-symbol-per-word system.

He started work in around 1809, soon switching from word-symbols to syllables, ending up with eighty-six 'letters', later reduced to eighty-five. He took the letter shapes mostly from a mixture of Roman and Greek letters, though the sounds don't match the Roman and Greek ones. It took him about twelve years to devise, adapting it as he went, and pretty soon after it appeared, it's claimed that most of the Cherokee nation was literate. As a writing system, Se-quo-ya's syllabary is alive and well amongst some 10,000 Cherokee people. Newspapers, books and websites are being written with the syllabary, and there's a readily available keyboard 'cover' to type it with.

Another example of an indigenous inventor of a script is Solomana Kante who, in 1949, invented N'Ko, meaning 'I say' in the Manding languages of West Africa. Kante created this writing system as part of the increase in what the poets Léopold Senghor and Aimé Césaire called 'négritude' – a rising awareness of the need for indigenous African peoples to assert their identity and culture for themselves rather than being written 'for' or 'about' by the colonial powers. I would like to think of Kante's invention as an earlier literal (pun intended) way of 'writing back' too. Today, his script is used in Guinea and Côte d'Ivoire.

Other kinds of invented alphabets are: those introduced by missionaries from outside; technical alphabets such as the International Phonetic Alphabet (IPA) with specific technical purposes (see 'S is for Signs and Sign Systems'); shorthand alphabets invented in order to write more quickly (see 'P is for Pitman'); asemic alphabets (made-up writing with no direct relationship between specific signs and specific meanings); fictional alphabets to fit fictional languages as with Klingon (*Star Trek*), Aurebesh (*Star Wars*), D'ni (Myst computer game) and from the daddy of fictional scripts, J. R. R. Tolkien, who composed at least nine – in chronological order: Tengwar of Rumil or Sarati, Gondolinic Runes, Valmaric, Andyoqenya, Qenyatic, the New English Alphabet, the Goblin Alphabet, Tengwar of Feanor, and the Cirth of Daeron.

When Captain Cook was the first European on the island he called 'Owyhee' in 1778, he and the merchants who followed him were fascinated by the islanders' dialect. American Protestant Missionaries arrived in 1820 determined to learn the language and construct a working alphabet. Initially using twenty-two Western letters, they discovered that the sounds of Hawaiian could be transcribed accurately (and taught much more easily) with just thirteen letters and a special letter to represent the glottal stop crucial to Polynesian dialects – the 'okina'. Their aim was obvious, to convert the islanders to Christianity and (eventually) to translate the Bible into Hawaiian.

Other scripts devised by nineteenth-century Christian missionaries, include Cree, the major language of the Algonquian family
in North America; the Fraser script for writing Lisu, a Tibeto-
Burman language spoken in Yunnan province in China, and in
Burma, India and Thailand; and the Pollard script, devised for
the Ta Hwa Miao people of Yunnan province. They all represent
efforts to use an alphabet to convert people to a new way of
thinking. It also enabled one native wag to write: 'Once we had
the land and they had the Bibles. Now we have the Bibles and
they have the land.'

It is related to the motives behind horn-books, battledores
and primers (as in 'B is for Battledores'). These invented alphabets are like a lever, levering people into close, word-by-word
contact with the texts of a religion. If nothing else, this reminds
us that the religion in question prizes not only the word as a
concept – as John 1: 1 says, 'In the beginning was the word and
the word was with God and the word was God' – but also the
written word. Whether you're Christian or not, it is clear that
many ideas about the meaning, value and purpose of writing
originate in what Christians did with their sacred texts.

The point at which some Christians thought that it was necessary for everyone to read these is not only crucial in the history
of the alphabet and writing but it is also double-edged. On the
one hand, it involved drawing people into a set of ideas that
was considered to be absolute and true and that had to be
obeyed. On the other hand, the idea that everyone should
be able to read it and talk about it was itself dissident: both
authoritarian and subversive at the same time.

You can see this dual nature playing out in the ideas and
practices swirling around in the English Civil War. A newly
literate class overturned what had been thought of as divine
power – the monarchy – and replaced it with a centralized

republican power, while a pamphlet war unleashed ideas about equality of worth and power for the people. As we will see in 'P is for Pitman', the idea persisted that letters and writing can bring about equal status and it's no coincidence that Isaac Pitman's father also adhered to the form of Christianity followed by those who had overthrown the monarchy 150 years earlier.

I think it's probable that today the alphabet and writing are on a cusp. On the one hand, the alphabet is used to encode the language of power: governance, administration, law and business are conducted using the alphabet. Plus ça change. On the other hand, we've invented new ways for that power to be conducted, starting off with radio, film and TV; the storage of voice and imagery on discs, tapes and now digital systems; moving on to voice recognition on computers and smartphones, turning text to speech or speech to text; automatic translation; video conferencing . . . At present, most schooling handles these ways of passing information and ideas between us as ephemeral and trivial, and those who design education become interested in digital media only when the alphabet is used for word processing and surfing the internet for information for essays.

Something odd is going on here. People are governed through the medium of the alphabet *and* through digital media. People are initiated into the alphabet in mostly traditional ways going back hundreds of years. People are initiated into digital media through going to the movies, watching TV, listening to the radio and using their computers. In very short and irregular bursts, with an overwhelming emphasis on alphabetical methods, they are only initiated into digital media in low-status lessons in school. (Schools are not judged or ranked according to test scores in this area.) The idea that schools could spend regular and serious time critically examining digital media, or indeed developing new and creative ways of using them, is thought of as not 'rigorous' enough – even a bit off-the-wall. In recent years, this time has been squeezed by alphabet-based activities. Even the study of the digital alphabet itself – computer-programming languages – is a low-status activity.

Yet in my own work, for most of the time I operate in a dual world of alphabet-digital literacy, flipping between recordings and texts, comparing recordings, using recordings in order to speak without text and so on. YouTube recordings, DVDs, and JPEG voice recordings of speeches, readings and performances pass between me and my employers and producers. I am sent a digital copy of a politician's speech from last week, which I will be discussing live with two academics; I am sent copies of the 1931 German film *Emil and the Detectives* and the 1935 English version so that I can write a short essay for a DVD pack. This partly involves comparing the visual languages of the two films.

I made videos of myself performing my poems. In order to do this I used the alphabet to write the poems, and an autocue to read them. Children watch the videos without reading the poems. People 'grab' the videos on their computers and use software to chop up the videos so that I appear to be saying odd, crazy or obscene things. They use the literacy of computer language (which they don't need to learn) to create a new kind of art form. When the US and the UK decided that it was a good idea to invade Iraq, General Colin Powell used the editing of digital media at the United Nations in order to show the world that this was a necessary and desirable thing to do. He and his colleagues operated in this dual world. Through that dual world he convinced sufficient numbers of people in powerful positions to turn the idea of invasion into a fact. This was high-status digital alphabetical activity.

Inventing and using alphabets (or any other method of encoding ideas, laws, administration, business and feelings) involves the matter of power. The alphabet had exclusive rights on this from ancient Egyptian times up until the invention of radio, film and TV. At that point, the masses couldn't get their hands on the new forms. They were mostly consumers. In the present era, the majority of people can record images, speech and written words and then transmit them locally, regionally or even worldwide. Though the processes involved are owned by large corporations, the access is mostly open. Is this a Korean moment, where people in power have helped create a new 'literacy' so that the people not in power can express themselves? Or is it a Puritan moment, where the people learn the new literacy in order to be initiated into a doctrine – in this case consumerism? Either way, to me it seems suspect and absurd that education – the litmus paper of what a society prioritizes – is not yet about critically examining these questions, whether through investigation and analysis, or through creating similar or alternative forms.

I'll finish this chapter on invented and new writing with a mystery. Consider the Voynich manuscript. It dates from the early years of the fifteenth century, probably comes from northern Italy, and is named after the book dealer who bought it in 1912. It is a beautiful little book, looking like a 'herbal' with pictures of plants, each accompanied by some text. There are scientific pictures and diagrams that look astronomical, pharmacological and biological.

Two problems: the pictures and the text. Most of the plants are fictitious; the meaning of the diagrams is obscure; no one has ever been able to read the writing. The world's greatest codebreakers have been put to work on it, including Enigma specialists, but so far, nothing. Not a dicky bird, as my father would say in rhyming slang.

The alphabet is an invented one, drawing on about the same number of letters as ours, and the language, say the experts, has the feel of a real language. Every mark and combination of marks has been put to the test but so far, as I've said, nothing. Not a jot.

People are coming to the conclusion that the whole thing is an elaborate hoax. The problem is that no one knows why anyone would want to do such a thing. To my mind, it's case closed. Of course it's a hoax. At the height of the Renaissance, with every part of the literate and educated world intent on pushing back the frontiers of knowledge, along comes a joker, an elaborate form of the court jester, who thinks that he can produce a parody of the whole movement. He inverts the idea of discovering and creating knowledge. He creates a pseudo-scientific document, which no one can understand. What's more, no one ever will. He uses writing – the very thing that has evolved to reveal, explain, investigate and communicate wisdom; the very system devised in order to wield power, to encode and enact laws – only to block that process and prevent it happening. It doesn't communicate. It doesn't convey wisdom. It doesn't encode crucial knowledge which will enable someone to exploit resources, or secure great wealth, which in turn will help him to enslave thousands in order to go on exploiting those resources and running governments.

The Voynich manuscript looks as if it could be a handbook for a merchant venturer, someone waiting at court in order to secure monopoly rights to dig valuable stuff out of a bit of land or to collect the fruits of the earth in order to sell them. At the very moment that it looks as if it's doing the job that a book should do, the author doesn't allow it to happen. With one beautifully executed volume, he causes instability and doubt at the heart of the production, ownership and use of knowledge. It's a carefully constructed absurdist joke.

I salute the hoax alphabet of the Voynich manuscript.

THE STORY OF

● **IN ANCIENT SEMITIC** inscriptions from around 1800 BCE, there appears a hook-shaped letter called 'el' meaning 'god'. The Phoenicians straightened out the hook and reversed it, calling it 'lamed' ('lah-medd'), meaning the stick you stuck into cattle to get them going. And you could certainly prod cattle with a stick looking like a 'lamed'. The ancient Greeks took 'lamed', facing in what we would think of as the wrong way round, flipped it over when their writing settled down as running from left to right and by 725 BCE renamed it 'lambda'. Up till Roman times, the bottom stroke tended to run upward at a diagonal, but the Romans turned it into a right angle and in their classic inscriptions added the serifs and the thin-thick strokes.

l

The lower-case 'l' derives from Charlemagne's scribes and their 'Carolingian minuscule' lettering. Across twelve centuries this letter varies from being an austere little single unadorned line to being decorated with various kinds of top or bottom serifs, tails or angled lines. Helvetica, the sans-serif typeface I am using on my word processor, creates some strangely ambiguous-looking words where the capital 'I' is the same as the lower-case 'l', both of which could at first glance look like the number '1'.

PRONUNCIATION OF THE LETTER-NAME

Incredibly, the name has survived from ancient Semitic times but as the sound of the letter can be made continuously, it may have had this long life so that people could point it out clearly: 'I said, "elllll".' In medieval times, in some European languages it was 'ellay'.

In some modern British accents, the final 'l' is more like a closing 'w' sound so the letter for them is pronounced as a very compressed form of 'e-oo-w' (where the 'e' is like 'e' in 'bed'.)

PRONUNCIATION OF THE LETTER

For many speakers of English, this is one of the letters whose pronunciation depends on where in a word or phrase it sits. Very few speakers will pronounce the 'l' at the beginning of 'lake' in the same way as they pronounce the 'l' at the end of 'Paul'. This means that the letter 'l' signifies two very different sounds. This is unmysterious to native speakers and very baffling for some non-natives. Meanwhile, 'milk' and 'film' are pronounced by many with another slightly different sound, so that they tend towards a compressed form of 'mi-ook' and 'fi-oom'. 'Bottle' and 'little', as said by some, can sound to non-natives as if we are saying 'bottoo' and 'littoo'.

Words and syllables can end with a double 'l': 'hall' and 'palliative', though not if there is another consonant following after, as with 'melt' or 'kiln'. In British English you write 'travel, travelled'. In US English you write 'travel, traveled', the rule being that the last syllable of 'travel' is unstressed. This was a 'spelling reform'. It's 'pull, pulling, pulled' but 'pile, piling, piled' because of the 'long vowel' sound before the 'l'.

We have produced a variety of ways in which 'l' combines with other consonants: 'please', 'slow', 'flow', 'glad', 'Kleenex', 'clot' and 'blue'. We can pronounce 'Vladimir' without much difficulty and at one point we could pronounce 'zloty' (Polish money). Rather mysteriously, Alfred Noyes wrote in his poem 'The Highwayman' that horses made the sound of 'tlot' as they came along the road. Other ways to put consonant sounds before 'l' give us 'thistle', 'dazzle', 'ruffle', 'rabble', 'tickle' and 'ripple'.

In Welsh, there is the double 'l' sound which is made by making the tongue take up a similar position adopted by a native English speaker for saying an initial 'l' but then instead of voicing, you blow air round the tongue. As the places and people of Wales are frequently spoken of as part of Britain, then this 'll' sound has to be counted as one of the sounds of British English.

Word-play with 'l' gives us 'lull', 'lullaby', 'la-la land', 'doo-lally', 'lolly', the 'Lilo' bed, the way to sing a tune – 'la, la, la, la . . .', 'Lola', 'Lily', 'Lulu', 'Tallullah', 'Hallelujah', 'lily-livered', 'Lilibullero', 'loll', 'lollop', the Scots' word 'peely-wally', 'willy-nilly', 'silly-billy', 'hill-billy', the Australian word for a tiny tornado – a 'willy-willy', Sir Toby Belch's exclamation – 'Tilly-vally, lady!', the children's literature character 'Milly-Molly-Mandy', 'pell-mell', 'dilly-dally', 'jelly-belly', 'mellow-yellow', 'live and let live', 'let sleeping dogs lie,' 'Polly-wolly-doodle all the day . . .'

'He who laughs last laughs longest' or 'he had the last laugh'.

 IS FOR LSD

As CHILDREN WE are taught our letters and then taught how to stretch them into longer and longer words ('A is for Ant and Apple and Aardvark' and so on). As adults we go back the other way and scatter our speech with letters to represent the long words and complicated things we can't be bothered to say. Much initials-use is a kind of slang. They are popular, colloquial ways of speaking and writing, sometimes as a private lingo, sometimes as a way of marking that you and your listeners are in the know, sometimes as a way of excluding those who don't. Of course, some are so widespread they have moved into the mainstream – so much so that saying the full term sounds pedantic. There are very few occasions in Britain when you would say 'Automobile Association', other than to distinguish it from Alcoholics Anonymous – 'I broke down on the M25 and called the AA' isn't likely to mean that I had had a panic attack and wanted a drink. As with a lot of use of initials, a subtle dance of the 'articles' ('a', 'the', or neither) is going on here. 'The AA' is cars, 'AA' is alcohol.

Initials represent objects in an adult world not to be mentioned in front of the kids. Swear words are defused and drugs are coded when reduced to single letters. The first few times I heard people talking about LSD in the 1960s, I thought that they had simply switched from using the contemporary slang for money – 'bread', 'dough', 'readies', 'dosh' – to £sd. I knew several people at that time who transformed their speech overnight and I often felt I was off the pace. I was eventually told that LSD was lysergic acid diethylamide, a name that I can never remember and had to look up to write here. Those initials work: they do their job so well that I don't have the ability or the will to maintain their link to words.

Invented as a cure for depression, LSD was once trialled as a weapon. My last job as a BBC trainee involved looking through film archives of anything or anyone connected to chemical warfare. I came across a black-and-white clip that showed a US soldier on an assault course, being given LSD by his officers, repeating the assault course and then being interviewed. It was distressing to watch because the soldier started flopping about, stumbling and mumbling. When he was interviewed at the end, he talked gobbledegook. The clip was used in a programme called *The Toxic Club*, but – to use another set of famous initials – the US government got in touch and asked for it be removed for the next showing. Talking about LSD being administered to US soldiers was too toxic.

The £sd symbol had become so detached from its roots that I don't think I ever knew what the letters stood for. I'm not even sure that I thought '£' was a letter. I thought of it more as a magic sign, symbolic of loads of dosh. Because we're not in the Eurozone, the symbol survives, a strange desiccated version of the curly upper-case 'L' it once was. The letters stand for 'librae', 'solidi' and 'denarii', and the reason why the coinage bore Latin names is down to Charlemagne who decreed it as part of his role as the Holy Roman Emperor. As one wag said, the Holy Roman Empire wasn't holy, it wasn't Roman and it wasn't an Empire but Charlemagne still seemed to have acquired enough power for people to do what he told them to to do.

That's why my daily arithmetic lessons derived from the fact that according to Charlemagne – as decreed in around AD 793 – twelve denarii equalled one solidus, and 240 denarii equalled one libra. With the £ sign being, to my mind, magic, and the 's' standing for, as I thought, 'shilling', my problem was with the 'd'. How could it mean penny? 'P' for penny, surely. It was an adult screw-up, I decided, but went along with it. We saw '8d'; we said 'eightpence'. I never heard anyone saying, '8D'. But then no one said 'denarii', 'solidus' and 'libra'. Money in Britain was once mostly in the hands of Latin- and French-speaking people yet the lower-class names won out: penny, shilling and pound. For a while, it must have been a deal: we'll have the names, you can have the initials; just as we rear 'hogs', you eat 'pork'.

The Romans were keen initializers and abbreviaters. All Roman numerals are represented by letters. 'IC' was 'Julius Caesar' (pronounced 'Yoolius' with the 'Y' sound at the beginning indicated by the letter 'I'). Roman memorial stones are covered in initials and through the long use of Latin there are hundreds of examples.

Today, Latin phrases pass about between us obscured behind initials. 'AD' is 'anno domini'; 'pd' is 'per diem'; 'PS' is 'post scriptum'; 'a.m.' is 'ante meridiem'; 'BA' is 'baccalaureus artium'; 'e.g.' is 'exempli gratia'; 'i.e.' is 'id est'; 'NB' is 'nota bene'; 'RIP' is 'requiescat in pace' and so on, ad infinitum or ad nauseam. The Periodic Table, learned by heart and recited by millions of secondary-school students, is made up of Latin initials. Important for old Hollywood movies: 'SPQR' on the Roman banners is

'Senatus populusque Romanus', with 'que' – meaning 'and' – on the end of 'populusque' getting full status as 'Q'. It means 'the Senate and People of Rome', which doesn't sound terribly militaristic.

For Christians, the initials 'INRI' derive from 'Iesus Nazarenus Rex Iudaeorum' ('Jesus the Nazarene, King of the Jews'). John 19: 20 states that this was written in three languages – Hebrew, Latin and Greek – and was put on the cross of Jesus. Quite who thought that Jesus really was the King of the Jews is another matter. My father once tried to convince me that 'INRI' was the cockney version of 'Henry'.

Initial letters as intricate, decorated, emblematic images in themselves appear on illuminated manuscripts throughout the medieval period. When we look at them hundreds of years later, the scribes' illumination seems at least in part about making the letters themselves sacred. Surrounding them with saints, animals, mythical creatures and ornate designs and patterns puts the letter on a pedestal. I don't suppose this is the immediate intention; the manuscript or volume as a whole is what is sacred, and the initial letters are the means to producing that end.

Today illuminated manuscripts are usually in glass cases in museums or churches with two pages on show, where we see perhaps only one or two illuminated letters. As a result, a solo letter takes on a special importance, displaying (showing off, perhaps) a bewildering range of skills. Was there something special about the beginning of a page or paragraph? Was there a particular importance in the idea of being an initial? In the historical root of writing, initializing names of things was one of the ways in which writing developed. Mythically and religiously, the idea of first and last, alpha and omega, has a particular importance. Jesus's words, as reported in the Gospels, have several key references to beginnings and ends and John famously starts: 'In the beginning was the word.' The gilded manuscripts appear to be saying, 'In the beginning was the illuminated initial.'

In Shakespeare's *Twelfth Night*, Malvolio the Puritan is mocked for his stereotypically Puritan attempts at interpreting letters and handwriting. He comes across a letter which he thinks has come from his employer, the gentlewoman Olivia, but the letter is a forgery placed there by the group who want to pull him down a peg. First, like Thomas Phelippes (see 'C is for Ciphers') he tries to crack the code of the letters 'M', 'A', 'O' and 'I', which he assumes represent his own name, Malvolio. He reckons he can spot Olivia's distinctive hand as he reads out the letters 'C', 'U' and 'T' to which he adds: 'and thus makes she her great P's'. Shakespeare's audience laughed as the Puritan is made to speak of things that he would normally repress. Puritans believed that talking out loud of the body and its functions caused lust, lasciviousness, lechery, debauchery and idleness.

Shakespeare's sonnets are dedicated to 'Mr. W. H.', a person who has never been identified. This may be a joke, a cunning disguise or a misprint. At the bottom of the page there are two more initials, 'T. T.', which correspond to the printer's name, Thomas Thorpe. All this has given rise to Initials Frenzy. Thousands of scholars, writers and celebrities have pored over the dedication, offering reasons, stratagems, jokes and candidates. These last include a string of people whose initials are W. H. (of course), also an H. W., and even a W. S., namely Shakespeare himself. For those who prefer to see Shakespeare devoting himself to aristocrats, there is the problem of that irritating 'Mr' slotted in before the 'W. H.' which rather suggests that W. H. was a commoner like Shakespeare himself. The idea of a commoner writing sonnets to another commoner or being grateful to another commoner, as the dedication suggests, is a step too far for some.

The modernist poet, Hilda Doolittle, published her work as 'H. D.' and, around the same time, George William Russell published his poems as 'Æ' (sometimes written as 'AE' or 'A. E.'). This seems to have been less a matter of disguise, more a matter of modernist minimalism.

More usually, the role of initials for writers, politicians and people in the public eye is as decoration of the surname. In showbiz, the clash of cymbals or a quick chord is called a 'sting'. Perhaps initials in the following names are a verbal sting: H. G. Wells, N. F. Simpson, W. H. Auden, C. S. Lewis, J. K. Rowling, P. J. Harvey and let's have an extra sting for J. R. R. Tolkien. Americans have been fond of slotting in a middle initial – Franklin D. Roosevelt, Dwight D. Eisenhower. George W. Bush's middle initial became so important that it became him: 'Dubya', thereby distinguishing him from his father, George Bush, but, unfortunately for him, suggesting a kind of baby-talk.

Part of the complex systems of naming that rap stars use is a set of symbolic and playful initials: P-Diddy, Run-DMC, Ice-T, LL Cool J., Jay-Cool, Jay-Z and thousands of others. Eminem (Marshall Bruce Mather III) plays with at least two jokes with his name: it's a spelling out of a version of M. M. (his own initials); and M&Ms are iconic sweets in the US. If there is one thing that Eminem most definitely is not, it is some kind of colourful candy. Of course writing out 'Eminem' is a playful disruption of the usual way of writing initials, anyway. His use of the 'mf profanity' in his lyrics won him the nickname 'Eminef'. His constant writing and singing about relatives and friends has won him something else: a raft of law suits where he can't pretend that he's not Eminem.

Some people suffer from another kind of initial-itis and their career or status calls on them to display their qualifications, awards and membership of professional associations, most of which come as initials, with the occasional non-initial abbreviation thrown in. Occasionally these are bogus or meaningless. One of the oldest worthless ones is 'MA Oxon'. It sounds as if it's a Master of Arts, a high honour from my old university, Oxford, whereas it is no higher than a BA. You just potter back to university a few years after collecting your BA and buy yourself an MA.

If you or I list the initials we've known and used in our lives, they act as markers of who we are. You could tell the history of your life through the initials of: your own name, the names of others in your family, your schools and colleges, items of technology that came into public view during your life, your qualifications, the associations, clubs and political parties that you've belonged to, the names of authors, performers, musicians you've followed, your diseases and medicines.

Highlights of mine include the fact that my brother's initials B. R. coincided with the 'BR' of British Railways, which meant that the antimacassars hanging over the seats in first-class train carriages were a temptation for him. Our uncle was in on the early days of colour TV technology and was invited to the House of Lords to demonstrate the latest advances. It seems that he and his colleagues were left alone in a room to wait for their lordships to see them, and the sight of a heavy-duty ashtray with the insignia 'GR' was a lure for one of them – obviously not for my uncle. However, it somehow or another came into our possession and it sits on the desk next to me as I write now. It was a few years before I discovered that 'GR' wasn't 'grrrr' but 'Georgivs Rex'.

When I first went to work at the BBC, it hadn't yet become 'the Beeb' – an Eminem-type/Dubya-type transformation of initials into a pseudo-word. Every management position benefited from a set of distinctive initials. 'HST' or 'head of staff training' is the one I remember the best, partly because he was technically my boss but also because of the most stressful sign I know: 'HST STOP', which you see on the platform at Euston Station. It means 'High-Speed Train, stop,' which I think a driver ought to know when to do without having to read a sign telling him to.

My first stint at the BBC coincided with Mao Tse-tung's switch to mass induction into the wisdom of his *Little Red Book*, and we saw on TV millions of Chinese people using the book to salute the Great Helmsman, whilst chorusing 'Little Red Book'. As part of BBC staff training, we were issued with a training book, and for some reason one of my co-trainees stood up in class and saluted our own great helmsman with it, calling out: 'HST! HST! HST!' He went on to become an eminent TV producer, novelist, playwright and screenwriter. I'm sure that moment was seminal for him.

A moment in left-wing political history turned what I knew as 'the Party' or 'the Communist Party' into 'the CP' at about the same time that a flowering of initialled parties and journals appeared, disappeared and went on appearing: SLL, IS, CPB (M-L), WRP, RCP, SWP. This goes back to the time of Karl Marx and William Morris and organizations such as the Socialist League and its successor the SDF, the Social Democratic Federation, which my father's grandfather belonged to. No matter how seriously I and others might take this, the constant juggling of the words 'socialist', 'communist', 'workers', 'labour', 'league', 'party', 'federation', 'revolutionary' and the like has proved to be a fruitful source of comedy. There was an opportunistic echo of this in the naming of the Nationalsozialistische Deutsche Arbeiterpartei. 'Nazi' is nothing to do with initials, though (or with workers and socialists), as 'Nazi' comes from lifting the first two syllables of the phrase as pronounced in German. NSDAP is the initialization.

Medicine is an example of how the professions proliferate initials. In education, we have the names of institutions, qualifications, reports, punishments, subjects, teaching methods and more. These change. I was taught 'PT' and 'RI' ('Physical Training' and 'Religious Instruction'). These are now 'PE' and 'RS' ('Physical Education' and 'Religious Studies'). 'BFL' can be 'Behaviour for Learning'; 'C3' can be a detention because it's the third level of punishment or 'consequence'. The National Literacy Strategy, or the NLS, ruled over education with an iron hand for about ten years until it was suddenly abolished. Likewise the Language in the National Curriculum Project, or LINC. Perhaps being given initials in education is a stipulation that has its own built-in death sentence.

Doctors are said to produce an underground language of initials to describe patients behind their backs. Have they really marked patients' notes with 'NFN' ('normal for Norfolk'), 'FLK' ('funny-looking kid'), or 'GROLIES' ('*Guardian* reader of low intelligence in ethnic skirt')? Are these true or apocryphal? There is also 'LOBNH' ('lights on but nobody home'); 'CNS-QNS' ('central nervous system – quantity not sufficient'); and 'PP' ('pumpkin positive') meaning that if you shine a pen-light in the patient's mouth, their head lights up as there is no brain.

As children we played with the initials 'PLP'. We would lean on someone and say, 'Are you a PLP?' If the person said, 'No,' we would say, 'Then you're not a proper living person.' If they then said, 'Yes,' we would say, 'Then you're a public leaning post.' I hear, 'It needs a bit of TLC' ('tender loving care') and 'But are there any PLUs?'('people like us'). As long as initial-clusters like these are code, they work as includers-excluders but once they've been decoded and appear in stand-up comedians' routines, they are damaged goods.

Initials are also useful for graffiti – they're quick to paint, and are instantly recognizable, performing a similar function to dogs' wee on walls. The geography of football and political affiliation can be charted in the initials drawn on the country's public surfaces. The rebus of a heart or the phrase '= scum' have proved to be the most useful additions. It's said that the number of times you graffiti your initials on walls is in inverse proportion to the amount of power you think you have.

If there was a prize for surprising me with a use of initials, I would have awarded it to J. D. Salinger for having his characters say, 'Jesus H. Christ'. At the time, I thought that he invented it as an irreverent absurdist joke, but not so. Mark Twain was on to it long before, claiming that one of his pals in the print shop where he was working was ticked off for writing 'J. C.', for 'diminishing' Jesus Christ's name. He replaced it with 'Jesus H. Christ', thereby aggrandizing it, presumably. People have been on the hunt for the word behind the 'H' with about as much chance of success as working out who 'W. H.' is – unless it was solved when the film *Jesus Henry Christ* came out in 2012.

Christianity was an underground religion for a couple of centuries. The early Christians used a visual acronymic pun to show those in the know where they were. They used the symbol of a fish, which possibly worked like this:

The Greek word for 'fish' is 'ἰχθύς' ('ichthys') or 'ΙΧΘΥΣ'.

Ι ('I', 'Iota'): ΙΗΣΟΥΣ ('Iêsoûs') is 'Jesus'.
Χ ('KH', 'Khi'): 'ΧΡΙΣΤΟΣ' ('Khristòs') is 'Christ'.
Θ ('TH', 'Theta'): 'ΘΕΟΥ' ('Theoû') is 'God'.
Υ ('U', 'Upsilon'): 'ΥΙΟΣ' ('Huiòs') is 'Son'.
Σ ('S', 'Sigma'): 'ΣΩΤΗΡ' ('Sôtér') is 'Saver'.

In short, it's devotional wit.

History lessons about Charles II were momentarily made more enjoyable when the coincidental acronym of 'cabal' was pointed out to us. The word itself is of Hebrew origin – 'cabala', 'Kabbalah', 'Qabala', etc – meaning the mystical interpretation of Judaic texts. Charles II's ministers were Clifford, Arlington, Buckingham, Ashley and Lauderdale, and the gag was that they were a 'cabal' or 'The Cabal', probably because they were thought to have sympathies for Roman Catholicism. Part of the Protestant narrative about Britain is that Catholics get into secret huddles and plot how to get in league with Catholic countries. Huddle or not, this particular cabal wasn't very cabal-ish as they fell out with each other, though they did secure a treaty with France, thereby proving the point that they were a cabal.

Acronym-spotting purists declare that the 'true' acronym must be made up of the initial letters of the words in question – and only the initial letters. Nothing else. Like 'scuba' – self-contained underwater breathing apparatus. Perfect. Reluctantly, they admit to the club the mongrel form: acronyms made up of initials along with bits of other words in the phrase – like 'radar' – radio detection and ranging. In 1901, the National Biscuit Company labelled one of its products as Nabisco and this has stuck. Some acronyms only work if you leave out initials of words that are in the original phrase: 'laser' – light amplification by stimulated emission of radiation. C'mon, guys, it should have been the much catchier 'labseor' as in 'There was a fantastic labseor light show in town last night.' Serious pedants object to 'PIN number' as it unpacks as 'personal identification number number'.

Any campaign worth its salt (Strategic Arms Limitation Talks) has to call itself a name that works both in its full version and as an appropriate-sounding acronym. It's a foul libel that activists have sometimes spent more time inventing the acronym than campaigning. ASH comes from Action on Smoking and Health.

• **A VERTICAL WAVY** line with five peaks appears as a hieroglyph in ancient Egypt some 4,000 years ago. It meant 'water' and indicated the sound 'n'. In ancient Semitic inscriptions from 1800 BCE, the number of waves has been reduced to three. It is thought these people borrowed the meaning, calling it in their language 'mem', meaning 'water' and indicating the 'm' sound. The Phoenicians in about 1000 BCE reduced the number of ripples to two, retained the vertical arrangement and curled the waves even more. It was still 'mem', meaning 'water' and carrying the sound 'm'. By 800 BCE, the sign has started to become horizontal and the waves have become zigzags, so that by the time the Greeks borrow it from the Phoenicians in around 725 BCE, it looks like a modern printed 'm' with a long right-hand tail. It is now called 'mu' and is voiced as 'm'. The Romans added the serifs, and made the letter entirely symmetrical.

m

Charlemagne's scribes borrowed a curvy Latin 'm' from the fifth century for their 'minuscule' and this was the lower-case 'm' that the Italian and French printers borrowed in the 1500s.

PRONUNCIATION OF THE LETTER-NAME

Like most of the other continuous consonants, 'em' enables a speaker to emphasize the letter sound, distinguishing it from its near neighbour 'n'.

PRONUNCIATION OF THE LETTER

'M' can appear at the beginning, middle or ends of words,

inviting us to close our lips and hum for a mini-second. Lexicographers decided that a 'terminal m' should be doubled when we add '-ing' or '-ed', as in 'hum, humming, hummed', to distinguish it from the pronunciation of 'fume, fuming, fumed'. The same goes for the distinction between 'tum, tummy' and 'gloom, gloomy'. In the extraordinary word 'mnemonic' it's silent, and when followed by a 'b' as in 'numb', 'thumb', 'jamb' and 'comb' we pretend the 'b' isn't there. 'Damn' was once written as 'd—n' as it was so rude (or not written at all). It retains the 'n' from its parent words 'damned' and 'damnation'; and we write 'condemn' and 'hymn' without voicing the 'n'.

'M' is rather uncooperative when it comes to combining with other consonants. We like words that end with '-mp', '-mping' and '-mpy', as in 'bump, bumpy, bumping', and the same with 'clump', 'dump', 'damp', 'clamp' and 'jump'. We are OK with it being near a 'b' when we can put it next to a new syllable as in 'combine', 'timber', 'remember' and 'imbue'. When African anti-colonial movements came to London in the 1950s, we learned how to say Tom Mboya. Migration and global news services have helped us learn this sound ever since. Placing consonant sounds before the 'm' gives us 'rhythm', 'film', 'pragmatic' and 'capitalism'.

Mostly, though, we like 'm' to be followed by a vowel sound: 'ma', 'me', 'my' and 'more' are amongst our first sounds. The words we have for talking quietly or inaudibly include 'murmur', 'mumble' and 'mutter'.

'Mmm' means 'something nice is happening'; 'hmm' means 'I'm thinking'; 'hmph' means disgust or contempt. Mothers all over the world have 'm' in the words for 'mother' – 'mum', 'mom', 'mummy', 'mammy', 'mommy', 'mama' and 'mamma', and babies make this one of their first consonants as they learn that their lips can close and open.

Sound-play with 'm' also gives us 'Mimi', 'mime', 'me-me-me', the 'Moomins', *Mamma Mia*, 'M&Ms', 'Eminem', 'money-men', 'mind over matter' and 'make a mountain out of a molehill'. 'There's method in his madness' and Malvolio's midnight cry, 'Masters, are you mad?' are Shakespearean 'm'-phrases. My brother's imitation of an underground train waiting in the station is: 'miniminiminiminiminiminimini . . .'

IS FOR MUSIC
AND MEMORY

ONE OF THE ways we are inducted into the alphabet is through the 'Alphabet Song'. Its verses go like this:

ABCDEFG
HIJKLMNOP
QRSTUV
WXYZ
Now I know my ABCs
Next time will you sing with me?

Eagle-eyed, eagle-eared followers of the song will have spotted many moons ago that singing this in the British-English zone ruins the rhyme scheme. 'Z' doesn't rhyme with 'G', 'P', 'V' and 'me'. It also needs a bit of crotchet work in line two and some creative pausing in line four. As people don't usually say 'my ABCs' any more, it rhymes even better with just 'ABC'.

No matter, it works. I always thought that it was one of those songs that was obviously composed by one or two people who disappeared into anonymity some time ago. Not so.

The Boston music publisher Charles Bradley laid claim to the song in 1830 when he copyrighted it. The tune is the same as the tune for 'Baa Baa Black Sheep' and 'Twinkle Twinkle Little Star' – another set of words that many think of as anonymous but is not. The tune, known as 'Ah! vous dirai-je, Maman?', first appeared in France in 1762 and Mozart mucked about with it in twelve variations in 1781/2.

Sayers of 'zed' have produced an alternative ending to the faintly moralistic 'Now I know my ABCs'. It goes like this:

X-y-z
Sugar on your bread
Eat it all up
Before you are dead.

This sort of thing is too irregular for the present movement that teaches reading, which is 'phonics'. You can find on YouTube (along with 15 million other people) the original alphabet song, fired out like a rap, with a souped-up version of 'Ah! vous dirai-je, Maman?' playing quietly in the back-ground. This is followed by the letters being 'sounded' rather than named, which is not without its problems: the letter 'l' is 'sounded' as something like 'erll'; as 'q' is sounded as 'kw', it's written as 'kw' and 'x' is written as 'ks', yet these are not the 'graphemes' the children will see. This is quite apart from the age-old problem of 'sounding' which may involve making a sound that doesn't exist in real words, like 'ber' or 'ker'. When we read 'ball', we don't say 'ber-all'. This, say the phonics experts, they have overcome with 'synthetic' phonics which combines letters and builds syllables and words, so that children learn how to lose the extra 'schwa' sound following the consonant. Yet, miraculously, consonant-plus-schwa creeps back in when children spell out their names: 'Fer, rer, er, der – Fred.'

Another musical or chanted way of using letters is through mnemonics. The Greek goddess of Memory was called Mnemosyne. She slept with Zeus for nine nights, one after the other. The result was nine children who turned out to be the nine Muses: Calliope – epic poetry; Clio – history; Euterpe – flutes and lyric poetry; Thalia – comedy and pastoral poetry; Melpomene – tragedy; Terpsichore – dance; Erato – love poetry; Polyhymnia – sacred poetry; Urania – astronomy. Mnemosyne lived in Hades, the under-world, where she sat by the pool named after her. When dead souls arrived in Hades, if they drank from the river Lethe, they forgot everything they had known in life, so when they were reincarnated they would remember nothing of their previous lives. But if they drank from the pool of Mnemosyne, they would remember . . .

Mnemonics have a long, shadowy history involving memory theory and practice, wizards and someone called von Feinagle but they emerge as a traditional aide-mémoire for anyone trying to remember sequences: the colours of the rainbow, the order of the planets, the order of the great lakes, the reactivity of metals, the first twenty elements of the Periodic Table, the colour code for resistors, geological eras, Henry VIII's wives, common-law felonies, the order of taking the derivative of a quotient, the bones of the wrist, guitar strings, the notes on the treble clef, Ionian philosophers, the apostles, the microwave wave-lengths, spelling rules and metric prefixes.

The main principle is the acrostic-acronym one, but occasion-ally something more musical appears:

Henry VIII's wives were 'divorced, beheaded, died; divorced, beheaded, survived' and if you can't remember which way to tighten and loosen taps and screws, say 'Righty-tighty, lefty-loosey'.

To not remember the months you can always say:

> Thirty days hath September,
> All the rest I can't remember.

And for calculus you may find this useful:

lo-di-hi
minus
hi-di-lo
all over
lo squared.

And for spelling:

I before E, except after C
Or when sounded 'A' as in 'neighbour', 'weigh' and 'weight'
Or when sounded like 'eye' as in height
And 'weird' is just weird.

Alphabetical ones include:

My Very Educated Mother Just Served Us Nachos
HOMES
Pregnant Camels Ordinarily Sit Down Carefully; Perhaps
    Their Joints Creak
Mrs Baker
Simply Learn The Positions That The Carpus Has
Every Average Dude Gets Better Eventually

The Lad Zappa
Richard Of York Gave Battle In Vain
BAPTIIIIISSM
Dashing In A Rush, Running Harder Or Else Accident
King Henry Died By Drinking Chocolate Milk
ASS SID

If you can remember all these, all you have to remember is what subjects they apply to. From the top, they are:

order of the planets in the solar system starting from nearest to the sun
order of the Great Lakes in the USA starting from the west
order of the geological eras
common-law felonies
bones of the wrist
guitar strings
names of Ionian philosophers
colours of the rainbow
names of the apostles (provided you let 'I' be 'J')
how to spell 'diarrhoea'
metric system, counting downwards from 'kilo' and including 'B' for 'base unit'
how to remember adding negative and positive numbers

And then you have to remember what names, nouns and principles they are attached to.

That's your knowledge base sorted, so you can go on to any pub quiz and get a few points, all thanks to acronym, acrostic and alphabetical principles.

One more: Every Good Boy Deserves Fish; Fat Albert Can Eat; Good Boys Do Fine Always; and All Cows Eat Grass.

That lot will sort you out for the treble and bass clefs, lines and spaces.

We can make music without giving the notes names but once people decided to do this, the question arose of which principle to use. The one I'm familiar with (in the sense of 'familiar' but I can't read music well enough to play) goes A to G and then starts again. Many hundreds of years ago there was a scale that ran A to O to cover two octaves.

In France they use 'solfa' or what Julie Andrews called 'doh-re-mi' which started out a thousand years ago as the first syllables of some of the words in an ancient Latin hymn. So, musical notes in the Western tradition are, one way or another, intertwined with letters. At one time, the 'ti' in the octave was 'si', but Sarah Glover (1786–1867) from Norwich decided that in the doh-re-mi system all the names should begin with different letters. Sarah Glover is one of the hidden names of culture. She adapted the continental 'solfa' system for a capella singing and it's her version that Julie Andrews is singing in *The Sound of Music*. She also invented the Glass Harmonicon, a kind of glass xylophone to help people establish pitch. The sol-fa and the Harmonicon were part of her plan whereby all social classes could get in perfect harmony with God – not just the rich.

The ancient Latin hymn goes:

Ut queant laxis
*re*sonare fibris,
*Mi*ra gestorum
*fa*muli tuorum,
*Sol*ve polluti
*la*bii reatum,
*Sa*ncte Iohannes.

('So that your servants may, with loosened voices, resound the wonders of your deeds, clean the guilt from our stained lips, O Saint John.')

The words 'ut', 're', 'mi', 'fa', 'so' and 'la' fall on the notes of the original sol-fa scale. It took a few hundred years to change 'ut' to 'doh' and to add the seventh note which Sarah Glover went on to swap from 'si' to 'ti'. So sitting behind the doh-re-mi system is a kind of ancient mnemonic.

THE STORY OF

- **'N' PROBABLY STARTED** its life 4,000 years ago as an Egyptian hieroglyph with one very small ripple and one large one, meaning a 'cobra' or 'snake'. The ancient Semites took this diagonal squiggle, smoothed it out a bit, and gave it the sound 'n' from 'nun' meaning 'fish'. This may have been logical if, as a people, their word for water-based snakes and fish was the same. By the year 1000, the diagonal had become vertical and the sign contained just one wave. The ancient Greeks took it from the Phoenicians, calling it 'nu', and it now looked like a 'v' added to a long vertical tail on the right-hand side. The Etruscans copied it and passed it on to the Romans who shortened the tail so that it was now a 'v' attached to an inverted 'v' or 'downstroke, upstroke, downstroke'. By the time Imperial Rome was carving it on its victory arches, it was the 'N' we know today.

n

The lower-case 'n' appears in around AD 800 amongst the letters standardized by Charlemagne's scribes with their 'Carolingian minuscule'. This was adopted by the Italian printers in the 1500s as their lower-case 'n'.

PRONUNCIATION OF THE LETTER-NAME
Like the evolution of 'em' for 'M', 'n' derived from a late Roman, early medieval 'ennay'.

PRONUNCIATION OF THE LETTER
'N' likes vowels sounds, so we surround it with 'a', 'e', 'i', 'o', 'u' and the vowel 'y'. At the ends of syllables and words we can use sympathetic consonants to make 'end', 'rent', 'rinse',

'lynx', 'sink', 'Winslow' and 'envy'. Preceding the 'n' with consonant sounds we can make 'isn't', 'kiln', the name 'Milne' and the 'ichneumon fly'. With the prefixes 'in', 'an', 'un', 'con' and 'en', 'N' becomes more cooperative, as with 'enrol', 'condition', 'under', 'untoward', 'anxious', 'unbelievable' and so on. The '-nik' ending of 'beatnik' and 'sputnik', borrowed from Russian, introduced a new way to use 'n' though I knew of 'nudniks' ('fools' in Yiddish) when I was a child.

As with 'm', 'n' doubles or stays single on the same basis: 'run, running', 'tune, tuning'.

Like the initial 'M' in names and words in some African languages, an initial 'N' appears in names like 'Nkosi' and 'Ngaio'. The world's most popular name is the Chinese name 'Ng' and English speakers are learning how to say it.

'N' on its own has had a new life in a pseudo-mathematical way where we talk of 'the nth degree' or even of 'n number of cases' as if it is an abbreviation for 'any'. Another way that 'n' survives on its own is the now acceptable way of writing 'rock'n'roll', though 'rock'n'roll' has now solidified as 'rock'.

Modern phonics teaching tells children that the 'kn' of 'know' and the 'gn' of 'gnome' are 'ways of making the "n" sound', rather than saying that the 'k' or the 'g' are 'silent', which certainly makes it less mysterious and sinister. I was once so interested in 'knock', 'knack' and 'knuckle' that I regularly wrote 'neck' as 'kneck'.

Word-play with 'n' gives us 'ninny', a 'no-no', some people's word for a 'dummy' – a 'num-num', 'nanny', 'nan' and 'nana'. John Donne said, 'No man is an island' which gives you a 'no', an '-n is', and an '-n island'. (Alliteration sometimes works by linking the ends of words to the beginnings of the next.) Feste sings, 'Hey nonny nonny . . .'

N IS FOR NONSENSE

NONSENSE ISN'T REALLY no sense. It makes a different or a new kind of sense. Pity it wasn't called 'new-sense'. Most of it depends on creating new worlds, new creatures and new language. In this sphere of language, nonsense writers are keen on playing with or 'disrupting' things that we accept as normal – like words themselves, songs that we've been taught and school routines.

Alphabet rhymes have been around for over 300 years. They seem to have started out in a robust and boisterous way. Iona and Peter Opie in their magnificent *Oxford Dictionary of Nursery Rhymes* quote John Eachard from 1671 who writes of:

A Apple-pasty,
B bak'd it,
C cut it,
D divided it,
E eat it,
F fought for it,
G got it . . .

By 1712 rhymes like this were doing the rounds:

A was an archer who shot at a frog
B was a butcher, and had a great dog.
C was a captain, all covered with lace,
D was a drunkard, and had a red face . . .

A hundred years later things had got much more strait-laced:

A Apple, a

The APPLE with its rosy cheek,
Doth first begin this pretty toy;
How sweet it tastes! and oft is made
The prize of each good natur'd boy . . .

K King, k

This is the man who, next to God,
Is plac'd to keep mankind in awe;
Happy the people whose good King
Is judg'd and judges by the law.

That came in a little book that was for the 'amusement and instruction of GOOD CHILDREN'. Presumably, if they weren't good, then reading this would make them good.

Nonsense feeds off stuff like this and the first author to take up the challenge was Edward Lear. He was the twentieth of twenty-one children, the son of a stockbroker who went bust. He suffered from epilepsy and depression all his life, calling one the 'Demon' and the other the 'Morbids'. His first interest was drawing, which took him to London Zoo, painting exotic animals and birds. He found his nonsense voice through entertaining the children of aristocrats when hired to paint the Earl of Derby's menagerie.

His first alphabet comes from about 1846 and he went on writing alphabets for specific children for much of the rest of his life. He began doing these rather non-nonsensically: ants, butterflies, cobwebs and ducks doing what ants, butterflies, cobwebs and ducks usually do.

By 1870, he was talking of 'The Absolutely Abstemious Ass, who resided in a Barrel, and only lived on Soda Water and Pickled Cucumbers. The Bountiful Beetle, who always carried a Green Umbrella when it didn't rain, and left it at home when it did . . .' He coped with the letter 'X' by writing, 'The Excellent Double-extra XX imbibing King Xerxes who lived a long time ago.' He seems to have realized that he could put in imaginary creatures by the time he writes: 'The Yonghy-Bonghy-Bo, whose Head was ever so much bigger than his Body, and whose Hat was rather small.'

This comes several years after the publication of *Alice's Adventures in Wonderland* which had been full of parodies of Sunday School songs. Children's literature was offering Lewis Carroll and Edward Lear a space in which to subvert some of the certainties of Victorian life. Lear produced one alphabet for very young children whose nonsense is to do with how it plays with the sounds of English, much as children do as they teach themselves how to talk:

A was once an apple pie
Pidy
Widy
Tidy
Pidy
Nice insidy
Apple-Pie!

He also wrote one where the convention is that the letter 'A' is a person or creature and every letter responds or acts through the poem:

A tumbled down, and hurt his Arm, against a bit of wood.
B said, 'My Boy!, O! do not cry; it cannot do you good!'

Just as Lear animated his physical and mental problems with the 'Demon' and the 'Morbids', so he animates objects and letters:

W said, 'Some Whisky-Whizzygigs, fetch some marbles and a ball!'

Z said, 'Here is a box of Zinc! Get in, my little master!
We'll shut you up! We'll nail you down! We will, my little master!
We think we've all heard quite enough of this your sad disaster!'

As is often the case with Lear, the whole thing ends in some kind of physical disruption, dismemberment or constraint.

Children themselves get up to all sorts of disruptive things with letters and spellings. For example, spelling difficulty – or spelling 'difficulty':

Mrs D
Mrs I
Mrs F, F, I
Mrs C
Mrs U
Mrs L, T, Y.

This may have come from a mnemonic for spelling 'Mississippi':

Mrs M
Mrs I
Mrs Double S, I
Mrs Double S, I
Mrs P, P, I.

There are many versions of a 'name game', a kind of mock-spelling, mock-sounding-out of letters. Ones I've collected go something like this:

You start with the person's name: Lucy. You then rhyme it by taking off the 'L' and replacing it with 'bomb', after which you say, 'Sticker Lucy, Fi-fucy', reverse that, and tie it all up with a 'That's how to spell Lucy':

Lucy Bombucy
Sticker Lucy, Fi-fucy.
Fi-fucy, Sticker Lucy.
That's how you spell Lucy.

When Lucy told me that, Toni said:

Toni Hiphoney
Stickaloney, Biboney
Hiphoney, Stickaloney
That's how
you spell Toni.

This reminded me of the game I was taught where you take a word and chop off one letter at a time. When you get to the last letters, you can switch to saying the name of the letter to make it go with a zing. I do it with the word 'everybody':

Everybody
verybody
erybody (say: erry-body)
rybody (say: rye-body)
ybody (say: why-body)
body (say: body)
ody (say: oddy)
dy (say: die)
y (say: why?)

All these work best if you can say them so quickly that people can't hear what you're doing. They just hear words being pulled apart and put back together again – a kind of mock spelling-out – in ways that they don't recognize. That's the point.

Shampoo
hampoo
ampoo
mpoo (say: em-poo)
poo
oo (say: ooo)
o (say: oh!)

Alphabet poems were intended to help children learn to read and I can't think of any reason why they wouldn't. The principle lying behind them is that familiarity with one letter at a time – in use in real words – will familiarize new readers to the alphabetic principle. Repetition of a single letter in use leads you to alliteration and assonance. Put it into a verse with rhythm and rhyme and you have a challenge for readers: can you say this without stumbling? Can you learn it off by heart?

Something similar is going on with this old gag:

A new teacher says that she's going to find out everybody's name.

'What's your name?' she says.

'Pitsmiff, Miss,' the boy says.

'Sorry?'

'Pitsmiff, Miss,' he says.

The teacher turns to the boy next to him.

'What did he say?'

'His name's Pete Smith, Miss.'

'Right,' said the teacher, 'I see that we've got a bit of a clarity problem round here. When I ask you your name, I want you to say clearly:

'"P, E, T, E, that's Peter, S, M, I, T, H, that's Smith, Pete Smith."

'Now, boy, what's your name?'

'A, R, C, H, there's your Arch.

'I, there's your I.

'There's your Arch-i.

'B, A, L, D – there's your bald.

'There's your i-bald.

'There's your arch-i-bald.

'A, R, S, E, there's your Arse.

'There's your bald Arse.

'There's your i-bald Arse.

'There's your Arch-i-bald Arse.

'O, L, E, there's your Ole.

'There's your Arse-ole.

'There's your bald Arse-ole.

'There's your i-bald Arse-ole.

'There's your Arch-i-bald Arse-ole.

'I, N, there's your in.

'There's your ole-in.

'There's your Arse-ole-in.

'There's your bald Arse-ole-in.

'There's your i-bald Arse-ole-in.

'There's your Arch-i-bald Arse-ole-in.

'Archibald Arseolein, Miss.'

Whatever their humour, these rhymes, jokes and tongue-twisters have another function: they draw attention to letters. Perhaps this is because letters are mysterious. There is nothing f-ish about 'f', nothing 'u-sounding' about the particular shape of a 'u'. We learn in this 'speech community' of English speakers that each letter has a name, it has 'values' (sounds we can make when we see it), and, more importantly, when we combine the letters, and see them on a page, we make them sound like words and phrases that make sense. It's obvious, but it's only obvious because we've learned it. It isn't obvious for any rational reason like, say, a bike is a bike because people invented it, modified it and you can see the way it works.

One of the reasons why we have a genre of disruptive, non-sensical rhymes and jokes is that it brings to the surface our feelings of mystery or our state of unknowing and relieves us of any anxiety or irritation we might have.

The best disruption of 'spelling-out' that I know is 'key-jug', as taught me by an Australian child. Just spell a name or phrase the usual way, but as you say each letter add 'key' quickly after it and 'key-jug' at the end of each word. It makes a nonsensical, alphabetical jazz.

THE (TRUE) STORY OF

- **RATHER WONDERFULLY, 'O'** starts out its life 4,000 years ago as the Egyptian hieroglyph for 'the eye'. Ancient Semites borrowed this and called it 'ayin', meaning 'eye' in their language. The sound at this stage was one of the Semitic 'guttural' sounds, the 'ch' you make at the back of your throat. This was the true initial sound of 'ayin', much as the Hebrew name 'Chaim' begins that way too. The Phoenician 'ayin' in around 1000 BCE reduced the eye to the outline of the pupil – an 'o' shape. It still meant 'eye'. In around 650 BCE, the ancient Greeks adopted this 'o', calling it 'mikron' (meaning a small 'o'), and to the Greeks it was a vowel, making the short 'o' as in our word 'hot'. They already had the long 'o' with their letter 'omega' as pronounced in our word 'owe'. The Romans created a thin-thick form of the 'O'.

o

The early medieval scribes produced a small version of 'O', which was adopted by the early printers as their lower case.

PRONUNCIATION OF THE LETTER-NAME

The Norman French seemed to have arrived in England calling this letter by its 'long o' sound and it has survived intact in both French and English.

PRONUNCIATION OF THE LETTER

On its own in words 'o' can give us the 'short o' in 'pot', and the 'long o' in 'no'. It can give us the 'oo' of 'do' and the 'short u' sound in 'son' and 'some'.

With other vowels, the letters 'r', 'y', 'w' and the 'e'

following a consonant, it can give us: 'boat', 'toe', 'neon', 'neo-gothic', 'quoit', 'riot', 'youth' and 'snout'. We use it to write 'Mao' and 'miaow' and it works in names like Chloe and Noel (with or without a dieresis on the 'e'). It can do service in 'lord', 'boy', 'low' and 'cow', and as the suffix '-or' as in 'actor' and the US version of the '-our' ending: 'color' and 'favorite'. When we double 'o' it can be shorter as in 'foot' or longer as in 'coot'.

'O' is an abbreviation in 'three o'clock' ('of the clock') where it's pronounced more as an 'a'. It lives on in thousands of Irish names like 'O'Connor' and 'O'Driscoll' where it means 'descendant of Driscoll'.

'O' entirely on its own is of course the exclamation of surprise or delight with or without the 'h' of 'oh'. Poets and playwrights were very fond of 'O' and 'Oh' right up until the 1960s, when it was quietly dropped on the grounds of being naff. It survives where it always thrived, in songs where it merges with 'uh' and 'ah'.

It's also the only letter which is exactly the same symbol as a number, enabling car registration-plate enthusiasts to work wonders with the numbers if they are lucky enough to have an 'o' in their name.

With 'this wooden O', Shakespeare was almost certainly referring to the Globe Theatre (of which he was a part-shareholder) in the prologue of *Henry V*, and the 'O' of *The Story of O* can be taken to mean a metaphor for anything from zero to sex and back.

'Ooooo' can mean very different things depending on the notes you hit. It can indicate 'you're looking good', 'you're acting a bit above yourself', 'this is exciting' and so on.

In combination with consonants, you can say you've hurt yourself: 'ouch' and 'ow'.

 IS FOR OK

. . . BUT IS IT OK to write OK, Ok, Okay and ok? And should people who say, 'Okily-dokily' be given a custodial sentence?

When zoologists looked at the duck-billed platypus, they had problems. They had their way of classifying animals but this beast didn't fit. What's more, it looked like a hoax. The duck-billed platypus was fine – it's still fine; it just goes on being a duck-billed platypus. It doesn't wonder what kind of animal it is.

OK is a duck-billed platypus.

We have no fixed way of writing 'OK' because we don't know whether it is two initials or a transcription of a non-English word. Either way, it sounds like two letters. It may well have started out in life as an 'interjection' – like 'uh-huh' – but it has now risen to the status of a word. Look at it: one moment, it's being adjectival and the next, adverbial:

'You're an OK sort of a guy.' (adjective)
'If you can run OK, you'll be picked for the team.' (adverb)
'I've given him the OK to run.' (noun)
'I've okayed him for the race.' (verb)

Unlike the platypus, OK lives everywhere. There are few places left in the world where an 'OK!' accompanied by a smile and a nod would be misunderstood. And unlike the platypus, it can acquire appendages: A-OK, okey-dokey, hokie-dokie and the aforesaid okily-dokily.

It is clearly a popular, useful and powerful word. It works. It even has its own hand-sign: tip of the first finger on to the tip of the thumb to make an o-shape, the other three fingers raised, though that seems to be an OK-plus, a better-than-just-OK kind of OK. You might have thought, with all that going for it, that we would be proud that humanity had invented a noise that could do so much for so many. Not so. In many circles, it is a despised little expression, seen as lazy, imprecise, slangy and – in some countries – an unwelcome Americanism. It's a low-status word even when used by high-status people. If a prime minister or president wants to sound informal, he or she will use 'OK'. In a formal setting, as in a news broadcast, it won't make the grade. You'll be told to not use it in a job application or in an essay on the causes of the First World War.

There isn't a clear answer why 'OK' hasn't been allowed into the academy that is formal prose writing. I suspect it's a cluster of connotations to do with its origins and its sound. I'll get on to the theories of its precise origins in a moment, but whatever these are, 'OK' took up a regular posting in the informal speech of non-posh Americans just as 'gee!' and 'wow!' have. Once a word is situated in a place like that, it's hard for it to fight its way into formal writing. Whatever its virtues, standard English is also a code which signals that the writer has had a particular kind of education. A rule like 'Don't use "OK" in your essays' does this job.

I think something else is involved: the sound. Though using initials for organizations, posts, qualifications and awards can be formal (CNN, MP, BA), initializing of expressions is often more colloquial or euphemistic (KBU: 'keen but useless', 'sweet FA'). Perhaps we see some initialled expressions as not being the full or real thing – OK for note-taking and chat but not for proper writing. No matter what its true origins are, we hear 'OK' as two letters and that's part of how we think of it. The irony here would be that 'OK' may be a 'loan word', 'borrowed' from another language and kept, and fully entitled to keep its place alongside 'robots', 'verandahs' and 'culottes'.

My first go at the etymology of 'OK' was when I was about six. I knew then that the word 'OK' came from sauce bottles. By the time I was putting it on my chips, it had been around for over thirty years and, along with Christmas pudding, is the distant descendant of Middle Eastern foods brought to Europe by returning Crusaders. Reading 'OK' on OK Sauce bottles was part of how I learned to read. At the time, did I but know, the sauce was being made in the kind of factory that was being hailed as the utopian future of British industry: clean, chimney-less, tiled works placed by the side of a bypass or 'arterial road'. Fans of art deco, brown sauce or the word 'OK' can support their interest by taking a trip to number 265 Merton Road, Southfields, London, where a plaque marks the building's history.

However much I would like my bottle of OK Sauce to be the explanation of the word's origins, wishing it won't make it so. There is a whole bunch of contenders for the real origin: from a Greek expression, 'ola kala' (meaning 'it's good'); as a loan word from the American Choctaw nation, 'oke' or 'okeh' (meaning 'it's so'); a French dockers' expression, 'au quai' (meaning 'it's all right to send to the quay'); another French dockers' expression, 'aux Cayes' (meaning 'to or at Cayes', a place renowned for good rum); the initials of a railroad freight agent, Obadiah Kelly, who put his initials on documents he had approved; an expression meaning 'all right' circulating in the languages of West African peoples; an anglicization of the Scots expression 'och aye'; and finally – the one I was told when I wondered about brown sauce labelling – that it was a mock initializing of the misspelled 'orl korrekt' or 'oll korrect', something that young swells from Boston liked to do in the 1830s.

Its first written, testified use is by the Democrats during the presidential election of 1840. Their candidate, Martin Van Buren, had the nickname of 'Old Kinderhook' (after his birthplace in New York State), and his supporters called themselves the 'OK Club'. This may have helped the spread of the expression but it didn't help Martin Van Buren. He lost the election.

I have another suggestion: it comes from all these sources. The theory I'm working to here is that some expressions and words don't come from one source alone. As one example amongst thousands, the expression 'the full monty' can claim several origins. Perhaps what happens is that a word or expression starting out in one place chimes with the same or a similar one in another, and together they snowball into widespread usage. One of the main causes of language change is that people hear something that sounds like something that they already say and they add that to their vocabulary or 'linguistic repertoire'. Colloquial words often catch on when you think that saying a given word will make you sound good to others when you say it.

In the case of 'OK', the main cause of its spreading has been 'mateyness'. If I say it I will sound more matey, more affable, more 'with you' than indifferent or hostile to you. One of the key times and places to indicate mateyness is when peoples who perceive each other as different meet up and wish to be friendly. A shorthand way of saying 'things are fine' is very useful. Saying 'good' in someone else's language is an excellent way of showing friendliness. My first visits to France as a teenager were constantly sprinkled with me saying 'bon'. In the list of possible contenders for 'OK's origin, there seem to be thousands, if not millions, of small encounters in which saying 'OK' would have done that job very well. If I'm right, 'OK' would be a symbol of 'interculturalism', the way peoples of different origins share culture.

Even so, let's hear it for the Boston wags. According to Allen Walker Read, there was a fad in the 1830s for abbreviations of expressions said in local accents and dialects: 'KY' for 'know yuse', 'NS' for 'nuff said', 'OW' for 'oll wright', and even initials for misspellings: 'KG', for 'know go' and 'NC' for 'nuff ced'. It sounded funny and cool to say 'OK' for 'orl korrekt'. As it happens, it seems as if plenty of peoples were saying something like 'OK' well before that but it would be the encounters between these peoples, along with the snappy sign 'OK', which made it stick.

THE STORY OF

- **A DOUBLE-LINED** V-shape appears in early Semitic from 3,800 years ago. It's thought that this was 'pe' meaning 'mouth'. By 1000 BCE, the Phoenicians were writing it as a diagonal hook shape, and also calling it 'pe' meaning 'mouth'. It took the sound of 'p' as the initial letter. The early ancient Greeks adopted it and called it 'pi', with the hook on the left in their right-to-left inscriptions. Early Roman inscriptions kept the upright stroke and started to curl the hook over but by around 200 BCE the curl had closed up, the letter reversed for left-to-right writing and the 'P' was fully formed. The inscriptions of Imperial Rome added the serifs and the thin-thick lines.

p

A smaller 'p' appears in the early medieval manuscripts and this leads to the shape taken up by the later standardizers of the letters; and, following their design, there is the lower-case type of the early printers, bringing the small 'p' below the line.

PRONUNCIATION OF THE LETTER-NAME

The ancient Greeks pronounced this letter as 'pee', though Phoenicians and Romans probably pronounced it 'pay'. That's how it came into England with the Normans and then, following the Great Vowel Shift, this turned into 'pee'.

PRONUNCIATION OF THE LETTER

This is 'B's close relative, as it is the 'unvoiced' form of 'B', a sound made by using the lips as a kind of dam, which then open, pushing out breath.

'P' combines with 'r', 'l' and 'h' to make 'pray', 'play' and 'phone'. It combines silently with 't' to make 'ptarmigan' and with 's' in the prefix 'psycho-'. One of my surprises when speaking French, is pronouncing the 'p' in 'pneu' and 'psycho'. Modern phonics teaching doesn't call these 'silent' but says that 'pt' and 'ps' are rare ways of making the 't' and 's' sound. Before a 'p' you can put other consonant sounds to write words like 'jump', 'lisp' and 'pulp'. One of my favourite books when I was a boy was called *Kpo the Leopard* which I rather enjoyed saying.

Like most other consonants, 'p' can end words without being doubled, as with 'cup', but it is then doubled in 'hop, hopping, hopped' though not in 'hope, hoping, hoped' because of the long vowel preceding the 'p'.

'P-words' can indicate smallness: 'pip', 'peep', 'pop', 'pup', 'pap', 'pee-pee', 'plip', 'plop' and 'pitter-patter'.

Other sound-play can be found in 'Pippa', 'the Pied Piper', 'poo-poo', 'Poppy', 'pip-pip' and 'he's a people person'. We seem to like saying, 'Pity the poor person who . . .'

Printers had to 'mind their ps and qs'. Moveable type is in mirror form. It's very easy to select a 'p' for a 'q' and vice versa when picking out the letters to put in the press. That's one story, anyway.

IS FOR PITMAN

THERE'S A GRAVE in Sydney on which there is the following inscription:

IN LUVING MEMORI OV JACOB PITMAN, BORN 28 NOV. 1810 AT TROWBRIDGE. ENGLAND, SETELD IN ADELAIDE, 1838, DEID 12th MARCH 1890

ARKITEKT INTRODIUST FONETIK SHORT HAND AND WOZ THE FERST MINISTER IN THEEZ KOLONIZ OV THE DOCTRINZ OV THE SEKOND OR NIU KRISTIAN CHURCH WHICH AKNOLEJEZ THE LORD JESUS CHRIST IN HIZ DIVEIN HIUMANITI AZ THE KREATER OV THE YUNIVERS THE REDEEMER AND REJNERATER OV MEN GOD OVER AUL. BLESED FOR EVER.

It's a testimony to some extraordinary projects. The gravestone, erected by Jacob Pitman's brother Isaac, is a tribute to four of them: the world's first phonetic shorthand, a phonetic alphabet, the 'New Church' and the world's first correspondence course. The inscription is itself written in Isaac's new phonetic alphabet; and the fact that it was possible to introduce shorthand to

Australia was a result of his realizing that if he could cram his shorthand textbook on to one small card, he could benefit from the newly invented Penny Post and send it all round the world, including to his brother Jacob in Adelaide.

If we roll this up into one ball of human energy, we can see that Isaac Pitman devoted himself to a utopia: with his phonetic alphabet, a new kind of written word would relate directly to the way in which people spoke. This would mean that everyone would be able to read and write easily. With another writing system he devised – phonetic shorthand – the way people spoke could be accurately transcribed and the transcription would keep up with the speed of speech. Nothing need be missed. As a result of both systems, the word of the true God (Jesus Christ) would be universally available and we would all be redeemed. As great literature would become accessible to all, everyone would become enlightened. If people could write faster, it would save time and, as Isaac Pitman said, 'to save time is to prolong life'.

Just to be clear – Pitman grew up in a world unlike ours in one particular respect: no means existed by which speech could be preserved and played back. The nearest that people could get to it was in writing dialogue in novels, plays and poems. A thing spoken was a thing gone. Of course, people had memory and they could imitate each other, but, unlike us, they didn't live in a world surrounded by electronically recorded speech. So, Pitman's two inventions were revolutionary: with strokes of the pen, everyone would be able to write down, in a much more consistent way than using the alphabet, the sounds of their speech ('phonemes'); and specialists would be able to learn a shorthand which for the very first time captured every phoneme as it was spoken.

Isaac Pitman was born in 1813, in Trowbridge, Wiltshire, the son of a hand-loom weaver. He left school at the age of twelve, because he couldn't cope with the tiny classroom jam-packed full. It seems as if there were words he couldn't pronounce – or thought he couldn't pronounce – but he joined what was one of the first lending libraries and proceeded to educate himself. One key book for him was *Walker's Critical Pronouncing Dictionary and Expositor of the English Language*.

When you read the opening pages of this book, it's easy to see how Pitman's reading of it set him on the path he chose for the rest of his life and, as a result, he changed the lives of millions of people – especially working-class women. The title page of Walker's dictionary is a statement of intent, showing how meaning, pronunciation and standardization were parcelled up together under the guidance of ancient Greek and Latin – two languages that no one knew how to pronounce anyway! The alphabet's life in Britain had never before received such a going over. Young Pitman pored over how Walker undertook to explain meaning, indicate how words should sound and why, define rules of pronunciation, examine the influence of ancient languages, lay down specific rules for the Scots, the Irish and Londoners, and even give advice to foreigners on how to use the dictionary.

Pitman set himself the task of learning the words and the right way to pronounce them. He would have seen very quickly that Walker hadn't tried to reform spelling with the purpose of ensuring that the twenty-six letters of the alphabet would represent sounds more consistently. What he had done was extend the use of the letters by adding a host of little signs ('diacritics') placed over letters to indicate what their 'accent and quantity' should be. It doesn't seem to have occurred to Walker that the 'natives of Scotland, Ireland and London' might not want to 'avoid their respective peculiarities' or, indeed, that they might find it too much bother to unlock his adapted alphabet purely in order to talk the way he thought they should.

The young Pitman seems to have been transfixed by the book and he proceeded to learn all 2,000 words and their correct pronunciations. By 1837, he had devised and written down in his notebook the world's first ever phonetic shorthand system. I was able to see this notebook in the Pitman Archive at Bath Spa University and I can admit to 'having a moment'. One of the mysteries about my mother was that she could listen to what we were saying, fill a page with little squiggles and then read back to us exactly what we had said. Though she was a 'scholarship girl' and had gone to the grammar school, her parents didn't think that staying on in the sixth form or going to university was the right thing for a working-class Jewish girl to be doing. So she went to secretarial college and learned shorthand and typing, which enabled her to work as a secretary first at a newspaper and then at the Kodak factory. My holding Pitman's notebook was to look at what had enabled my mother, exactly 100 years after Pitman's invention, to get her first job, to delight her sons with her scribbles and to turn my father's extempore thoughts into beautifully typed lectures.

Pitman published his shorthand in a twelve-page booklet in 1837 as *Stenographic Sound Hand*. By 1840, it was called *Phonography*. He reduced the information required to learn it so that it fitted on to a single piece of paper and in 1840, when the Penny Post came in, he began sending these out around Britain and all over the world.

By 1844, Pitman (along with A. J. Ellis) had produced a reformed spelling alphabet that looked like this:

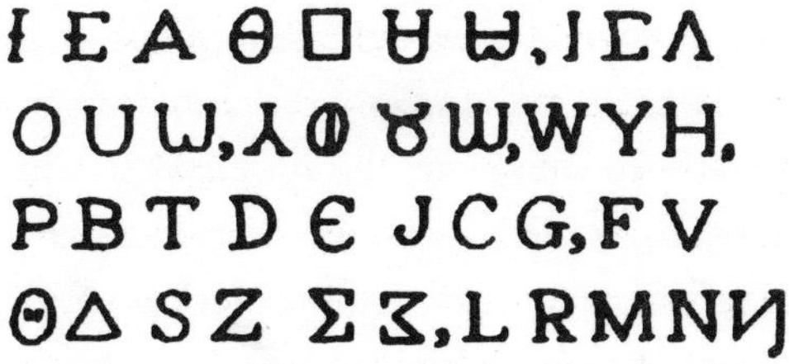

With these two alphabets (the shorthand and the reformed spelling alphabet), coupled with his prodigious energy, Pitman now pursued what he himself called the 'cause'. He travelled and lectured, published books, edited journals. He canvassed support, wrote letters and articles; he organized a 'Phonographic Festival'. He tried to convince educators to teach both the shorthand and his 'Pitman Alphabet' of 1844 – 'short hand will be the common hand,' he proclaimed.

Pitman drew some praise but more fire from various quarters, including a reverend and a Quaker poet, seeing respectively the hand of Satan in the new system or calling it little more than 'parrot lore'. The vegetarian, teetotal, non-smoking, heavily bearded Pitman pressed on, driven by his desire that 'every boy should have the opportunity of acquiring the art'. One blot on the page was that his second wife found out that a young woman admirer was writing to him in shorthand. Mrs Pitman engaged the services of a trained practitioner and put a stop to it. In the great alphabetic struggle, we know now that Pitman shorthand won; the Pitman alphabet lost. It seems as if you can 're-form' the alphabet for specialists but you can't reform the alphabet for everyone.

In the Pitman Archive, they have many documents which chart these battles but one item trumps the lot. In 1891, Pitman was due to give an address to the National Phonographic Society but he was busy elsewhere, so he recorded an address on the new technology of the wax cylinder. In his strong Wiltshire accent – with what sounds to my ear a bit like a mix of Irish and American – he talks of the 'combined labours of very enthusiastic phonographers who have worked with me for fifty-four years perfecting a brief representation of the sounds of speech' and adds that these labours have extended 'phonography to all parts of the earth where English is spoken'.

I wonder if Pitman had any sense that the apparatus on which he was recording his voice would over time drastically reduce the number of people who would use his phonographic short-hand. Dictaphones, 'telediphones', 'rapid transcription services', reel-to-reel tape machines, cassette machines, minidiscs, digital recorders, PCs, laptops, iPads and iPhones would all eat away at the need for shorthand. My students record their lessons on something that's the size of a pen, put earphones on and tran-scribe it. A journalist from a newspaper interviews me and puts what looks like an alloy packet of cigarettes on the table between us. Shorthand teachers bewail the loss of the skill, pointing out that the journalist who uses shorthand is the one who listens and notes what's important. Perhaps Pitman should have sent his message to the National Phonographic Society in shorthand.

Looking at Sir Isaac Pitman from the vantage point of today, we can see that he stands in two alphabetical streams: one concerns the wish or need to write quickly (usually called 'short-hand'); and the other is the wish or need to make writing easier (usually called 'spelling reform', though this might involve reform of punctuation or of the letters of the alphabet).

As I've said, the point about Pitman shorthand was that it was the first attempt to write quickly by using symbols for sounds we make ('phonemes'). Before and since, most short-hands have involved inventing squiggles or abbreviations to make the business of writing words shorter. I can remember sitting on an underground train in the 1950s looking at an advert which addressed us passengers with 'Gt a gd jb nd mre py.' I think it was called 'Speedwriting'. Pity they weren't more wholehearted about it and called it 'Spdwrtng'.

The term 'shorthand' has alternatives: the actual process of writing in any kind of shorthand is 'stenography', though it has also been called 'brachygraphy' and 'tachygraphy' (three Greek prefixes are more than enough for anyone in one sentence but 'stenos' means 'narrow', 'brachys' means 'short' and 'tachys' means 'fast'), each of which indicates some sense of what was intended.

The Parthenon in Athens can claim to hold the oldest short-hand. A marble slab dating from the mid-fourth century BCE indicates that the Greeks used a shorthand based on vowels. I'm not sure that would work in English. That Speedwriting ad would read: 'E A OO O A OE A'. Two hundred years later, in Hellenistic Egypt, we hear that it will take one Apollonios two years to learn shorthand. That method was to take 'word stems' with signs for word endings. An equivalent in English would be to take a 'stem' like 'play' and use a sign on the end for 's' when it's 'plays', another for '-ed' when it's 'played' and another for '-ing' when it's 'playing'. These three signs could then be used for all verbs with '-s', '-ed' and '-ing' endings.

Thanks to the author Robert Harris's trilogy about Cicero, the figure of Marcus Tullius Tiro (103–4 BCE) has become better known than he was. He was a slave and then a free man, employed by Cicero in order to write down the orator's speeches. The system he used and probably invented came to be called 'Tironian notes' and it consisted of 4,000 to 5,000 signs. It was a great survivor, lasting through the medieval period, and it was on occasions still being used in the seventeenth century. Anyone fluent in Gaelic or Irish will know that in those languages, there is a symbol looking like a '7', meaning 'and'. It's a Tironian note.

In his letters, Cicero frequently referred to Tiro whose job it was to take dictation, figure out Cicero's own handwriting, wait at table, do a bit of gardening and handle Cicero's accounts. Clearly, every philosopher should have a Tiro. It's thought that devoted old Tiro collected Cicero's writings and published them after his death, as well as turning his hand to a bit of writing himself, including works on the Latin language which, sadly, haven't survived. Tiro suffered from ill-health, which Cicero records in his letters. Goodness knows who did the dictation, table-laying, gardening and accounting when Tiro was throwing a sickie. It seems Tiro wrote a biography of Cicero too but this hasn't survived either. For many years in western Europe, Cicero was a kind of core curriculum in himself, studied for his thoughts on philosophy and politics along with his prose style. Some suggest that it's his prose style which helped create the formal prose style of Western languages.

As a vocal republican, Cicero found himself on the wrong side of Mark Antony following the assassination of Julius Caesar and was then assassinated himself. Tiro then bought an estate and, in spite of his record of ill-health, he survived till he was ninety-nine years old. As we've seen, his shorthand lasted for many years more, particularly amongst the early medieval monks. The system went into decline in the eleventh century, though the Renaissance saw a revival of interest in it.

Some hundred years later in the wild and windy North of England, Roman soldiers, wives, merchants and slaves would write and receive messages, written on wooden tablets with pen and ink (an iron nib with carbon and gum arabic for ink), not all of which are letters, though. Some 1,300 tablets have been found so far in and around Vindolanda, a fort on Hadrian's Wall, and they include: travel expenses – '2 wagon axles, 3.5 denarii'; along with: 'a friend sent me 50 oysters from Cordonovi, I'm sending you half' (did he know nothing of food poisoning?); and a note to the Emperor Hadrian: 'As befits an honest man I implore Your Majesty not to allow me, an innocent man, to have been beaten with rods.' There is no record of what Hadrian did about this, but my money would be that he ignored it. Why should innocence have stood in the way of a public beating?

Amongst these are some tablets written in a hitherto undeciphered shorthand. Because no one knows what they say, we have to imagine what kind of note, from or to a fort on Hadrian's Wall, would need to have been written at speed and to someone who could read shorthand. Clearly, this was correspondence between Tiro-like servants and slaves, full of vital political and military action, dictated by their masters but secretly laced with an odd subversive postscript which their lordships would never see. General Flavius to General Brutus as dictated to Septimus: 'Hail Brutus. Can't find Ninth Legion. Last seen heading for Bath. Send more troops. Regards, Flavius.' (Ye gods, can't the old twit figure out that they've gone native? Hope you and yours are well. Send more plonk, best wishes, Septimus.)

It's quite possible that China in the Imperial period invented a shorthand earlier than Tiro, used for court proceedings and criminals' confessions. In 1572 one Timothie Bright was in Paris – not a great place to be at that moment if there was a possibility that you might be mistaken for a Protestant; an English accent would certainly suggest you leaned that way. Even so, he escaped the St Bartholomew's Day massacre by taking refuge in the house of Francis Walsingham whom we find earlier in this book cooking the goose of Mary Queen of Scots. Bright qualified in medicine at Cambridge and practised in Ipswich. He wrote *A Treatise of Melancholy* which may or may not have been the reason why he became a priest, a calling he practised in Yorkshire.

His book on shorthand is called – delightfully – *Characterie*. It was of course dedicated to Queen Elizabeth – you wouldn't want to risk doing otherwise. He told her that he had invented a 'speedie kind of wryting', with 'every character answering a word'. He too had the intention that it would be used to record orations or public speeches verbatim and would be 'secret'. He also hoped it would allow 'nations of strange languages' to communicate with one another, even if they did not share a common language.

Bright's system involved 500 signs, each representing one word. I make that 500 words. I'm guessing that the main reason why it didn't catch on is that we communicate with many more words than that, as exemplified by his great contemporary, Mr Shakespeare of Stratford-upon-Avon. Given that Bright's book appeared in 1588, a date well known for other reasons, I'm guessing that it was just too late to have been known by Drake for dictating messages about how the day was going.

Bright's book was followed by a number of others, including the most famous and long-lasting from this period, Thomas Shelton's *Short Writing* in 1626 (later reissued as *Tachygraphy*). It's thought that Shelton was, as they say, one of the Sheltons of Norfolk, big-time landowners who fought on the side of Parliament in the English Civil War. If so, he would be neither the first nor the last person mentioned in this book who was much influenced by Puritanism in his zeal about the alphabet.

Shelton actually made a living out of shorthand and wrote several books and handbooks on the subject. His system 'borrowed' some ideas from one of his predecessors in this field,

John Willis. Every consonant was an easily drawn symbol which sometimes resembled the corresponding alphabet letter. Vowels depended on where the following consonant was written. Think of 'ball', 'bull', 'bell', 'bill' and 'boll'. Write your letter 'b'. In order to make 'ball' you write your letter 'l' above the 'b'. To write 'bull' you write the 'l' below your 'b'. If you think of the 'b' sitting in the middle of a clockface position, put your 'l' at the 'ten past the hour' position (i.e. top right) and you have 'bell'. Position the 'l' at a 'quarter past' (i.e. at the mid-point), and it'll be 'bill'. 'Twenty past' will give you 'boll'.

A range of other methods gave practitioners vowels at the ends and beginnings of words. Further symbols designated frequent prefixes and suffixes. You will know that the vowel letters do not by themselves designate all the vowel sounds. Still with 'b–l' words, we have 'bale', 'Baal', 'bile', 'boil', 'bowl' and even 'boules'. Shelton wasn't much help here, if it was accurate transcription by sound you were after. You just had to guess from context. Even so, it was extremely popular which suggests that people found it easy to learn. It was used by Isaac Newton, Thomas Jefferson and, most famously, by Samuel Pepys, though when things got particularly personal and potentially self-incriminating, he complicated matters by adopting a hodge-podge of non-English words. I don't suppose the Puritan Shelton had in mind his shorthand being used to aid the concealment of accounts of Pepys's encounters under the table with the family maid.

Other shorthanders muscled in on the scene, with some of their titles coupling the notion of improvement to a particular form of writing. Throughout the history of people discussing how to write, how to write quickly or how to write more neatly, it is virtually impossible to disentangle the teaching and the learning of these physical attributes from a quasi-religious and egalitarian purpose and intended outcome. Indeed, one of these shorthanders, Jeremiah Rich, produced a tiny volume of the Psalms in metre, written in stenographic characters, which was published in 1659. He also worked with the great radical fighter for freedom and equality during the English Civil War, John Lilburne, who was hauled before the courts many times for defending the principle that we are born with rights and do not have to be given them by people deemed to be greater than us. During at least one of these trials, Jeremiah Rich was present using his shorthand to note proceedings. Lilburne was so impressed, he offered to give Rich a certificate for his labours.

Pitman had many such predecessors but he breaks with them when he introduces a purely phonetic shorthand – and one that corresponds to most of the phonemes for English. Unlike the work of any of his forebears, his shorthand survives, though others since him have developed shorthands which are not purely phonetic.

Perhaps the last word on shorthand should rest with Dickens. Though some would claim that Dickens' ear for dialogue and character can be traced back to the hours he spent in parliament and in court, writing down in shorthand the real speech of hundreds, if not thousands, of people, he shows himself in his semi-autobiographical novel, *David Copperfield*, a reluctant learner:

I bought an approved scheme of the noble art and mystery of stenography (which cost me ten and sixpence); and plunged into a sea of perplexity that brought me, in a few weeks, to the confines of distraction. The changes that were rung upon dots, which in such a position meant such a thing, and in such another position something else, entirely different; the wonderful vagaries that were played by circles; the unaccountable consequences that resulted from marks like flies' legs; the tremendous effects of a curve in a wrong place; not only troubled my waking hours, but reappeared before me in my sleep.

The second stream that Pitman stands in is spelling reform. Essentially, these revolve around an idea we've already met: that the way English has evolved is that the alphabet does not represent phonemes in a consistent way. To recap: some sounds can be represented in several different ways, e.g. the 'e' sound in the middle of 'bed' can also be indicated with the 'ea' of 'threat', and, arguably, by the 'eb' of 'debt'. Meanwhile, the 'ea' of 'beat' is the same letter combination in the middle of 'threat'. So we can say that some letters or letter combinations indicate sounds which differ from word to word.

The sixteenth century was a time of great debate about English spelling, which was still in flux. There were no national dictionaries, education departments or mass-media language police dictating how to spell. The modern linguist David Crystal gives the example of the word we now spell as 'disparagement'. Should it have been 'dispargement', 'dispergement', 'disparragement' or 'disparadgment'? The comic writers Sellar and Yeatman parodied this in their book *No Bed for Bacon* by having Shakespeare debating with himself on how to spell his own name, something which in real life he doesn't seem to have fixed.

As early as 1582, the writer Richard Mulcaster said that all this was shaming: 'Foreigners and strangers' were in a state of wonderment at the 'inconstancy of our letters' – only he spelled 'foreigners' as 'forenners'. Mulcaster's reforms included getting rid of 'ignorant superfluities' like the two Ds in 'didd' ('did'). However, he also thought that some words didn't have enough letters because the letters used weren't clear, unambiguous indicators of the sounds to make. That's why a 't' was put before the 'ch' of 'fech' to make 'fetch'. And it's Mulcaster who gave us what he called the 'marvellous' letter 'e' indicating the difference between 'mad' and 'made' or 'fat' and 'fate'.

Another kind of spelling reformer turned up in the seventeenth century who 'improved' our words by showing how they owed their origins to Latin. David Crystal traces these back to *The Writing Scholar's Companion* of 1695, with 'Infallible rules for Writing with Ease and Certainty'. (Not.) This anonymous person handed out rules for 'silent consonants' which 'must be written'. (Such writers are not only certain, they are also bossy.) 'Anon.' figured that the word 'det', 'dett' or 'dette' (as it had been written before 1549) should be spelled 'debt' because it owed its ultimate origins to a Latin word 'debitum'. 'Doubt' had been 'dute' and 'doute' but earned a 'b' on account of its Latin 'root' 'dubitare'. The same sort of pathways can be found for the 'b' in 'subtle', the 'c' in 'indict', the first 'c' in 'arctic', the 'p' in 'receipt', the 'l' in 'salmon', the 'l' in 'falcon', the 'l' in 'fault' and the 'h' in 'habit'.

All this was right but wrong. That's to say, it was etymologically right but didn't take heed of how the word reached the mouths of the people saying it. These words arrived as spoken or written French words in which these consonants didn't appear either in speech or in writing. Introducing these consonants is a good example of why language shouldn't be legislated on by real or imagined experts. David Crystal is too good a linguist himself to fall into this trap or indeed to knock his colleagues, but who can resist a giggle at the examples he has found of the scholars not simply being wrong in their pedantic method but just plain wrong?

It was decided that the word 'scissors' should be spelled with a 'sc' at the beginning because its origins lay with the Latin word 'scindere', 'to cut'. But they didn't. The word originates with the Latin 'cisorium' – a 'cutting instrument'. 'Scythe' had to have a 'sc' too because it too supposedly came from 'scindere'. But it didn't. It came from Old English 'siðe' (pronounced 'see-thuh'). 'Ptarmigan' was given a 'pt' beginning because it supposedly needed the same Greek prefix you see in 'pterodactyl' meaning 'wing-shaped'. But it didn't. It came from a Gaelic word 'tarmachan'.

Apart from the pratfalls I've already described, these little stories are warning shots to all spelling reformers: you may succeed but end up creating more problems than you solve. The other side of the same coin is that you may invent something so perfect that no one wants it.

The examples already cited are successes of a sort. In 1662 James Howell turned 'logique' to 'logic' and was a successful anti-doubler, turning 'warre' to 'war' and 'sinne' to 'sin', as well as 'toune' to 'town'.

There have been hundreds of such efforts across the centuries. These are a few examples, taken fairly randomly.

After the 'International Convention for the Amendment of English Orthography' that was held in Philadelphia in August 1876, societies were founded such as the English Spelling Reform Association and the American Spelling Reform Association. That year, the American Philological Society adopted a list of eleven reformed spellings for immediate use. These were: are→ar, give→giv, have→hav, live→liv, though→tho, through→thru, guard→gard, catalogue→catalog, (in)definite→(in)definit, infinite→infinit, wished→wisht. In 1898, the American National Education Association adopted its own list of twelve words to be used in all writings. These were: 'tho', 'altho', 'thoro', 'thorofare', 'thru', 'thruout', 'catalog', 'decalog', 'demagog', 'pedagog', 'prolog' and 'program'.

The Simplified Spelling Board was founded in the United

States in 1906. The SSB's original thirty members consisted of authors, professors and dictionary editors. Andrew Carnegie, a founding member, supported the SSB with yearly bequests of more than US$300,000. In April 1906 it published a list of 300 words, which included 157 spellings that were already in common use in American English. In August 1906 the SSB word list was adopted by Theodore Roosevelt, who ordered the Government Printing Office to start using it immediately.

In December 1906 the US Congress passed a resolution and the old spellings were reintroduced. Even so, some of the spellings survived and are commonly used in American English today, such as anaemia/anæmia→anemia and mould→mold. Others, such as mixed→mixt and scythe→sithe, did not survive. In 1920, the SSB published its *Handbook of Simplified Spelling*, which set out over twenty-five spelling reform rules. The handbook noted that every reformed spelling then in general use was originally the deliberate choice made by a single writer, who was followed at first by a small minority. In this spirit it encouraged people to 'point the way' and 'set the example' by using the reformed spellings whenever they could. However, with its main source of funds cut off, the SSB disbanded later that year.

In Britain, spelling reform was promoted from 1908 by the Simplified Spelling Society which attracted a number of prominent supporters. One of these was George Bernard Shaw and much of his considerable estate was willed to the cause. However, the conditions of his will gave rise to major disagreements amongst the members of the board and this hindered the development of a single new system. Even so, a Shavian system exists.

Over a two-month spell in 1934, the *Chicago Tribune* introduced eighty re-spelled words, including 'tho', 'thru', 'thoro', 'agast', 'burocrat', 'frate', 'harth', 'herse', 'iland', 'rime', 'staf' and 'telegraf'. An editorial in March 1934 reported that two-thirds of readers preferred the reformed spellings. Over the next forty years the newspaper gradually phased out the respelled words.

In 1949, a Labour MP, Dr Mont Follick, introduced a Private Member's Bill on spelling reform, which failed at the second reading, although in 1953 he again had the opportunity and this time it passed the second reading by 65 votes to 53. Because of anticipated opposition from the House of Lords, the bill was withdrawn after assurances from the Minister of Education that research would be undertaken into improving spelling education. This led in 1961 to James Pitman's Initial Teaching Alphabet (ITA), which was introduced into many British schools in an attempt to improve child literacy. Some people reading this book will have been taught ITA. Although it succeeded in its own terms (people learned to read ITA texts), the advantages were lost when children transferred to conventional spelling and after several decades the experiment was discontinued.

In 1969, the engineer and linguist Harry Lindgren proposed Spelling Reform 1 (SR1), which called for the short /ɛ/ sound (as in 'bet') to be spelled with <e> (for example friend→fr<e>nd, head→h<e>d). For a short time, this proposal was popular in Australia and was briefly adopted by the Australian government.

Fully worked-out alternative alphabets include Benjamin Franklin's phonetic alphabet, the Deseret alphabet, the Initial Teaching Alphabet, Interspel, the Romic alphabet, the Shavian alphabet revised into Quikscript and Unifon. Great names attached to spelling reform also include: John Milton, Samuel Johnson, Noah Webster, Charles Dickens, Alfred, Lord Tennyson, Theodore Roosevelt and H. G. Wells.

Wholesale spelling reform today is doomed for the time being because all present texts are in 'traditional orthography', i.e.

present-day spelling. A switch to a new spelling system would require people to develop a new kind of bilingualism: old and new reading.

That said, there may be another theoretical problem dogging the whole movement. What if we don't read alphabetically? Or, to modify that, what if people read only partially alphabetically? What other systems do such people use to read? Ultimately we read with and for meaning. That's to say, we make sense of the squiggles. We may use alphabetical clues, we may on occasions – or even quite often – sound the parts of a word, but for it all to matter, we use other systems. In short, these systems are grammatical and semantic.

One grammatical way is that we use the grammar we know to help us anticipate what comes next. We can do this to eliminate impossible combinations or include others. So if I am reading 'It will . . .' and, let's say, those are the last words on the page, I know for certain that the next word is not going to be 'the' or 'a' or 'an' or 'some' or 'both'. Without necessarily knowing what a 'verb' is, I will also have a sense of what kinds of words come after the expression 'It will . . .' These kinds of predictions about category go on all the time while we're listening, talking, reading and writing.

Also involved is a myriad of predictions to do with meaning. Meaning spreads even more widely than grammar. That's to say, I will bring all the ideas, feelings and information that precede the words I'm reading to bear on those particular words I am reading. That phrase 'I will . . .' is embedded in who this 'I' is earlier in the book, what this 'I' has done, and is likely to do – according to my judgement of them prior to this point. What's more, as I read and figure out what goes on in books in general, I have another, wider set of predictive powers to do with what characters do and how they do it, what heroes and villains do, what it means for a story to be 'first-person narrative', what happens in realist books, what is described in non-fiction books, memoirs, letters, ads and so on.

If I – and others who think like this – am right, then what we need is not so much spelling reform as reading reform. This involves making attractive reading matter much, much more available. It involves freeing up time in education and in life for people to get hold of this reading material. It involves a commitment to reading, to personal choice in reading, and to free discussion about what we read – assisted educationally, locally and nationally by our representatives. Historically, people have seized opportunities for themselves, most notably in the societies created by working people in the nineteenth and twentieth centuries. It's possible that digital communication has opened up new possibilities. Interestingly, as these have expanded, people have instituted their own spelling reforms in order to make reading and writing more enjoyable. They get the alphabet to do the work they choose it to do.

As ever, change in language comes about when the requirements and the technology change. Pitman succeeded with his shorthand because he was on the cusp of two major changes: political change, and the growth of the popular press and publishing. Pitman shorthand was a key tool for the masses to gain access (via the shorthand-using reporters) to what was really being said in courts, parliament and 'on location' where news was being made. As industry became more complex and bureaucratic, the dictating of letters and reports became more necessary. The 'shorthand typist' like my mother provided a means by which those letters and reports were distributed and, in turn, she used those skills and sense of herself to become greedy for more information about society and literature to develop herself intellectually and socially.

Pitman failed with his spelling reform because it was out of kilter, out of synch with the culture and technology of written material. He could theoretically reform the spelling of what someone might write tomorrow but he couldn't reform the spelling of what was written the day before – unless he had been able to hire thousands of copyists of all previous written material for decades on end. In theory, the internet could do just that. It could 'translate' any text into a reformed alphabet if there was a popular political and cultural will to pick up where Pitman left off. Even if this were to be enacted, though, I'm not sure that by itself it would solve the question of how and why our levels of literacy and our uses of literacy vary so widely. That matter is, I believe, cultural rather than alphabetical.

THE STORY OF

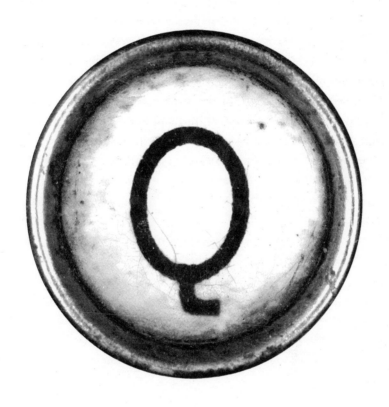

- **THE PHOENICIAN 'Q'** from 1000 BCE was 'qoph' which possibly meant 'monkey', possibly 'a ball of wool'! It was a circle with a line running down through it and on down: a monkey with its tail, or a ball of wool? Those who say that this letter was a ball of wool say that it was inspired by an ancient Egyptian hieroglyph. The ancient Greeks adopted it around 800 BCE calling it 'qoppa'. Whereas the Phoenicians distinguished between the 'k' of their 'kaph' and the 'q' of their 'qoph', the Greeks did not, and so they dropped 'qoppa'. But the Etruscans, with their long-standing connections to Greece, adopted it, kept it and passed it on to the Romans with a pronunciation more like 'kw'. A recognizable 'Q' appears in Roman inscriptions as early as 520 BCE.

It was the Romans who seemed to have invented the first form of the '"u" after "q"' rule. It was needed whenever the 'q' sound came before a vowel even if that vowel was 'u' as in the famous 'equus'. Amongst the various struggles that took place between the Germanic settlers of Britain and the Romance-language-speaking Normans, one was over the 'kw' sound. As we know now, Romance 'qu' beat Germanic 'cw'.

q

A 'q' without a flick-up at the end of its tail appears in Latin manuscripts in the AD 600s; Charlemagne's scribes liked that and adopted it for their 'Carolingian minuscule' and, following the usual pattern, the Italian printers adopted this form for their lower-case 'q' in the 1500s.

PRONUNCIATION OF THE LETTER-NAME

With the modern French pronunciation of 'q' as being like a tight-lipped version of our 'cue' sound, we can assume that the Normans brought it in as that sound – more or less. As all French children know, the letter-name for 'q' is identical in sound to the word 'cul', meaning 'bum', a word that appears in English in the phrase 'cul-de-sac'.

PRONUNCIATION OF THE LETTER

When it is the first letter of a word, in English 'q' is always followed by a 'u', to create usually an initial 'kw' sound, as in 'queen'. 'Liquor', with its internal 'qu', is not usually pronounced 'lick-kwor' but 'liquid' is 'lickwid'. 'Q' also appears occasionally as a final sound as in 'torque' and 'bisque' where it's a simple 'k' sound. It appears in some loan words like 'risqué', 'pique' and 'parquet' (all three from French) where it is also a 'k' sound. I've never been sure whether to say 'kw' or 'k' in the craft of 'marquetry'. In Arabic and Hebrew imports it appears without a 'u' as in 'Qatar' and 'Qabbala'. One modern way of transliterating Chinese is to use a 'q' for the 'ch' sound as in 'Qin'.

In the preposterously spelled 'queue' (and the name of the letter itself), the 'q' sound is neither a lone 'k' or 'kw' but is sounded as 'ky' as if the word were written as 'kyoo'. Only one word I can think of has two Qs in it: 'quin-quireme', the most popular use of it being in the poem 'Cargoes' by John Masefield, where it comes from Nineveh. This was compulsorily recited by the seven- and eight-year-old children of Pinner Wood Primary School in 1953.

The 'quick', 'quiet' and 'quite' words give people a bit of alliterative play: we like the sound of being 'quite quiet' and 'quite quick' and ducks go 'quack-quack'.

IS FOR QWERTY

THOUGH I MEET up with the alphabet every day, it doesn't come in alphabetical order. It is presented to me as QWERTYUIOP. Prior to the invention of the qwerty keyboard on the early typewriters, the word 'alphabet' meant two things at the same time: the letters that we use and alphabetical order or 'the ABC'. Both physically and mentally, the alphabet was stored alphabetically. The peoples who used the alphabet didn't really have another way of conceptualizing it.

Now, though, I sit down and select letters from a store that is arranged completely differently. One peculiarity of this is that I can recite the alphabet in a few seconds, I can touch-type, but I can't recite qwerty. So I know these two methods of storing the letters in different ways. If you arranged a dictionary or register of people at a conference in qwerty order, most of us would be lost. Yet I can't help feeling that qwerty, in its own way, subverts the orthodoxy of the alphabet. Day after day, for millions of people worldwide, it demands that we go to it and to its own special way of ordering literacy. The ABC alphabet has bitten back, though: the keyboards on our phones are in alphabetical order. As a qwerty-trained typist, I find it confusing to collect my pre-paid tickets from a machine on a railway station if the on-screen keyboard, looking exactly like a qwerty one, is arranged in alphabetical order. I can't find the letters to punch in my code!

Qwerty people have a hidden side: we have had relationships with different machines all through our lives, sometimes loving, sometimes resentful, sometimes dominant, sometimes being dominated. Part of our biography is in the play of our fingers over keys.

The story of the qwerty keyboard is intimately connected to a man called Charles Latham Sholes, who was one of the forces behind the abolition of capital punishment in Wisconsin. In 1851, John McCaffary, an Irish immigrant, had been sentenced to death and before a crowd of some 2,000–3,000 people he was hanged from a tree. McCaffary remained alive for some twenty minutes before eventually dying. This spectacle gave added strength to the campaign to abolish the death penalty, led by Sholes, first as a newspaper man for the *Kenosha Telegraph* and then as a senator in the Wisconsin Assembly. When the abolition bill was passed on 12 July 1853, John McCaffary became both the first and the last person to be executed in the state of Wisconsin.

It was Sholes and his friends who first created a typing machine that could be exploited commercially and it was Sholes in conjunction with a business associate, James Densmore, who first came up with the qwerty keyboard in 1873. By then, the patent was in the hands of Remington and the world's first qwerty typewriter – or QWERTY typewriter (it was upper case only) – appeared on 1 July 1874. It was the 'Remington No. 1', also known to aficionados as the 'Sholes and Glidden' after its designers.

Clearly, 'qwertyuiop' on a top row, 'asdfghjkl' on a second, and 'zxcvbnm' on a third, is a long way from 'ABCDEFGHIJ', 'KLMNOPQRS' and 'TUVWXYZ'. This layout came about because the model of typewriter Sholes, Soule and Densmore were playing with, using 'ABC', caused the 'typebars' (the thin metal arms on the end of which were the letters) to collide and jam. Densmore figured that the problem lay in letter frequency, the number of times a letter was used in English writing. He asked his son-in-law, a school superintendent in Pennsylvania, to tell him which letters and letter combinations appear most frequently. The trick to avoid the clashing was to place the most commonly occurring letters (on the end of their respective type-bars) as far apart as possible. The easiest way to make this happen mechanically, was to arrange the keyboard like this:

```
2   3   4   5   6   7   8   9   -   ,
  Q   W   E   .   T   Y   I   U   O P
    Z   S   D   F   G   H   J   K   L   M
      A X & C V B N ? ; R
```

Remington adjusted this, so that by 1878 it was:

```
2   3   4   5   6   7   8   9   -   '   _
  Q   W   E   R   T   Y   U   I   O   P   :
    A: S   D   F   G   H   J   K   L   M
      & Z C X V B N ? ; . !
```

Mistakenly, some people have said the qwerty layout enabled people to type faster. In fact, it was designed to slow typists down, requiring them to use different fingers or different hands for letters which were likely to appear together. What's odd is that it's survived. An electronic keyboard won't jam. There are no 'typebars'. Given that most people's quickest fingers are likely to be the index finger of each hand, one way to make typing faster would be to situate high-frequency letters within the orbit of those two fingers and the least frequent in the orbit of the third and fourth fingers.

If you can touch-type, you can expose yourself to a disconcerting experience by trying to touch-type on a keyboard with a slightly different arrangement. In France they use the 'azerty' keyboard which is arranged like this:

A Z E R T Y U I O P
Q S D F G H J K L M
W X C V B N

as opposed to (to remind you):

Q W E R T Y U I O P
A S D F G H J K L
Z X C V B N M

No one knows exactly why France adopted 'azerty' and any efforts to alter it have failed.

As Sholes sold the patent to Remington he made very little money out of his contribution to typewriting and keyboards. He is recorded as saying: 'Whatever I may have felt in the early days of the value of the typewriter, it is obviously a blessing to mankind, and especially to womankind. I am glad I had something to do with it. I built it wiser than I knew, and the world has the benefit of it.' Densmore was more canny. He retained a royalty and died with half a million dollars to his name.

As with most technology, the typewriter and the keyboard can be seen as both emancipating and oppressing at the same time. It enabled millions of women to earn money independently, and to see worlds other than their homes. On the other hand, it put those same women into what used to be called 'the typing pool', where, all day and every day, they pounded typewriters to 'write' what wasn't their own writing on the machines that weren't theirs. I can now see the importance of my mother owning her own typewriter. It enabled her, in the 1940s and 50s, to write what she wanted to write and present it with the same quality as the best around.

The first typewriter I saw belonged to my mother. My mother was Mum, to my father she was 'Con', to friends she was 'Connie', to children and colleagues at her school she was 'Mrs Rosen', but in a disconcerting way, every so often she was a 'typist' and a 'secretary'. She became this because of a locked black box stored in our 'front room' along with a furry square mat. This was her Remington typewriter, which she could sit at for hours, threateningly ignoring the rest of us, typing away without looking at the keys, at a rate of clacketty-clacks matched only by the speed she clacketty-clacked with her knitting. We could see that there was an inaccessible, unreachable part of Mum working away in there that wasn't very Mum at all. It belonged to some earlier pre-Mum era when we didn't even exist.

I liked to sit next to her and watch how her long fingers hammered away, how the metal letters stuck on their thin arms flailed to and fro, how the ribbon jumped up and down, and the ribbon's wheels jigged round. I liked the way things got stuck every so often and she would hesitate for a moment, poke her finger into the jangled arms, release them and carry on.

And the page of type: how could it be so perfect, its titles underlined, the margins so neat, the lines of type spaced so evenly? She explained how the 'return' could be altered, how you could arrange it so that the margins were regular. She showed us how to change the ribbon and – best of all – she let us clean the metal letters with a toothbrush. The tiny metal flanges of the letters would get a build-up of ribbon fibre and ink, and the toothbrush would get them sharp and shiny again. I loved the keys themselves: each letter was printed on to the cream-coloured disc of the key, looking as if it was under glass, surrounded by its own circular ridge of metal. Then the noise would stop. She would put the machine back in its box and slot it back in the alcove.

We weren't allowed to use it on our own. This was a special and expensive machine. For letters to appear on a page as cleanly and beautifully as this, she couldn't risk my brother and me just playing about on it. It was too important. This way of producing letters on the page had its own black box. This kind of alphabet was under lock and key. This kind of alphabet was handled by someone extremely clever who had gone to a special college to learn how to do speed clacketty-clacking.

The mystique was dented when my parents found us an old typewriter. It had no case. There were one or two letters that didn't type. The right-hand margin clip was broken. So? It was a typewriter and my brother and I spent hours on it. First as one-finger typers and then as two-finger typers, then as two-finger-and-a-thumb-for-the-space-bar typers. Because it didn't have a case, it grew fluff. Fluff got in amongst the thin arms that held the letters and under the keys. Norman and Butt, the estate agents in the shop beneath our flat, threw their old typewriter ribbons into the dustbins in our yard. My brother and I went through the bins and found two-coloured ribbons – half black, half red – and we put these on our typewriter so that we could write in two colours. Our forefingers were learning qwerty. We could make pages of print – of a kind – just like a professional, just like Mum. Or nearly. We knew that it wasn't as good as hers. But hers had to be better than good.

Once she wrote and typed a story about a girl she taught and sent it off to the BBC. The BBC said they liked it and she was on the Home Service reading it. I asked the head teacher if I could go to the Physics lab to listen to it. He said, 'No.' I was disappointed. He said, 'No, you can listen to it with me in my study and I'll get someone else to do assembly that morning.' So I sat with the headmaster, on a chair old enough for Shakespeare to have sat on, he said, and we listened to my mum reading the story that she had typed on her typewriter. 'Very good,' he said. 'She was very good.'

My brother broke through a barrier. He got an Olivetti. It was slim and sleek. It didn't clacketty-clack, it puttered. It was made of a serene dark green metal. The keys were like flat dice: black, square, plastic, with white letters. Everything worked. And when he finished, he could slot it into a case and carry it about with him. It was a 'portable'. With his Olivetti, my brother threw out the pre-war heaviness of qwerty and brought in something as neat and as hard-edged as Bridget Riley's art and Mary Quant's hairdo. If I typed on it, he would tell me not to type so hard. You don't bang down the keys, like Mum has to, he said.

I spent my twenty-first birthday money on a portable too. I went German. It was an Adler: black and cream. Here the keys were like chunky cream lozenges. It wasn't metal. It was bendy plastic. It didn't putter. It clucked. What was I thinking of? I had foregone style for lightness. This was a writing machine I could take anywhere. It wasn't much thicker than a Dickens novel. I moved up a notch. I was doing two fingers on each hand and two thumbs now. I remember sitting in the dressing room of the Nuffield Theatre, in Southampton, dressed in my costume of Obadiah for a production of *Tristram Shandy*, with my Adler. I had a deadline for an article to write for the student magazine, *Isis*. If I could bash it out, while waiting to go on stage for the matinée, get it into an envelope and into the post on the way home after the show, it would meet the deadline and get into the magazine. Cluck cluck cluck. I knew then that I was in charge of qwerty. Qwerty did what I told it to do.

Even better, in the student magazine office was a big Olivetti. Like a real professional one. As big as my mother's old Remington but as stylish as my brother's. Over the summer, the news was that the office was closing, and we were moving to a new office that someone had kitted out. There was a rumour that Robert Maxwell was involved. The Olivetti went into the back of a car and found its way home. It sat on the desk I got for my twenty-first birthday, and I sat upstairs in my parents' house in the holidays back from college, typing the poems that would end up in my first book for children, *Mind Your Own Business*. I used triple-carbonated paper, three copies in one go. Even my mother was impressed. She had never liked the mess of the old carbon paper you had to slot in by hand between the sheets.

And wasn't the typeface rather snazzy too? Didn't my mother's seem rather quaint? Even as she was sending off her scripts to BBC Schools Radio, didn't it make her writing seem old too? I was Olivetti qwerty man.

Someone mentioned electric typewriters. What's the point of that? It doesn't make you type any faster. Someone mentioned that you didn't have to go back over a mistake and whack it with an 'x'. You now pressed a delete button and the letter disappeared. What! You could make a letter disappear? There's a ribbon, and it lifts the letter off the page. The letters aren't ink. They're more like Letraset. They're like . . . stuck on to the page. So the little ribbon unsticks them. I was up for it. By making qwerty less permanent, it was making qwerty look perfect on the page. Scripts, articles, poems would have no more mistakes. I had to upgrade myself. This four-finger, staring-at-the-keyboard thing had to end. I had to learn how to touch-type.

So I enrolled for a two-week typing course at a typing college in an upstairs room in Camden Town. All day, I sat with young women who had just left school, sixteen-, seventeen- and eighteen-year-olds. All day we did the exercises, 'frf', 'juj', 'kik', 'ded'. Hours and hours forcing my mind, fingers, keys and letters to work along in synch. I loved it. And in the evenings, after school, I came home and forced myself to type what I had to type using what I had learned. Qwerty started to disappear from being something I stared at. Now it was something that my fingers knew. Because I did so much typing in the evening, I found the daytime class easier and easier. I became annoying. At least two people in the class stopped talking to me. I didn't mean to sound like a qwerty show-off though it must have looked that way. I'm sorry.

The electric typewriter was supposed to be portable. Like a suitcase is portable. And, like a fat black plastic suitcase, it stayed put. The letters it made were strangely thin and weaselly. People said I had to get a golf-ball. Everyone was talking about golf-balls. I was going to get a golf-ball, when someone else said that it was going to be computers. What you're going to be able to do now, they said, is type something and store it in the machine. Then you can call it up again, change it as many times as you like and only when you're happy with it do you have to print it. You get this printer where you put in these sheets that are all joined up, press a button and it prints it all out in a great long sheet, which you tear into pages.

No thanks, I said, I'll stick with the electric. I'm loving erasing my misdemeanours with the delete button. I can even put up with thin, weaselly qwerty. My fingers know everything now. I rule qwerty like the King of Ruritania rules the peasants. Every letter does just as I tell it to. Well, mostly. 'Z' and 'X' give me bother. That quick change from the little finger to the third finger of the left hand. Don't ask me to do it quickly. And another thing, I didn't do a third week, when I would have learned how to touch-type the numbers. I have to look. But apart from all that, I'm Mr Qwick Qwerty Guy now. My electric typewriter sounded like jazz: te tutter, ta ta ta tutter, tutter te ta ta ta. The bebop of qwertyuiop.

I bought an Amstrad. Why were the letters green? Not when they were printed. On the screen. The screen was green, the letters were green. And with whopping great big serifs. No one does serifs like that any more. But now, I had joined the era of letters on a screen. The page was starting to lose its dominance. Where once writing had been that permanent thing I did with something that made marks, now the mark was temporary. Everything was postponable. OK, if there was a deadline, something had to be fixed. Everything else could be changed. And I loved it that you could leave something for a year and then decide to change it. The imperfect screen page had only ever been seen by me. So where qwerty had once been permanent, as with my mother's typewriting, and where it had been semi-permanent, with pages of writing with the electric typewriter, it was now, potentially, forever provisional.

I was loyal to Amstrad. I stayed with it long after people were writing documents and playing that weird-coloured ping-pong game on the Apple, and after PCs came in and you could store thousands of documents and obliterate the universe or battle to the death in Japanese. I got an Apple. It was called a 'duo-dock'. You had a laptop which you docked into a loading bay which turned it into a desktop. Qwerty was now portable and office in one. One moment, I could type small on a tiny laptop keyboard and the next I could be big and old-style on the PC-like keyboard. It was like slipping from recorder to saxophone. The fingers just knew what to do.

And that's how it is for me now, promiscuously moving from laptops to PCs, taking my portable qwerty skill with me. Typing with my eyes shut works as a party trick for five-year-olds. Talking about one thing while typing something else is one of the most annoying things you can do with your friends and loved ones. It still seems incredible that my mind and fingers can own a knowledge which enables me to produce pages of perfect script.

There is a drawback. Of course there is. There is always a drawback. If I write on to paper, the scribblings-out stay there. Bad for looking good. Good for staying in sight just in case I want to use something that I didn't want before. Corrections on the screen disappear. The delete button was invented by employers who wanted their secretaries to produce perfect documents. If these machines had been invented by writers, there would have been a 'correct' button which would turn the word red and bung it in the margin. Yes, I know there's an application like that that's been invented, but I want a key. I want 'correct' to be of the same status as qwertyuiop. Just something that my right-hand little finger could learn. Bebop and dop on, Correct!

Today, there are millions of keyboards and printers in homes, schools and libraries. 'Qwerty' still reigns in the office but it has escaped. Many more people than there were in my mother's time have the means of producing documents and writing of all kinds in a form that looks and feels professional.

I am curious about one thing, though. There is still enormous emphasis placed by governments and education departments on the presentation of correct writing. Schools spend millions of hours teaching children handwriting, spelling, punctuation and general orthographic neatness – with a pencil or pen. Quite a bit of time is spent doing 'IT', none of which involves learning 'qwerty'. If 'qwerty' was on the curriculum, millions of children would be able to write nearly as fast as they think, and go back and edit pages of their writing so that they could present them immaculately. Instead of learning spelling and grammar as something that exists only in textbooks, they could learn how to use the spell- and grammar checks. They're not failsafe but they are a modern data-bank on which we can base our work. It's only a modern way of using a reference book. I have a feeling that in fifty years' time, people will look back with bemusement at this era in which electronic 'qwerty' was so dominant, while schools still spent so much time on pen and paper. By the way, the longest word that you can write from the top row of a qwertyuiop keyboard is 'typewriter'.

THE STORY OF

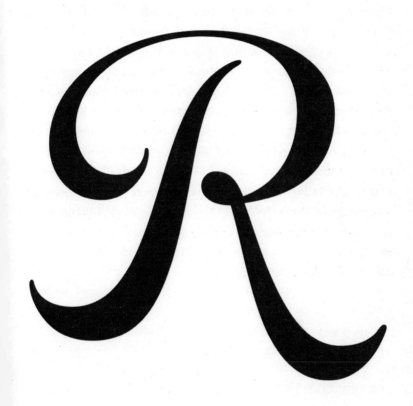

- **AN EARLY FORM** of 'R' appears in ancient Semitic inscriptions as a probable 'resh' meaning 'head' with 'r' being the sound it signified. At this stage it looked like a simplified profile or outline of a whole human head. This shape (but not the word or sound) was a possible copy from an ancient Egyptian hieroglyph. Around 1000 BCE the Phoenicians turned it into a backwards or reverse 'P' shape. This is the early form of the Greek 'rho' letter appearing around 725 BCE. This passed to the Etruscans, who handed it on to the Romans, who reversed it and added the beginnings of R's tail, probably to distinguish it from 'P'. Classical Romans from Imperial Rome produced the letter as we know it today.

r

This appears first in Latin manuscripts from around AD 500 and was adopted first by Charlemagne's scribes with their 'Carolingian minuscule' lettering and then by Italian printers in the 1500s as our lower case.

PRONUNCIATION OF THE LETTER-NAME

This is one of the vowel-consonant names like 'eff', 'ell', 'em', 'en', 'ess' and 'ex'. The theory again is that this was once 'erray' and contracted initially to the first syllable of that word. From there it could have evolved into any of the vowel-plus-'r' combinations so quite why it ended up sounding the same as we pronounce the word 'are' is not quite clear. Modern French – which is sometimes a guide to how the Norman French may have spoken – pronounce it in more or less the same way as we do: 'air'.

PRONUNCIATION OF THE LETTER

Speakers of English have many ways of pronouncing or not pronouncing this letter. As a native of southern Britain, I'm one of the frightful gang who don't voice it at all in words like 'card', 'mother', 'fire' and 'fur'. When a vowel is the next sound to follow it, though, I do sometimes make a non-growly sound by rolling my tongue up on to the roof of my mouth as in 'for a laugh', 'foreign' and 'fire on deck'. I even commit the heinous crime of inserting a non-existent 'r' sound when I say 'draw-r-a picture', 'saw-r-a man'. Some who have grown up selecting which Rs to pronounce and which not also pronounce their Rs as a 'rw' or a 'w'.

Those who always voice the 'r' in 'card', 'mother', 'fire' and 'fur' vary in several different ways, rolling their tongue so that it vibrates against the roof of their mouth, growling at the back of the throat, or making quite a marked 'r' as in the stereotypic pirate-voice saying 'arrrr'.

As an initial letter in words, 'r' appears with an 'h' in 'rhino' and 'rhythm' or with a consonant or consonants preceding it as with 'tram', 'pram', 'dram', 'gram', 'cram', 'brim', 'thrill', 'stream', 'krill' and Anna Karenina's lover 'Vronsky'. I know someone with the surname 'Nri' and people of my age have learned how to say 'Sri Lanka'. It combines with vowels to make (in my pronunciation) a vowel sound as in 'card', 'herd', 'third', 'lord', 'curd', 'board', 'peered', 'feared', 'tired', 'bored', 'fared', 'stair', 'stare', 'mere', 'pier', 'pour', 'our', 'lure', 'poor', 'dinosaur', 'are', 'coir', 'fleur de lys' and 'heart' . . . For all pronouncers of 'r' these are vowel-plus-consonant sounds. Following the 'r', we use consonants to make words like 'hurt', 'carp', 'curse', 'lord', 'barf', 'large', 'ark', 'snarl', 'furze', 'arc', 'curve', 'curb', 'turn' and 'harm'.

'R' also appears with 'w' in 'playwright', 'write' and 'wrong', which I'll look at under 'W'.

It doubles in 'purr' so that we don't have to double it again to make 'purred, purring' but 'bar' doubles to 'barring, barred' so that we can distinguish it from 'bare, baring, bared'.

It provides a key part of our growl sound, 'grrrr', and our 'filler' sound, 'er', 'err', 'eer', 'air' or 'erm' depending on where you come from. Sound-play with 'r' gives us 'Around the rugged rock the ruddy rascal ran.' When we're cold we are supposed to say, 'brrrr', and lions 'roar'. We sing, 'A ring a ring a roses' (which, while we're on it, has no documentary evidence to link it to the Plague). Some people used to be called 'Ra-ra girls'. There are the 'three 'Rs' which are in fact 'r', 'w' and 'a' as in 'reading, writing and arithmetic'. We like putting the phrase 'right or wrong' on the end of statements.

Perhaps, then, we can claim that 'r' is our most adapt-able letter.

R IS FOR RHYME

EVERY DAY, I make or discover a rhyme. I'm writing what you're reading now a few hours after writing my 'Q is for Qwerty' chapter. I told my children what I was doing and my daughter said, 'What's qwerty?'

'It's the first six letters on a keyboard,' I said, 'and so it gives its name to the kind of keyboard we use; I had mastered qwerty, by the time I was thirty.' This isn't true, but rhyme's a bit like that. If it works, it works.

Rhyming also draws attention to the fact that language is a made thing. It's not a transparent hole through which we look at reality. It's a tool we make and use in order to then shape reality, rather as if we kept making chisels in order to sculpt. One of the peculiar things about language is that we often forget we're making it and using it. We do have explicit ways of discussing it, which is what I'm doing now, but we also have many furtive ways of drawing attention to it, without saying, 'What I'm doing now is talking about language.' The poetical word for this is 'prosody', meaning the musicality of speech or writing or, more specifically, of poetry. Anything that patterns a piece of speech or writing is prosody. It's the aesthetics of language. Rhyme, rhythm, alliteration, assonance, repetition, stress, intonation (in speech) – or some or all of these in combination with each other, are the main colours that writers have on their palette to work with. The alphabet is the brush. And, to grind this metaphor into the ground, the same brush will sometimes give you different strokes. And sometimes the same stroke can be produced by different brushes.

Both problems can be found in the days of the week: Sunday and Monday are perfect rhymes but the 'un' of 'Sunday' does not have the exact same letters as the 'on' of Monday, and most of us will pronounce the '-day' part of the name as 'day' or 'dee'. We can make the same letters do different jobs. When we line up words together that look unalike to make them sound alike – as with rhyme – we draw attention in a small way to the making of words and the use of letters. A good deal of the time, though, we can take thousands of words and find rhymes for them where the rhyming part of the word is identical: 'cup' and 'pup', 'hill' and 'pill'. We notice this stuff in different ways: it may make us laugh, it may be the means by which one idea or feeling is linked to another; and the neatness and completeness give us pleasure:

Had we but world enough, and time,
This coyness, Lady, were no crime.
Andrew Marvell

The alphabet in the original spelling gave the rhyme as 'tyme' and 'crime' – the same sound produced by different letters – but in modern print, the spelling adds to the symmetry. The rhyme links 'time' and 'crime' but in one sense there is no link between time and crime. A crime is still a crime whenever it happens or no matter how long it takes to commit.

In the opening couplet and with its opening rhyme, the poem announces that it will be paradoxical, that era's favourite poetical stance. A paradox yokes together unlikely partners, usually playing on the irony that these two unalike elements are so close. ('What goes round the world but stays in one corner?' a child asks me. 'A stamp.'). The implied meaning of Marvell here is of course that the Lady's coyness *is* a crime and it is precisely because, or so he claims, of a problem with time: the impossibility of human beings having all the time in the world. Without announcing itself, the rhyme draws attention to the paradox and theme of the poem: the crime of coyness in contrast to the time available.

In poetry, rhyme has company: some kind of rhythm or beat, regular – as here – or subverted, as with, say, Ogden Nash or John Hegley. Either way, there is usually a quality in the air of running up to take a jump, leading up to the rhyme. In this poem, Marvell does this with four metrical 'feet', each containing a 'te-TUM'. If you were writing it musically, each foot would be a crotchet-quaver. This means that as we read the poem, we get to know when the jumper is going to take off, when the rhyme is going to happen: 'te-TUM, te-TUM, te-TUM, te-RHYME, te-TUM, te-TUM, te-TUM, te-RHYME'. And here the alphabet plays tricks on us. It conceals as it reveals. There are no specific letters to help us see the rhythm, but by pronouncing the letters of the words according to custom, we make the rhythm: 'Had WE but WORLD eNOUGH, and TIME . . .' By the time we get to the end of the second line, the last foot is waiting to trip the 'Lady' up. The foot says it's 'no crime' when the poet means that it is.

The alphabet has yet another job to do here. The pulse of poetry before Andrew Marvell's day was marked and aided by alliteration and assonance. In each line of the poem – or, in the case of Old English poetry, in each half-line – there were sounds, consonants or vowels which were repeated. Here from the middle of the fifteenth century are the opening four lines of a poem about blacksmiths:

Swarte-smeked smethes [black-smoked smiths], smattered with
  smoke,
Drive me to deth with den of here dintes [their blows]:
Swich nois [such noise] on nightes ne herd men never,
What knavene [what workmen] cry and clattering of knockes!

By Marvell's day, with rhyme in the ascendancy, the alliteration and assonance (repeat of vowel sounds) was quietening down.

Had We but World enough, and time,
This Coyness, Lady, were no Crime.

This kind of repetition of sound can do all sorts of things but here, I suspect, it works like the bassist in a band, helping to hold together the melody and rhythm. When you hear the alliteration or assonance, there is a sense in which you have been bounced from one sound to another. Just as that runner, running up for the long jump, does that stuttering and rhythm of the run, so alliteration-assonance marks out the 'feet' of the poem's lines. Or put another way: I've underlined the alliteration – alliteration is like an oral underlining. It's also a way of showing the 'letter-i-ness' of letters. It shows off what any given letter can do. If we want to exaggerate it, we can give those Ws a real elongated quality, lengthening them into the vowels that follow: 'weeee' and 'worrrrld', like time, can go on for ever. And if we want to curse the Lady's coyness then we can be as guttural and phlegmy as we like with 'cccccoyness' and 'cccccrime'. Or we can just hint at it and let the alphabet do its work.

The word 'rhyme' is a screw-up. It should be 'rime'. It once was 'rime'. This spelling showed the roots of the word in both Old English and Old Irish, but someone thought that 'rime' was related to 'rhythm'. 'Rhythm' is spelled like that because of its origins in Greek. But the origins of 'rhyme' aren't Greek. To sum up: someone very clever changed 'rime' to 'rhyme' because he thought everyone was ignorant. But they weren't. He was. But he thought he wasn't. And his view won the day. Result: the alphabet misapplied. If you're disturbed that I've taken twenty seconds out of your life to explain that, please spare a thought for my children who have all in their time had 'rhyme' on their lists of words for spelling homework.

To complicate matters further, 'rime' still exists as a technical term. Many teachers of early reading find it useful to show children that there are two parts to a syllable: the 'onset' and the 'rime'. In 'bat', 'b' is the 'onset' and 'at' is the 'rime'. Maybe, the person who came up with 'rime' to mean something that isn't 'rhyme' could have thought of another word. Apart from anything else, 'rime' already existed as a word. It means 'frost'. I think I could make an argument for saying that 'rime' (meaning a part of a syllable) is the alphabet misapplied too.

Rhyme is so much with us and in us that it's easy to think that it's 'natural' or 'inborn'. But some cultures get by without it. The ancient Greeks knew about it, didn't do it much, and when they did, it was often for comic effect, as in a play by Euripides, where Hercules speaks in rhyme when he's drunk. There are two short moments of rhyme in *The Iliad* but *The Odyssey* doesn't rhyme. If you're looking for a rhyme for 'Odyssey', 'theodicy' would work:

Homer wrote about Odysseus
his hubris and his Odyssey.
Voltaire wrote about Pangloss,
his idiocy and theodicy.

The ancient Egyptian, Chinese, Arabic and Persian poets were rhymers, and rhyme for most of these writers was one of the defining characteristics of poetry. The Roman poets Virgil, Horace, Ovid and Catullus gave it a go but didn't stick with it. How and why it became the dominant form of poetry in the West has never been fully explained. One possibility is that the Arab presence in Spain helped create the hugely successful rhyming troubadour poetry. The Church became enthusiastic rhymers in religious song, perhaps influenced by Irish verse. By the thirteenth century in England there were rhymes appearing in the shape of ballads.

The first rhymes I remember were when my mother read me Beatrix Potter's *The Tale of Squirrel Nutkin* where the cheeky squirrel (and surrogate child-reader) is rude to Mr Brown the Owl, peeping in through his keyhole and singing a riddle:

A house full, a hole full!
And you cannot gather a bowl-full.

My father meanwhile took on the responsibility of delivering anything from Shakespeare to rude rhymes, from Virgil to Yiddish comedy. The first I remember was:

Herrel Shmerel [the foolish little man]
went to the races,
lost his gatkes [long johns or trousers]
and his braces.

Once rhyme was embedded and we had become acculturated to it, he could subvert our expectations:

The higher up the mountain
the sweeter grows the grass
the higher up the donkey climbs
the more he shows his face.

At school we sang rhyming hymns ('There is a green hill far away'), and learned rhyming poems by Robert Louis Stevenson ('Faster than fairies, faster than witches'). Out in the playground we said:

Inky pinky ponky
The farmer bought a donkey.
The donkey died,
The farmer cried,
Inky pinky ponky.

On the radio they were singing about the doggie in the window, the one with the waggly tail. Then Elvis said that he wasn't nothing but a hound dog, and my brother's friends had blues records from the Mississippi Delta that rhymed 'bed' with 'bread'.

There were some books that said you didn't have to rhyme. There were poems by Carl Sandburg and William Carlos Williams. It was a modern thing. Or an American thing. You could just say it. The grip of the alphabetical echo was loosened. D. H. Lawrence said that you could say that you went to a water-trough and saw a snake and so you threw something at it, and it went away and you felt ashamed. I wrote that I was in my room and saw a moth so I killed it and it made me think that we've been like that since prehistoric times. It didn't rhyme.

But then we did Gerard Manley Hopkins.

He noted that the two lines of 'Ding dong bell, pussy's in the well' have the same number of beats but a different number of syllables: three beats per line. First line: three syllables. Second line: five syllables. He invented 'sprung rhythm' where his poems would rhyme but the beat of the line would depend on where he stressed the syllable. And using the Old English effects of alliteration and assonance, he could knit the lines together. He got rid of the 'foot' that repeats itself along the line. So, on his own, in the 1870s he created a kind of jazz poetry where the beat loops over several unstressed syllables: BOOM ba-ba-ba-ba BOOM BOOM ba ba BOOM. He realized that some people just wouldn't get it, so as he wrote, he marked his poems with accents:

With swíft, slow, sweet, soúr, adázzle dím.
[Ba BOOM ba ba BOOM ba-BOOM BOOM]

With Hopkins' alliteration this became: Wa-SOOM sa sa SOOM, a-DOOM DOOM.

Needless to say, when he sent his first sprung rhythm poem off to be published, they asked him to take the accents out and then didn't publish the poem anyway. Hopkins was a Jesuit and perhaps the editor of a Jesuit journal wasn't the most likely person in the Victorian era to be hip to this sort of thing. Though these rhythms became all-important to Hopkins, he went on rhyming. Sometimes the rhyme-words almost disappear in an unstressed or half-word limbo:

I caught this morning morning's minion, king-
dom of daylight's dauphin, dapple-dawn-drawn Falcon, in his riding.

To my ears, this sounded like play, jazz, experiment and impro.
Miles Davis on the page. Not that I saw it at the time: it's shot
through with alphabetical dance. In French, we were taught that
some writers spent whole days or weeks looking for 'le mot juste'
– the right word, but the rightness of the word would depend on
it being right in meaning for that place and time. Here was another
kind of search for the right word, to find the one that chimed
with the ones next to it. Again and again. Poem after poem.

The poet laureate of the time, Robert Bridges, didn't know
what to make of it and sat on the stuff that Hopkins sent him,
until 1918. Hopkins had died of typhoid in Dublin not long
before his forty-fifth birthday in 1889.

I spent two years trying to write like Hopkins and although
it worked for Dylan Thomas, Seamus Heaney and Ted Hughes,
I wasn't good enough at it. I went back to free verse which is
called by its detractors 'chopped-up prose' or 'tennis without
the net'. Looked at that way, it is poetry at its least alphabetical,
rarely drawing attention to its letters in any consistent way,
except in the experiments of e. e. cummings, Apollinaire and
concrete poetry. It draws on timing, and the length of the line
as its 'foot' or basic unit. It's been around for a long time: ever
since people translated the metrical Hebrew verse of the 'Song
of Songs' and the Psalms into non-metrical verse. Greek and
Latin were the first languages for that, followed by the various
vernaculars, like Old English, gothic and on into the modern
era. The Wycliffe Bible of 1382–95 does free verse pretty well
– here I've arranged the lines:

Lo! my love, thou art fair;
lo! thou art fair,
thine eyes be the eyes of culvers [doves].
Lo! my darling, thou art fair and shapely;
our bed is fair as flowers.
The beams of our houses be of cedar;
our couplings be of cypress.

As the Wycliffe translators show, repetition is the most useful tool in the box for free verse poets. It's 'free' because you decide what to repeat and when, rather than be bound by the demands of a 'foot' or of a rhyme. It's in the repetition that the prosody creeps in and the letter-i-ness of letters assert themselves.

In my own writing I've mixed and matched, noting that children love rhythm and rhyme but that sometimes means that they don't hear the words or that the words tell the rhyme but not the truth. Sometimes the youngest ones don't hear these things either.

I do a poem that says:

Down behind the dustbin
I met a dog called Jim
He didn't know me
and I didn't know him.

One sharp lad says, 'How did you know his name was Jim then?' I don't know the answer. I say to very young ones:

Down behind the dustbin
I met a dog called Felicity.
It's a bit dark down here,
They cut off my . . .?

'. . . head,' they say. Well, it would be dark. One of them said:

Humpty Dumpty sat on the wall
Humpty Dumpty had a great fall
All the king's horses and all the king's men
Trod on him.

Which proves that a not-rhyme can do as much as a rhyme. I reply:

Roses are red
violets are blue
most poems rhyme
this one doesn't.

THE STORY OF

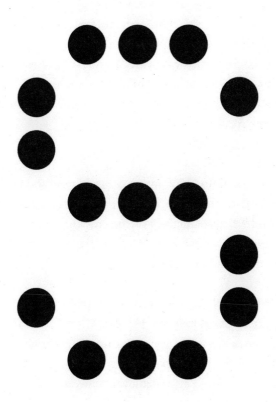

- **EARLY STAGES OF** 'S' written by the ancient Semites of some 3,600 years ago appear to be a horizontal, curvy 'W' shape, perhaps signifying an archer's bow. The Phoenicians of 800 BCE made it angular, looking identical to our 'W'. At this stage it was the letter known as 'shin' meaning 'tooth' with the value of 'sh'. The early ancient Greeks rotated it to the vertical and called it 'sigma' and it indicated the 's' sound. The Etruscans and early Romans took this and flipped it over so that it resembled an angular 'S'. The Imperial Roman inscriptions turned it into the thin-thick serif letter we know today.

s

Following the pattern of many other letters, the lower-case 's' starts off in the Latin manuscripts of the AD 500s, is taken up by Charlemagne's scribes for their 'minuscule' and is adopted by the Italian printers of the late fifteenth century as their lower-case 's'.

PRONUNCIATION OF THE LETTER-NAME

'S' is part of the family of 'F', 'L', 'M', 'N', 'R' and 'X' whose names are vowel plus continuous consonant (or, in X's case, continuous in part of its sound). This means that in late Roman and early medieval times it was called 'essay' and this became contracted to 'ess', perhaps to distinguish it from 'zed'.

PRONUNCIATION OF THE LETTER

At the beginning of words, but not combined with other consonants, it can be 's' as in 'simple' or a 'sh' sound as in 'sure' and 'sugar'. We combine it with 'h' to make 'sh' and it can also combine with consonants after it to make 'Sri Lanka', 'stew', 'swing', 'spin, 'ski', 'slow', 'scowl', 'Svetlana', 'snoop', 'smile', 'squeal', 'stroke', 'spring' and 'school'; and in various Yiddishisms as 'shlemiel', 'shmendrik' and the famous 'Oedipus, shmoedipus, what's it matter so long as he loves his mother?' In the '-sion' suffix it is usually pronounced as a 'sh' as in 'pension', though it can be 'zh' as in 'explosion' or 'erasure'.

In various places in words it can be a 'hard s' sounding like a 'z sound' as in 'exercise'.

It's the most common plural in English, with only a few words like 'oxen', 'children', 'women', 'men' and 'brethren' showing the Old Germanic plural. It's also the most common way in which we conjugate the third person singular, as in 'he eats' ('soft s') or 'she hums' ('hard s'). Non-natives find this hard to remember and if you're a spy, it's one of the ways you can spot that someone is unlikely to have been brought up speaking English as a first language. We don't like the 's' or 'z' sound abutting up to another 's' so we insert an 'e' or an 'e' sound to make it easier for ourselves. So it's 'cats', 'dogs', 'hits' and 'shops' but 'misses', 'mixes' and 'fizzes'. One kind of plural causes difficulties: 'potatoes', 'mangos', 'tomatoes', 'tangos', 'pinkos', 'lingoes', 'dingos', 'hellos' . . .

At the ends of single-syllable words, an 's' on its own is usually double: 'pass', 'boss', 'hiss' and 'mess', but we have the word 'pus' which is not the same as 'puss', and the words 'has', 'was', 'yes', 'bus', 'is' and 'as', and, since the popularity of *Les Misérables*, there are people saying 'Les Mis'. This seems to follow on from some other abbreviated words ending in a 'hard s' like 'biz' and 'showbiz', 'Pres.', 'des. res.' and the shortened names Les, Des and Baz.

Shakespeare's close friends called each other 'coz' for 'cousin'; we say 'cos' for 'because' but the Wizard of Oz is a wonderful 'wiz'.

The 'sh' combination gives us an 'imperative' 'Sh!' or 'Shhhhh!' which may come from the verb 'shush', as in, 'I shushed them up . . .'

Loan words allow us to borrow German ways of using 's' as in 'kitsch', 'schadenfreude' and the stunningly spelled 'Nietzsche'.

In some words the 's' is not voiced as in 'island', 'aisle' and 'isle'.

Sound-play with 's' gives us words like 'sizzle', the 'sssss' of hissing disapproval, 'sassy', 'sis' for 'sister', 'suss' as an abbreviation for 'suspect' or 'suspicion', and a host of words using the 's' combinations like 'shloosh', 'slosh', 'smash', 'splosh', 'splash', 'swish' . . . And there's 'I do like to be beside the seaside' which shares out Bs and Ss.

I look at the now-extinct 'f'-looking 's' in 'S is for Signs and Sign Systems', below.

S IS FOR SIGNS AND SIGN SYSTEMS

IN EVERYDAY CHAT, the words 'sign' and 'symbol' are used interchangeably but academics like to make distinctions between them. The word 'symbol' is often understood to be a picture or image (actual or literary) with two meanings: it has a literal meaning and at least one other. In the visual sphere, a symbol usually looks like something we recognize – a tree, a lion or some such – and we say that this tree or lion symbolizes 'life' or 'strength' and the like.

A sign is slightly different in that, in the visual sphere, more often than not it does not look much like something we recognize – as with an alphabetic letter, or a circle with a line across it on a road-sign – and yet we regard it as standing for or indicating something else. In the case of a letter, it's a sound; the circle with the line across is 'no parking', or 'if I park here for a short while, I might not get caught'.

In literature, the cited objects, living things, people and scenes tend to be described as being 'symbolic' of ideas, historical moments, feelings and the like: the demolishing of Saddam Hussein's statue was symbolic of the downfall of the regime.

The word 'sign' is used very often to indicate that a word has a set of meanings 'signified' by that word: 'cat' signifies a furry four-legged animal and is also used to signify a kind of whip. The sign of a letter indicates sounds.

So, the letter 'g', say, isn't really symbolic of anything. On the other hand it's a sign which indicates several different sounds in English. The word 'rabbit' involves putting letters (signs) together to create another sign which we take to indicate a particular animal. However, we can use the idea or image of the rabbit to be symbolic of other ideas, as with 'a rabbit caught in the headlights'. At this point the word 'rabbit' is the sign for 'rabbit', while also being a symbol for being scared.

These two notions are not quite as distinct as I have suggested, though. Our understanding of the word 'rabbit' (when it's working as a sign) is flavoured by its 'connotations'. These are all the experiences, references and language we know that are connected with rabbits. For us to be able to communicate with each other, we must have some shared sense of what a rabbit is, whilst having many personal, communal and ethnic variations. Some people rear and eat rabbits, some people don't. Some people have read *Peter Rabbit*, some people haven't. Some people remember the countryside full of rabbits dying of myxomatosis, some people don't. Some people may see the word 'rabbit' as being similar to 'habit', while others see it as similar to 'rabbi'.

Those who study signs and symbols often talk of them having 'systems'. Chess pieces may or may not be symbolic of kings, queens and knights – I'll leave that to your imagination – but they are surely signs for different capabilities or functions in a game. The game itself works because of how we agree that these different signs should be interpreted and function as an ensemble. Some argue that if letters are signs, the way they operate in different languages is in sign systems. These can be deduced by observing how we get them to behave.

An observant Martian looking at the passage I've just written might detect quite quickly that I don't ever seem to use any given letters more than two times immediately next to each other. It would notice that I've doubled some letters but not others and would therefore make a note to see if that selection of letters being doubled applied to all writing in English or just mine. The doubling of letters could then be described as one part of the sign system of letter-use. Having worked out that letters are put alongside each other in clusters called 'words', the Martian could try to see if there were any sign systems at work here too. For example, some combinations keep cropping up at the ends of words, like '-ed' and '-ing' and '-ion'. At the level of groups of words, a little dot clearly has some kind of function which would be quite hard to determine purely in terms of a sign system, other than that it seems to appear fairly regularly after a minimum and maximum number of words.

Once the Martian had been told that words can refer to things, actions and feelings, it might also wonder about the other words that seem not to do this so clearly, like 'the' or 'would'. This would take the Martian into the world of what systems are used to stick words together in these chunks between full stops, called 'sentences'.

Back with the alphabet, as a fixed sequence of twenty-six letters. When, say, we put it on friezes round children's bedroom walls, we are showing children that it is complete and finite. This is 'the alphabet', we say. It's not something that 'could be' the alphabet. It's not even 'an' alphabet. We are so certain and finite about this – and we learned it that way – that it's hard to accept that we have many alternative and additional signs and sign systems within the thing that we treat with such certainty. Some have faded from view.

Perhaps the oddest of the alternatives are lower-case 'a' and 'g'. We carefully teach children how to draw them, how to recognize them, what sounds we should say when we see them. There are As, we say, in 'cat', 'hare', 'was', 'water' and 'father'. There are the Gs in 'garage'. The 'a' and 'g' used in initial literacy teaching are known as 'single-storey'. Very carefully, educational publishers produce booklets and schemes where the only lower-case 'a' and 'g' in sight are the single-storey 'a' and 'g'. Meanwhile, the publishers of picture books carry on doing what they've always done, which is produce their books with the 'double-storey' 'a' and 'g'.

If you trace the story (!) of the letters back you can find the single-storey versions in most handwriting of the modern era such as 'cursive' or 'round hand'. You find them in one form of the 'Uncial' script which we may think of today as 'Irish writing'. In Roman 'minuscule' lettering (i.e. 'lower case' or 'little') we find a little 'a' looking dangerously like the 'u', not quite closed off at the top, co-existing with a double-storey version.

The story of 'g' is slightly different. There seems to have been general agreement that it had an umbrella-handle shape on its lower part and various kinds of hooks or loops for the top part. So it is for Gutenberg, the first printer to use a movable typeface, and so it is with Caxton, the first English printer. The divergence seems to originate in Venice with the da Spira brothers (who were German) in the 1460s. Their typeface has the double-storey 'g'.

So, we live with two signs for 'a' and two signs for 'g', with most print up until the 1920s showing us the double storey while most handwriting has been single storey.

Single storey in print turns up in Germany in its full finished form in 1927 with Paul Renner's 'Futura' typeface. He had been working on it for three years and it was a modernist reaction against the gothic or 'black-letter' script which dominated most German writing of the time. The Nazis recognized it as such and arrested Renner: nominally, for the crime of opposing Nazism; in reality for hanging out with lefties, being friends with the highly suspect novelist Thomas Mann, creator of the homoerotically obsessed hero in the novel *Death in Venice*, and protesting against the imprisonment of his colleague Jan Tschichold. Renner was dismissed from his position as an adviser to the German publishing association on the grounds of his 'national untrustworthiness'. According to Simon Garfield, the Nazis judged a lecture he gave on the history of letterforms as 'too sympathetic towards roman types' – meaning typefaces rather than guys from Rome. Futura was labelled as anti-German, though not anti-fascist. Mussolini loved it.

Ironically, in 1941 the Third Reich discovered that gothic lettering was anti-German too and banned it, though the real reason was probably the fact that the people in occupied Europe couldn't read the invaders' writing. Renner himself was able to keep out of jail, either by hopping across the border into Switzerland or by appealing to the father of his daughter's fiancé, a certain Rudolf Hess, who at that point had not yet fled Germany in a little plane. Futura survived and it's one of the ways you'll see the single-storey 'a' outside of your children's writing and early reading. At the moment, advertisers use it. Whenever they want to say that their product or company is nice, they say it with a single-storey 'a'. The single-storey 'g' goes beyond niceness; it's now in quite formal typefaces.

An older example of having two signs for the same letter was the long 'ſ', snaky 's' question. As with most 'rules' to do with English, the eighteenth century was when people tried to turn custom and use into commands. Thomas Dyche's *A Guide to the*

English Tongue (first published in 1707, and reprinted many times) said that: 'The long ſ muſt never be uſed at the End of a Word, nor immediately after the short s.' This seems like a negative rule telling you how you must not use the 'ſ' without telling you exactly when you *should* use it, leaving open the possibility that you could begin a word with 's' and that you could – if you really wanted to – write 's' in the middle of a word; in which case a second 's' would require you to write 'ss'. Others elaborated and refined this, determining rules on what to write before apostrophes and – a giveaway as to why the long 'ſ' dropped out – the rule that the long 'ſ' should not be used adjacent to an 'f'. I find this kind of pernickety stuff fairly tiresome, particularly when it concerns features of writing which people dispense with anyway.

In pre-print days, the long 'ſ' (always minuscule) seems to derive from one of the roman scripts. Gutenberg and the Venetian printers used both the long and the short 's', plus the double 'ſſ' in the middle of words. The King James Bible of 1611 is written in 'black-letter' or 'gothic' type with the long 'ſ'.

By the mid-nineteenth century in Britain, the long 'ſ' had pretty well dropped out and you can mark its demise by looking at the sequences of editions of the same book. In the case of the *Encylopaedia Britannica*, 'ſ' dropped out between the fifth edition in 1817 and the sixth edition in 1823. It survives for mathematicians as the symbol to indicate that they should 'integrate' in calculus. One possible reason for the death of 'ſ' is the printing of Ariel's song from Shakespeare's *The Tempest*, 'Where the bee sucks, there suck I'. I've heard that there are still people who enjoy reading pre-nineteenth-century editions of *The Tempest* and books of Shakespeare's songs for this very reason.

The tales of 'a', 'g', and 'ſ' remind me that the rules we tell children and which we repeat to ourselves weren't fashioned in an academy after long analysis. Quite the contrary: they emerged from custom and use as forms of tacit agreements between writers, printers and readers.

Lower-case 'a', 'g' and 's' are examples of variant signs from within the alphabet. Surrounding the alphabet, in its hinterland, we have created other symbols, which we have slotted into typefaces, often signifying whole words. Quite apart from mathematical symbols, a glance at the qwerty keyboard gives us '@' and '&', and at various times I've used symbols for 'therefore', 'because' and 'leading to'. Many of us in the Twittersphere borrow from maths for our tweets, with '+' to mean 'and', '=' to mean 'the same as' or 'is', '<' meaning 'less than', '>' meaning 'greater than'. The asterisk tells us that there's a footnote; the bullet point tells you that I'm someone who likes using bullet points. And of course there is the glorious hashtag which can signify 'this is the topic' or 'here is my ironic aside'.

The Twitter hashtag owes its origins to people in chatrooms marking the topics of their conversations. The first time it escaped from the chat world was when one Nate Ritter from San Diego, California, reported online on the fires in California, in October 2007. However, crediting Mr Ritter with the invention of the hashtag, as when he used it to say #sandiegoforestfire, would get up the nose of the many chatroomers who had been using it for at least the previous five years. It reached Twitter two years later, in particular in the hands of Iranian people protesting over the elections. Twitter started to hyperlink hashtags to search results on 1 July 2009, followed up by 'trending topics' (linked by the hashtag) in 2010. I'm not sure how I was able to function in life prior to the invention of the Twitter hashtag: #ironyalert.

The sign itself used to be called the 'number sign' because from at least 1900, people would use it to separate off a number in a piece of script – #5. It was also used to signify a pound in weight in the US; as the 'sharp' sign in music; and by proof-readers to mean 'insert a space'. It still sits on my phone's keypad: 'To return the call, press the hash key.' A sign with multiple meanings, then.

No one is quite sure why it's a 'hash', though cross-hatching in drawing may have something to do with it. Someone called it an 'octothorp' or 'octothorpe' or 'octotherp' – 'octo' because it has eight points while the 'thorp', 'thorpe' and 'therp' suffixes are shrouded in etymological jokes, one possibility being that it was invented by someone who was interested in the 1912 Olympic gold medallist Jim Thorpe; another that it was a joke coinage by telephone engineers in the 1980s; while others maintain that it owes its origins to map-making as a sign to show that a village ('thorpe' in Old Norse) was surrounded by eight fields. Or it's a joke.

The '@' can be called in English the 'at sign', the 'at symbol' or 'ampersat'. Because it is universal, it needs names in all languages, so in Dutch it's a 'monkey's tail'; in Danish it's the same word as an 'elephant's trunk'. Finns see it as a 'cat's tail'; Germans as a 'spider-monkey'. In Greek, it's a 'little duck'; in Hungarian, it's a 'worm'; in Korean, it's a 'snail'; in Norwegian, it's a 'pig's tail'; in Russian, it's a 'little dog'; in Czech and Slovak, it's a 'rollmop', which endears itself to me.

It is one of the most important symbols of our times, contrib-uting to the identity of millions of us through our email addresses, Twitter IDs and logins. It's the axis between our digital name and the company that stores and sends our messages. When we want to leave some part of ourselves that is contactable, we find ourselves saying, somewhere in the mix, the word 'at' and we all now know that this is '@'. 'Rosieface at server.co,' I might say – and that's a shorthand way for me to say who I am and for others to know me. It's a new piece of grammar, derived from centuries of accounting and abbreviated writing.

As you might expect, no one knows for certain where it comes from. I remember it some fifty years ago, sitting in the little blue accounting notebooks with its sheet of carbon tucked inside, where it meant 'each at' as in '100 bricks each at 4d'. Medieval monks saved time, vellum and ink by abbreviating words. In ancient manuscripts, it's been spotted as a substitute for 'ad', the Latin word meaning 'to' and 'at'. Bulgarian monks of the eleventh century used it to mean 'amen'. Spanish and Portuguese writing have long used it to signify a unit of weight – the 'arroba' which itself is derived from an Arabic expression meaning 'a quarter'. The sign has been spotted in a merchant's document which travelled from Seville in Spain to Rome on 4 May 1536. In Italy, it could signify the unit of weight of one 'anfora' ('amphora'). I know the first time I came across it: it was on my mother's typewriter, which was made in the 1930s, and it appears on at least one model of typewriter as early as 1889.

The '&' is the ampersand, meaning 'and'. In children's recitations of the alphabet in the eighteenth and nineteenth centuries, it used to be stuck on the end of the twenty-six letters – or twenty-seven if it included the long 'ſ', and you can see it alongside the letters on all the early means of teaching the alphabet (see 'B is for Battledore'). The word 'ampersand' may sound like direct borrowing from Greek or French but it's a squeezed-up form of the phrase 'and per se "and"'. Imagine thousands of children over hundreds of years reciting the alphabet and when they got to the end they said, '. . . X, Y, Z and per se "and"'. Apparently, the Latin 'per se' bit could be added when saying any letter or sign which 'on its own' was also a word – like 'A', 'I' and 'O'. The 'and' sign was 'per se', on its own. So, 'and per se "and"' ended up as ampersand. I have to say, I rather like it that such a technical and precise word owes its origins to children chanting and squashing a mixture of English and Latin words.

The ampersand sign itself is another story.

The Latin word for 'and' is 'et'. If you draw a curly capital 'E' and a small 't', joining and compressing the two letters into a kind of monogram, you can see the origin of '&'. It seems to have developed in the first century in Roman cursive handwriting, went into medieval manuscripts and thence into the first type-faces. The most common place I saw it when I was a child was in company and shop names, the most important by far in the life of someone wanting sweets and toys: F. W. Woolworth & Co. Ltd.

Semaphore with flags is a signalling-system based on the letters of the alphabet. When I was in the 'cubs' in the 1950s, we had to learn how to do it, in order to pass to a higher level of cubmanship. It involves holding two flags. The trick we were taught as a way of remembering the semaphore alphabet was to think of the positions of the two flags as if you were standing in the centre of a clock-face, and you pointed your arms holding the flags out from your body as if your arms were the hands of a clock. Though we used to signal to each other across a hall or yard, there were occasions when you could see sailors perform it for show. I'm not sure that I realized at the time that before the age of telegraphs, telephones and radio, any kind of visual signalling system could relay messages across vast distances, so long as each relay station could see the one it was picking up from.

Robert Hooke, the polymath scientist, figured this out and presented it as a viable idea to the Royal Society in 1684. As is often the case, the demand for such a system did not arise out of the need to improve the human condition but from a war, a particularly pressing matter, according to Hooke, on account of the Siege of Vienna the year before. The Fellows didn't nibble on Hooke's scheme, so it stayed on the back burner until Claude Chappe invented a visual signalling system in 1792, straight after the French Revolution.

Things didn't get off to a perfect start, because when he first demonstrated it in the Place d'Etoile, republican Parisians thought that he was secretly trying to communicate with the Royalists, and smashed it up. Once established, it worked by using 556 stations covering a distance of some 3,000 miles. Here again, the need was military, with the perceived or real enemies of the Revolution encircling France. The system depended on towers being placed some 10–20 miles apart, with two articulated arms placed on the top. The positions of the arms related to letters. The first line ran from Paris to Lille; other lines radiated out from Paris across France. Napoleon used it a few years later but it didn't bring much pleasure to Chappe who ended his life throwing himself down a hotel well-shaft.

Visual signalling systems had been around, probably for thousands of years, using fire or smoke. The Romans used a hydraulic system and during the first Punic War they sent messages between Sicily and Carthage. On each of two hills facing each other was an identical earthenware container, each with an identical plug and plughole. Each container was filled with water and a vertical rod fixed in it. Each rod was marked identically down its shaft with likely events in the war: 'cavalry arrived', 'infantry arrived' and the like. At one container on one hill stood the sender; at the other, the receiver. The sender would choose which message he wanted to send and raise his torch; the receiver raised his torch and this synchronized the pulling out of the plug of each container. Torches were lowered while the water ran out. When the water level sank to the point that revealed the desired message on the vertical rod, the sender would raise his torch again and stop the flow. The receiver would do the same, and read off the message on the vertical rod in his container.

All this was written up by the Greek historian Polybius who didn't spend his time in luxury hotels making up this stuff, but made great efforts to visit the places he wrote about and to interview the people who had witnessed the events. Some two thousand years after the Roman hydraulic signalling system, an English engineer called Francis Wilshaw proposed something very similar, except that the containers holding the water were to be connected. Unsurprisingly, it wasn't commercially viable.

Hydraulic systems are potentially quite secret. They are under water. Chappe's flailing arms on towers couldn't cope with bad weather and anyone with access to the code could read them. In other words, not secret.

Flag semaphore was in place by the time of the Battle of Trafalgar and it features in fiction, most notably for me and my imaginative life in Arthur Ransome's *Winter Holiday*, *Missee Lee*, *Pigeon Post*, and in no end of skulduggery – usually with smugglers in the China Sea, in the *Boy's Own Paper*. The semaphore method used here was flashing Morse code with a torch. On camping holidays, my friends and I would try to imitate this by using our rubber-coated torches, signalling from tent-door to tent-door, whilst trying to make sure that the enemies (our parents) couldn't see.

One way in which a flag semaphore signal was frozen and has since been reproduced a million times is with the sign that is variously known as meaning 'nuclear disarmament for Britain', 'peace' and 'no nuclear power stations'. It initially appeared on 500 cardboard lollipops on sticks on the first march from London to Aldermaston in 1958.

I ran away from home to join the third march and the origins of the sign were already in dispute. (I say 'ran away from home' but what happened was that I said I was going on the march, my parents said that at thirteen I was too young, I said I wasn't, my mother made me sandwiches and gave me a chicken while telling me that I most definitely wasn't going, and I went, partly inspired by the mystery and mystique of this new sign.)

I was told then that the lines represented the letters 'N' and 'D', standing for 'nuclear disarmament', and with my vast knowledge acquired through having been a cub (not that cubbing was very nuclear-disarmament-ish) I could confirm that. For others, tramping along the road from Aldermaston (where nuclear weapons were and still are manufactured) to London, singing, 'Kumbaya' and 'Have you heard the H-bomb thunder . . .?', this was far-fetched cobblers. They said that it was an ancient Sanskrit sign for peace. At school, some people drew it on their exercise books. Some of them got it wrong, and drew it like the company sign for Mercedes-Benz.

Half of the original 'lollipop sticks' with the sign were black-on-white and half white-on-green. Just as the Church's liturgical colours change over Easter, so the colours were to change 'from Winter to Spring, from Death to Life'. Black and white would be displayed on Good Friday and Saturday, green and white on Easter Sunday and Monday. The first badges were made by Eric Austin of Kensington CND, using white clay with the symbol painted black, and distributed with a note explaining that in the event of a nuclear war, these fired pottery badges would be amongst the few human artifacts to survive the nuclear inferno.

They were designed by Gerald Holtom, a conscientious

objector who had worked on a farm in Norfolk during the Second World War, and, according to the Campaign for Nuclear Disarmament, he 'confirmed' that the symbol uses the semaphore letters 'N' for nuclear and 'D' for disarmament. He wrote later: 'I was in despair. Deep despair. I drew myself: the representative of an individual in despair, with hands palm outstretched outwards and downwards in the manner of Goya's peasant before the firing squad. I formalised the drawing into a line and put a circle round it.'

So, was it Gerald Holtom's arms, semaphore for 'ND', or both?

Someone said that the whole thing was more sinister. It was the sign on the side of the tanks in the 3rd Panzer Division. Before the days of the internet, this was hard to confirm or deny. In fact, this was not only cobblers, it was nasty cobblers. The Panzer sign doesn't include the vertical line running all the way to the bottom of the circle. Holtom worked as a designer. The truth is that he incorporated both ideas – the outstretched arms of despair and the outstretched arms of a semaphore signaller. His first designs are now in the archive at the Commonwealth Collection in Bradford.

Morse code is an alphabetic sign system. Dots and dashes are produced by creating short or long electric impulses. Each letter has its own dot-and-dash configuration. 'A' is dot-dash; 'M' is dash-dash; 'Z' is dash-dash dot-dot. The numbers have dot-dash configurations too. The code is named after Samuel Finley Breese Morse (1791–1872), a highly accomplished portrait painter. He was born in Massachusetts to a Calvinist preacher who worked hard at drumming Calvinist ideas into his son. Samuel Morse studied at Yale and began painting. His interest took him to the Royal Academy in London where he practised life drawing and sculpture. In the years after this he became one of America's most respected and famous artists, once painting President James Monroe – he of the Monroe Doctrine of staying out of the US's backyard. On a visit to Paris in 1839, Morse chummed up with Louis Daguerre who had invented the daguerreotype, the first practical means of making photographic images.

In 1825, the city of New York commissioned Morse to paint a portrait of the Marquis de Lafayette, a republican hero. While Morse was painting, a horse messenger delivered a letter from his father that read one line: 'Your dear wife is convalescent.' Morse immediately left Washington for his home at New Haven, leaving the portrait of Lafayette unfinished. By the time he arrived, his wife had already been buried. For days Morse had been unaware of his wife's illness and her lonely death. This motivated him to turn away from painting and find some means of rapid long-distance communication.

In 1832, Morse met up with one Charles Thomas Jackson who knew a thing or two about electromagnetism. Morse watched Jackson at work and figured out the concept of a single-wire telegraph. By the time he got his patent, William Cooke, Charles Wheatstone and Carl Gauss had also developed an electromagnetic telegraph. Cheapness and convenience would determine which system would become the most popular and last the longest. At the time, what seems to have bothered Morse the most was whether he was the first. People who develop language systems frequently become extremely agitated by others in the same field. Leonard Gale, who taught Chemistry at New York University, helped Morse introduce relays into his system so that messages could be sent further, and with money coming in from one Alfred Vail, together they were able to put on a public demonstration at the Speedwell Ironworks in Morristown, New Jersey on 11 January 1838. The first publicly transmitted message was 'A patient waiter is no loser', which to my ear carries a touch of Morse's Calvinist background. After several tries Morse got backing from Congress for his system. Having won over his native land, he set up other telegraph lines in Istanbul for Sultan Abdülmecid. Latin America and the whole of Europe – bar Great Britain – adopted it, with Britain sticking with Cooke and Wheatstone's system for the time being.

Does 'SOS' mean 'save our souls' or 'save our sausages'? In fact, it is not an acronym or an abbreviation. The SOS's dots and dashes (short and long signals) were chosen because, as a combination, it was distinct and without ambiguity. In fact it is an example of the Morse code being non-alphabetic. It has been pointed out that it could also signify the message 'VTB'. But then, I'm thinking that this could be translated into 'Very troubled blokes' for all-male distress moments.

Paul Passy was an originator of another sign system. He was born in 1859 into a famous French family – his father Frédéric was one of the first people to be awarded the Nobel Peace Prize. Young Passy learned English, German and Italian, and went on to study Sanskrit at university. He spent ten years as a language teacher in state schools as an alternative to doing military service. In 1886, he gathered together a small group of language teachers to encourage the use of phonetic notation in schools to help children pronounce foreign languages and to improve the teaching of reading. The group originally called themselves Dhi Fonètik Tîcerz' Asóciécon (the FTA). By 1897, they were L'Association Phonétique Internationale (API), or, in English, the International Phonetic Association (IPA). The IPA's early peak of membership and influence in education circles was around 1914, when there were 1,751 members in forty countries. The First World War not only broke up the Association's activities, but French militarism and Passy's pacifism led to his dismissal from his chair at the Ecole des Hautes Etudes on the grounds that he opposed an extension to conscription.

It was the work of Passy's group of teachers which led to the creation of the International Phonetic Alphabet, the world's first truly universal alphabet, in which each symbol corresponds directly to a distinctive sound or 'speech segment'. It has been adapted and improved since the late 1880s, with its core sign system, the roman alphabet. There are many other symbols: inverted letters, diacritics, Greek letters, 'hooks' added to letters, along with signs like Ɵ, ʈ, ᴄ, ʒ, ǀ, ǃ, ǂ and ‖, making up some 150 symbols or so. It is most commonly sighted in Oxford dictionaries, as a guide to pronunciation; linguists all over the world use it, though Passy's pacifist and universalist ideals have not entirely won the day. The Americanist Phonetic Alphabet is an alternative system of phonetic notation originally developed by anthropologists for the transcription of Native American and European languages and still used by linguists working on Slavic, Indic, Uralic, Semitic and Caucasian languages. There are always alternatives. Perhaps that is the core meaning of this book.

As a dictum it certainly applies to the various sign systems used by blind and deaf people. Braille is a system of writing based on raised dots which readers feel with their fingertips and it too owes its origins to military endeavour. Napoleon wanted a secret code system for conveying messages and Charles Barbier de la Serre, a captain in the army, devised 'Ecriture Nocturne' – 'Night Writing'. It's based on a code that Polybius devised – the same Polybius who wrote up hydraulic semaphore. The basic trick with 'Night Writing' is to draw up a matrix, 6 × 6; then fill the matrix with letters or letter-combinations, and these letters can be represented by the numbers you read off the top and side, rather as we identify a particular street with map referencing. Barbier figured you could replace the letters with dots. The problem was that it needed so many dots that it was too complicated for people to learn. However, Barbier also figured that it was a system that blind people could use and in 1821 he took it to the National Institute for the Blind in Paris, where he met Louis Braille.

Braille was born in 1809 in Coupvray, a small town east of Paris, where most people were 'petits cultivateurs' (small farmers). His father was a leather-worker and saddler. Like all children of farmers and artisans, Louis spent time playing around his father's gear. When he was three he was in the workshop, trying to make holes in a piece of leather with an awl; he pressed down hard to get the point into the leather, and the awl skidded and stuck into one of his eyes. No treatment could save the eye; when it became infected, the infection spread to the other eye and, by the time he was five, he was completely blind.

His parents taught him how to get about using a cane and he was allowed to go to the local school. From there he went to the National Institute for the Blind's school in Paris where the children were taught to read by the 'Haüy System'. Valentin Haüy was born into a family of weavers, and was educated by monks at the abbey where his father rang the Angelus bells. He became a skilled linguist and interpreter to Louis XVI. In 1771, when he was having lunch in the Place de la Concorde, he was horrified to see blind people being mocked in the street during the religious parade known as 'The Fair of St Ovid'. They were given dunces' caps and giant cardboard glasses and were forced to play musical instruments that they didn't know how to play.

On impulse, he decided to set up a school for the blind and there he devised a system of reading based on the idea of raised letters, produced by embossing the paper. In 1785, he founded the Institute for Blind Youth. The republicans of the French

Revolution regarded him with some suspicion and 'retired' him albeit with a state pension. In 1806, at the request of Tsar Alexander I, he went to St Petersburg to found a school there.

Back at the National Institute for the Blind's school, Louis Braille grew frustrated by the tiny number of books – all very expensive and delicate – which had been given the Haüy embossing treatment. Even more frustrating was the fact that it wasn't possible to write this way. Meanwhile, Louis's father gave him letters made from leather and Braille was able to write home to his family. We can get some idea of what motivated him from his own writings later: '[It] is vitally important for us if we are not to go on being despised or patronized by condescending sighted people. We do not need pity, nor do we need to be reminded we are vulnerable. We must be treated as equals – and communication is the way this can be brought about.'

In 1821, Braille encountered Barbier's 'Night Writing' and decided that this was the system he could use to create a blind person's alphabet. He had pretty well worked it out by 1824, when he was only fifteen. Braille created his own raised-dot system by using an awl, the same implement which had blinded him. Later, he worked on the development of what would become the 'brailling machine' which children have used with me when I've done poetry workshops in blind schools. The non-electric kind was quite heavy-handed. It required a good old push on a group of keys to emboss the card with the right combinations of dots. Louis turned out to be a great student and ended up teaching History, Geometry and Algebra at the school. He was also a talented musician and went on to become a professional organist in two Paris churches.

You might have thought that the Braille method would have been hailed as a great breakthrough by the Institute but the system wasn't used there in Louis Braille's lifetime; in fact, the head teacher was sacked for transcribing a history book into Braille. Braille himself died in 1852 at the age of forty-three. Two years later, largely due to the pupils' demands, the Braille system was finally adopted at the Institute.

Having served many blind and visually impaired people extremely well for over 150 years, the system is in some decline, particularly in the face of computer-based speech recognition and screen-reader systems.

Much more complicated, but just as inspiring, are the many systems of signing that deaf and hearing-impaired people have developed all over the world over many centuries. As early as the fifth century BCE, Socrates refers to one of these and by the seventeenth century in Europe, people were trying to formalize the matter, basing signing on parts of the body whose initial letter would provide the letters of a word, while others used hand and finger shapes to represent letters and words. When I've worked with a signer in a performance, I often look across to them to see how they are turning my poems into signing. What always strikes me is how the system uses the entire body: fingers, hands, arms, chest, face and whole body movement.

Unlike the sign systems devised by sighted devisers of sign languages in the seventeenth century, most signing is not directly related to either a written or spoken language. So, rather than thinking of relating a sign to, let's say, a written or spoken form of 'hello', we should think of it as 'a greeting in sign language' and its 'meaning' is in the way the greeting is expressed with hand, face and body. However, that too is misleading if we just think of signing as a form of mime – nor are the signs equivalents to, or borrowings from, the gestures that hearing people use. Most signs in sign language are not related directly to the objects, descriptions and processes being communicated, just as the word 'apple' doesn't look, sound or feel like an apple. Though some mimetic features are involved, as a system it doesn't rely on mime.

Like all languages, the signs rely on mutual intelligibility. This means that where two deaf or hearing-impaired people get together, and no one is specifically teaching them a sign language, they will invent and develop their own – surely a great testimony to the fact that human beings need to cooperate and communicate with each other. In many circumstances, where families have a mix of hearing and hearing-impaired people, the family will adapt a given system or, where there is none, they will invent and develop their own. This has been observed all over the world. Different situations produce different requirements: two hearing-impaired people wanting to understand each other are not the same as a room of people, some of whom have impaired hearing and some who don't; they are different again from a hearing-impaired person wanting to be understood by someone who has no hearing impairment; or an international meeting of hearing-impaired people and so on.

Across small and large communities, many sign languages have developed and so the question of standardization has arisen many times. There are several front-runners and different countries have tended to develop their own versions, American, French, British and so on, though not all the deaf and hearing-impaired people in that country will use the 'national' system. What's more, different self-defining communities develop their own variants.

As with all disability matters, things have changed rapidly over the last few years, with deaf and hearing-impaired people wanting to take control of services and the systems of communication. Power has shifted. Some people working in this area have favoured lip-reading either as an adjunct to signing or as a substitute for it. The deaf people I've met use lip-reading only as an occasional alternative or additional way of interpreting but, famously, it is very open to misunderstandings. To say in English, in many English dialects: 'Where there's life, there's hope' looks very similar to 'Where's the lavender soap?', though your facial and body movement is not likely to be the same!

Now when I visit schools, I'm often given an amplifying system to wear round my neck and I'm told that the hearing-impaired children are using it in conjunction with lip-reading me. However, listening and reading are quite obviously not the same as talking and writing. Signing remains a key way in which deaf and hearing-impaired people can produce thoughts and feelings in language, not just receive them.

THE STORY OF

● **T'S ANCESTOR IS** found in ancient Semitic inscriptions from 1800 BCE as a sign looking like our simplest lower-case 't', i.e. without an upward tail-flick on the bottom. By 1000 BCE, Phoenicians were calling this sign 'taw' meaning a 'mark' and it signified the 't' sound. Placing a line across another to make an 'x' or a lower-case 't' is one of the simplest ways we can show that 'I was here'. A single line can be a scratch produced by mistake or by an animal. Cross the line with another line and it's clear that something has been intended by someone.

The ancient Greeks adopted the Phoenicians' 'taw' in around 800 BCE, calling it 'tau'. The Greeks put the cross-stroke on the top like our upper-case 'T', perhaps to distinguish it from 'X', which in rough writing can slip round to the vertical. The Etruscans adopted 'T' in around 700 BCE and passed it on to the Romans a hundred years later. By this point the Romans called it 'te' (pronounced 'tay') and on their most fancy inscriptions in Imperial times it acquired its serifs and thin-thick lines.

t

Charlemagne's scribes kept the 'hat' on 'T' but they started to curl the bottom of the downstroke in their 'Carolingian minuscule' script of the tenth century. The stroke across the downstroke doesn't appear until around 1200 and Italian printers in the late fifteenth century adopted this form as their lower case. The 't's were crossed.

PRONUNCIATION OF THE LETTER-NAME
The Norman French arrived in Britain calling it 'tay' and

by the process of the Great Vowel Shift this sound turned to 'tee'.

PRONUNCIATION OF THE LETTER

We make 't' in our mouths in more or less the same way as we make 'd' but without using our vocal cords. Because it appears in 'the', 'it', 'to', 'at', 'they', 'them', 'this' and 'that', it's in the top two words for frequency in English, only beaten by 'e'.

Consonants that come after it at the beginning of words give us most commonly 'tr' (as in 'tray') and the two kinds of 'th' sounds as in 'thorn' and 'this' (see 'D is for Disappeared Letters' for how English used to manage this). The word 'two' indicates an old pronunciation you can revisit with 'twice', 'twine' and 'twain'. The loan words 'tsar' and 'tsetse' give us a rare 'ts' start to a word.

At other places in words we can use consonants after the 't' to make 'hurtle' and plurals like 'bats'. Consonants in front of the 't' can give us 'start' and 'past', the chocolate firm 'Lindt', 'lift', the 'gh' words like 'right' and 'thought', 'empty', 'plenty', a loan word like 'diktat', 'silt', 'fact', 'apt', 'mint', 'next' and 'betwixt' (a favourite of mine), and the artist's name 'Klimt'.

A 't' on the end of some verbs gives us an alternative way to make the 'simple past' as in 'dreamt' and 'learnt'.

'Double t' appears when we make 'cut, cutting' and we can get through a lot of Ts for 'tut, tutting, tutted' though the sound is sometimes written 'tsk-tsk'.

We can end words with one 't' or two, and make distinctions in meanings that way: 'but' and 'butt', 'set' and 'sett'.

The diminutive '-let' enables us to have 'piglets', 'ringlets' and the like, and if we retain the French form we have 'omelettes' while Americans have 'omelets'. The '-tte' ending also crops up in the old word 'fytte' meaning 'a part of a story or poem', in the name 'Charlotte' and in 'St Mary-atte-Bow'.

A group of words play with the 't' sound as in 'tittle-tattle', 'tot', 'titter', 'tip-tap', 'totter', 'tatters', 'tiptoe and 'itty-bitty'. We say 'ta' for thanks, and 'ta-ta' for goodbye, and the various forms of 'tit', 'titty', 'teat', 'titty-bottle'. The song goes: 'Tea for two'.

IS FOR TXTSPK

ON THE OPENING night of his musical, *West Side Story*, the conductor and composer Leonard Bernstein received a telegram. It read:

NB460 PD=TDBB LOS ANGELES CALIF 26 1155AMP
1957 SEP 26 PM 4 33
:LEONARD BERNSTEIN
=WINTERGARDEN THEATRE=
IT WAS WORTH ALL THE DEXAMYL ITS A SMASH
YOUR A SMASH AND IM THRILLED FOR YOU
BLESSINGS AND LOVE=
:BETTY..

Next to 'BETTY..' is the name 'Bogart' written in ink. 'Betty' is the nickname of Lauren Bacall. Dexamyl is the trade name for an 'upper' that was much favoured in the 1950s.

By this time, people had had over a hundred years to develop a particular way of writing telegrams. The first, sent on 11 January 1838, read: WHAT GOD HATH WROUGHT. The last message to go out from the radio room of RMS *Titanic* before it sank forty minutes later read:

c/o SOS SOS CQD cqd – MGY We are sinking fast passengers being put into boats MGY

CQD means 'All Stations: Distress'; MGY was the *Titanic*'s call sign. The owner, Bruce Ismay, left the ship in a lifeboat, got himself on board the SS *Carpathia* and sent a telegram to Islefrank, New York City, which, by the time it arrived, read:

Deeply regret advise you *Titanic* sank this morning fifteenth after collision iceberg resulting from serious loss life further particulars later Bruce Ismay.

For the people concerned, a momentous telegram was one sent on 14 December 1941 to Miss Viola Wikoff, Brooksville, Kansas: 'Darling not coming Moving sooner than expected dont know where. Lefty 812 AM.' 'Lefty' was in the army; seven days earlier, Pearl Harbor had been bombed.

Quite apart from the drama in these messages, they all represent a special way of writing: much of the time they miss out the 'a' and 'the' that you would expect. Quite often they leave out the 'subject' of the verb – they don't bother with 'I'. Most of the time they are unpunctuated, don't even bother with the famous 'stop' and they omit prepositions like 'to' and 'with'. The last message to leave the *Titanic*'s radio room used abbreviations.

Most people who used telegrams just learned this way of writing in the same way as they learned how to speak: through custom and use. Even so, Nelson E. Ross thought that the population needed a guide. In his *How to Write Telegrams Properly* which appeared in 1928, he wrote:

Eliminating Small Words – At a slight sacrifice to smoothness, but with a saving in tolls which often more than compensates, small words may be eliminated from your telegram without impairing the sense.

The articles 'a' and 'the' are outstanding examples, followed closely by 'we,' 'I,' and 'that.'

Mr Ross then gives some very reasonable suggestions as to how to do this, followed by:

A press correspondent might first write this dispatch:

'The enemy has not yet been met or even seen on account of the entanglements thrown up during the night,' etc.

Revised for the cable, this dispatch might read:

'Enemy unmet unseen account entanglements upthrown night.'

Person-to-person dictation of telegrams over the phone or radio needed phonetic clarity so that's how the alphabet acquired the 'alpha-bravo' lingo much loved of 1960s and 70s TV cop shows. People sometimes call this a 'phonetic alphabet' – which it isn't, or a 'spelling alphabet', which all alphabets are, because you spell with them.

In the First World War, the Royal Navy's version ran (and I've written it out so that only proper names have capitals):

apples butter Charlie duff Edward Freedy George Harry ink Johnnie king London monkey nuts orange pudding Queenie Robert sugar Tommy uncle vinegar Willie Xerxes yellow zebra

The RAF from 1924 to 1942 used this one:

Ace beer Charlie Don Edward Freddie George Harry ink Johnnie king London monkey nuts orange pip queen Robert sugar toc Uncle Vic William x-ray Yorker zebra

Which is nearly a working sentence! The US version from 1941 to 1956 was:

Able baker Charlie dog easy fox George how item jig king love Mike Nan oboe Peter queen Roger sugar tare Uncle Victor William x-ray yoke zebra

which isn't. The RAF had adopted most of these by 1943. In 1951, the International Air Transport Association agreed on:

Alfa bravo coca delta echo foxtrot golf hotel India Juliet kilo Lima Metro nectar Oscar Papa Quebec Romeo Sierra tango union Victor whisky extra Yankee Zulu

This one feels the most poetic: I would like to visit the Alfa-bravo-coca Delta where you hear an echo. I don't fancy The Foxtrot Golf Hotel, but I know people who would. India Juliet Kilo has made a name for herself in art-house movies; the Lima Metro is the Peruvian government's big new infrastructure scheme; Nectar Oscar Papa is the kind of Papa we all want, and Quebec Romeo is hot. The Sierra Tango Union is a mountain dance troupe, Victor Whisky Extra is best avoided and Yankee Zulu is a good bet for a basketball team.

In different ways, telegraph and 'spelling alphabet' messages resemble some kinds of modern textspeak. Another source of abbreviated and slang writing was in the speech and messages passed between people in the armed forces of the First and Second World Wars:

LMF – lacking in moral fibre
MIA – missing in action
boko – a lot (from the French, 'beaucoup')
C3 – no good, worthless
Flak (from the German, 'Fliegerabwehrkanone'): 'aircraft
  defence cannon'
PBI – poor bloody infantry
Snip – the regimental tailor
SFA – sweet Fanny Adams and/or sweet f*** all
Tic-tac – the signaller
Z-hour – the time something was due to happen . . .

There were thousands more, including initialized names for equipment, ranks, places and people.

With their short, sharp, electrically generated pulses, Morse code machines mechanized abbreviated writing: 'SOS' was agreed on at the 1906 International Radiotelegraphic Convention in Berlin and adopted in 1908; the first ship to transmit an SOS distress call was the Cunard liner *Slavonia* on 10 June 1909.

Even the old telephone dial involved mechanizing the alphabet so that you could think you were dialling the first three letters of the name of the telephone exchange. In effect, it was a new alphabet of eight 'supra' letters into which were encoded three sub-letters. Following the number 1, which stood alone, the next eight possible dial positions contained the letters, in order:

ABC DEF GHI JKL MNO PRS TUV WXY

If I wanted to dial my grandparents who were on the 'Clissold' exchange, I dialled the first, the fourth and the third of these positions, to make the letters 'CLI'. My best friend David was on the 'Grimsdyke' exchange so I dialled positions three, six and three to make 'GRI'. The alphabet was being used to create a numerical code. The observant amongst you will have spotted that two letters are missing: 'Q' and 'Z'. This prejudice against two lovely letters was presumably in order to get the neat multiple of eight for the dialling positions. By the time our keypads came along, they knew they couldn't get away with this modified literacy, so they created the same number of keypads but squeezed the 'Q' in with the 'PRS' and put the 'Z' on the end of 'WXY'. As it happens, there's still an element of literacy illusion about it, because as we tap in 'letters', we are in fact tapping in signals that can be interpreted in a binary way – ultimately a series of number codes.

I don't remember people objecting to the fact that we shortened Clissold to 'CLI' and Grimsdyke to 'GRI' but shortening has been a long-standing bugbear of those who want to defend the language.

In 1712 Jonathan Swift published a 'Proposal for Correcting, Improving and Ascertaining the English Tongue', in which he reviled poets who used monosyllables, abbreviated words to fit them to their verses, and made sounds that 'none but a Northern Ear could endure'. Worse, they shortened words and syllables, their taste being 'depraved', with the result that even prose was now 'full of those Manglings and Abbreviations'. No one took any notice of Swift and fashions for playing with the look and sound of language keep cropping up. The linguist Allen Walker Read, whose serious academic research started from a toilet graffito, spotted the presence of a fad for abbreviating colloquial and misspelled expressions, running round the US in the 1830s (see 'O is for OK'). For the Boston wags, ' 'GTDHD' was 'Give The Devil His Due', and 'KKN' was 'Kommit Know Nuisance' ('commit no nuisance'). In the 1950s, the word went round the playground that signing off letters with 'SWALK' or 'BURMA' ('sealed with a loving kiss' and 'be undressed and ready, my angel') were 'dead cert' ways to smooth the path to bliss. In the adult world, initials like 'AGM', 'AOB', 'ASAP', 'AWOL', 'IOU', 'RSVP' and 'VIP' have been more or less official – in some cases – for hundreds of years.

Small ads for houses and cars for sale, and 'lonely hearts' have long been places where people have been able to reduce scores of customary or clichéd phrases to a set of initials: 'XDS' ('electronic cross-axle traction control system'), 'ONO' ('or nearest offer'), 'PAS' ('power-assisted steering'); 'SA/F, WLTM, GSOH' ('single Asian female, would like to meet, good sense of humour').

By the time people had learned how to use chatrooms, comment threads, feedback posts and 'social media sites' on the internet, we were ready to unleash all the compressions, elisions and abbreviations we knew already and invent thousands of new ones. Part of this informal world – where, in 2010, 6.1 trillion text messages were sent worldwide – is the proliferation of abbreviated professional-association and techno lingo. I'm not sure I ever knew what initialized phrases like 'URL', 'WAP', 'ISP', 'SMS' and 'PDF' stood for. I just started using them as if they were words whose etymology I didn't know either. And even if I did once know what 'LAN', 'JPEG' and 'HTML' stood for, I've forgotten.

I first came across digital-media speak in the mid-1990s, before texting had really taken off, and it felt at first like an English dialect I hadn't heard before. People were 'speaking' English – and a lot of internet chat feels as if it's being spoken – but there were all kinds of asides, jokes, and in-group sayings that I wasn't catching. In 2012, it was revealed that David Cameron thought that 'lol' meant 'lots of love'. Quite apart from the political significance of the message itself, it was a moment where we were reminded that we live in different text-communities which is obvious when we say things like, 'I don't understand "legalese"', but not so obvious when the lingo is so casual and informal.

Amidst all the vast list of 'wtf', 'ttfn', 'fwd', 'imo', 'rotflmao', 'IH8U', 'b4', 'iaotb' – you use and have made up hundreds more – is one that amazed me the first time I saw it. On the BBC Radio 4 programme *Word of Mouth*, we were looking at forensic linguistics and our expert was explaining that he had to keep up with the very latest textspeak. He showed us a transcript of a text conversation and fairly frequently through the chat was 'kmt'. He said that it means 'kiss my teeth' but that some people write 'smt' meaning 'suck my teeth'.

At first glance, this is just the same as all the others but something else has happened here. The phrase 'kiss my teeth' doesn't exist in conversations. It's something you do. (I don't, but you get what I'm saying.) A person sucks or kisses their teeth as a gesture or sign, as if I were to write 'oer' for 'one eyebrow raised' or 'cmt' for 'clearing my throat'. In case you haven't been around people kissing their teeth, it signifies contempt or irritation or both. If you're writing dialogue, you have to invent a few letters to indicate it. I've seen 'stchuuuuup'. Because this 'interjection' or 'exclamation' is part of how people talk to each other, then text or chatroom conversations needed a way of signifying it at speed, so someone somewhere just applied the abbreviation rule and put down 'kmt'.

Thirty years ago, people like me were trying to guess what

would happen to speech and language thirty years hence. I thought that, for many people, the need to write would fade away. I imagined a semi-literate society. The literate would have power and control over the machines that the non-literate used. It would be possible – perhaps even arranged deliberately – that millions of people would communicate through various kinds of instant micro-visual appliances which would mean that they wouldn't have to go through what they would see as the laborious business of putting words down on pages. Cameras, CB radio and means of recording and playback would get so cheap and lightweight that they would do the job. ('CB' is another one of those acronyms where I had forgotten what they stood for. I just looked it up: 'Citizen Band'. And of course the CB radio users – truck drivers in the main – invented a CB lingo or cant that was almost incomprehensible to outsiders.) The alphabet, as I saw it, was on the verge of returning to its medieval distribution, where only a tiny minority owned it, used it and ruled with it.

What I didn't foresee was that the internet and mobile phones would demand both old and new literacies. Side by side on the internet and other digital media, the alphabet carries on doing exactly what it's done for thousands of years: conveying philosophy, science, fiction, poetry, jokes, current information, opinion, instructions, memories, devotion, worship and much more. New systems of referencing have made access both easier and more widespread. Interchange between the users of different alphabets has never been greater. Alongside these traditional usages, there has grown up an unimaginably huge written conversation. Trillions of people write to each other. To do this they have incorporated aspects of their speech, aspects of older forms of humorous and jargon-like means of written language. When an earlier form of these instant written conversations was around (telegrams), it was too infrequent and expensive to affect us all. Children, students, cleaners and footballers didn't send telegrams every day. Today they do the equivalent.

The media have different ways of presenting this: it's awful because we are all becoming 'sloppy' writers; it's wonderful because it is democratic, no one tells you how to write, no one can tick you off if you make mistakes or invent new things, it's like an oral writing, a written speech. No, it's awful because it means people spread 'news' without corroborating it, so conspiracy theories, witch-hunting, bullying and abuse proliferate. No, it's wonderful because our machines have eyes which means that we can safeguard ourselves. No, it's awful because Big Brother has alphabet-reading machines which means that he knows where we are, what we're doing and, because we keep writing down what we want, love and hate, he knows what we're thinking too. The alphabet has become a means by which our identities are read, logged and stored. But that's wonderful, because there is so much of it, Big Brother doesn't know what to do with it. No, that's awful because ultimately it doesn't matter what Big Brother does with it. All that he cares about is that we buy the whole shebang off him; the digitization of mass alphabet-use has been a means by which Big Brother has become a trillionaire.

In the midst of this, I have to remind myself that there were times when the alphabet wasn't used for much more than inscriptions and sacred texts, legible to a tiny minority and written by even fewer.

THE STORY OF

● **THE STORY OF** 'U', 'V', 'W' and 'Y' is quite complicated, if not absurd. We might suspect this is the case given
that we are quite happy to call 'W' 'double-u' when it's
clearly a 'double-v'.

Roman or mock-Roman inscriptions use the 'V' shape to
indicate what we would think of as the 'U' sound:
'SEPTIMVS' and the like.

The Phoenicians had a letter that looked like our
modern 'Y' in around 1000 BCE. They called this 'waw'
meaning a 'peg' and it indicated a 'w' sound. The ancient
Greeks took this in around 700 BCE and called it 'upsilon'.
The Etruscans took the bottom stroke off the 'Y' to make
a 'V' shape and it was this 'V' that the Romans adopted,
shifting the pronunciation to an 'oo' sound before consonants but keeping the 'w' sound before vowels. So 'V' was
doing service as 'w' and 'u' sounds.

u

People writing by hand as early as the fourth century
started to round off the 'v' turning it into a 'u'. In the
Renaissance, the printers adopted the rounded 'u' as the
lower case for 'v'. Some writers by hand also made their
'capital' into a 'u' shape.

It took till the seventeenth century for printers to make a
distinction between 'u' and 'v' depending on the sound.
Early printers used the two signs interchangeably, with 'v'
words sometimes typeset with a 'u' as in 'knaue' for
'knave', or, in Roman style, 'vnder' for 'under'.

When the sound of 'w' began to develop in northern

Europe, including Britain, it was decided that this needed a 'double-u', which I'll look at in its own place!

PRONUNCIATION OF THE LETTER-NAME
In hindsight this could have been a sound like 'oo', or the 'u' sound in 'put', or even a 'woo'. Somehow it acquired a 'y' sound on the front. I haven't read a convincing explanation of how or why that came about.

PRONUNCIATION OF THE LETTER
As with all vowels, this depends on which part of the English-speaking world you come from, the historical origins of the word, the position in the word where the letter falls, and in what combination of letters it appears.

So, as a Londoner, I say the word 'sun' very differently from the local way of saying it in Yorkshire. However, when I say 'put', that rhymes with the way a northerner would say 'hut'. My 'hut' rhymes with my 'putt'! Some Scots speakers pronounce 'put' as I would pronounce 'poot'.

We can use it to make a 'yoo' sound as in 'use' and 'situation'.

'U' hardly ever doubles but when it does, it's most commonly in 'vacuum'.

We can combine it with other vowels and the letter 'r' (if you're an unvoiced 'r' speaker) to make the same or different vowel sounds, as in 'cue', 'sue', 'sour', 'ruin', 'course', 'fur', 'pure', 'tour', 'fleur de lys', 'wounded', 'wound up', 'through', 'thorough', 'though', 'enough', 'bough', 'brougham', 'conscious', 'radium', 'dinosaur', 'Guam' and 'duet' (which, for some speakers, has the virtue of asking the 'u' to make a 'you-w' sound!).

We have the sound 'uh-uh' which can mean 'watch out!' or 'something's not right'. A word for a 'fool' has appeared in the last twenty years which I think could be written 'wuss' to rhyme (in my speech) with 'puss', not 'fuss'. Rugby players kick an 'up and under'.

 IS FOR UMLAUTS

Two LITTLE DOTS and quite a kerfuffle.

One kind of two little dots is called an umlaut. An umlaut does the job of changing the sound of a vowel. There are two similar-looking words in German, one with an umlaut and the other without: 'schon' and 'schön'. One means 'already' and the other 'beautiful': 'schon' is pronounced 'shown'; 'schön' is pronounced (in my southern English speech) 'shern'.

Another kind of two little dots is called a dieresis. A dieresis does the job of separating vowels that look as if they are combining: 'Laocoön' doesn't rhyme with 'moon'. It rhymes with 'show on'.

A third kind of two little dots doesn't change the way things sound in any way at all, but it seems to have made brand-name execs think they're doing something cool: Häagen-Dazs (1961 – ice cream), Blue Öyster Cult (1970 – band), Motörhead (1975 – band), Mötley Crüe (1980 – band), Spinal Tap (with an umlaut over the 'n' which my computer won't let me do! – 1984 – satirical band name). Since then, the umlaut has crept into the names of products, cafés, shops and magazines: Füd, YogaMöm,

Seäsonal, Gü, hibü, däv, AÄRK, LÄRABAR, Bük – and thousands möre – apologies about the 'möre', I got stuck on it.

As it isn't doing what umlauts or diereses do, then it probably needs another name: the adlaut, perhaps. So what does the adlaut do? Does it lend a stylish European-ness to the product or business? Or is there a knowing irony: that they know and we know that the dots aren't doing anything but winking at us? Above a 'u' or an 'o' there is a hint of a smiley-face going on there, a kind of ad hoc emoticon. Mötorhead were flirting with something Teutonic as the name was written in gothic lettering. Given the success of Volkswagen, Audi, BMW, Bosch, Siemens and Miele, perhaps the umlaut brings with it a sense of Germans getting it right with metal machines.

It was Jacob Grimm of the Brothers Grimm who first gave the umlaut its name, a word meaning literally 'around-sound' or 'the other way around-sound'. So, in German the umlaut marks a change. The German name Hans is usually pronounced in English to sound like 'hands'. Germans pronounce 'Hans' sounding something like the way someone in the South of England would pronounce 'hunts'. When it becomes 'Hänsel' ('little Hans'), Germans say, 'Henzel'. The umlaut is busy. When Germans see it, it makes them want to pick up on it, so when they see the adlaut, doing nothing at all, they are likely to feel a bit irritated. It's like looking at an empty bottle of your favourite drink.

In the English-speaking world, people used to be quite fond of the dieresis. It was on 'naïve', 'Noël', 'coöperate', 'zoölogical', 'spermatozoön', Odysseus' father 'Laërtes', Perseus' mother, 'Danaë', along with some other Greek deities and heroes, but we're mostly trusted with managing to pronounce these words without it. Even Emily Brontë and her talented family are losing it. Most common sightings today are with Zoë and Chloë.

What seems to have happened is that at the very moment that branding has discovered the adlaut, orthodox printing has tired of the dieresis. The move away from the two dots in newspapers, magazines and books might be part of a general dislike of these over- or under-the-letter signs or 'diacritics'. For centuries, the English-speaking world has shunned the 'tilde' that the Portuguese place on São Paolo. We'd much rather write 'cafe' than 'café' (with its acute accent), we've stopped writing 'hôtel' (with a circumflex), and 'façade' (with a cedilla). The acute accent survives, if people are worried that you'll muddle 'lame' with 'lamé', 'expose' with 'exposé' or 'resume' with 'resumé' (or even 'résumé' if you're feeling français). It flourishes in food with 'glacé cherries', 'flambé', 'purée' (and a host of others), and in ballet with 'plié', 'allongé', 'jeté' (and a host of others). If anyone produces a cooking ballet (*Swan Cake?*), you wouldn't be able to move for acute accents.

The accent pointing the other way (grave accent) is a rarer species in the English-speaking world. Would you rather have a 'derriere' or a 'derrière'? It survives in an antique way for when pre-twentieth-century poets wanted to make sure that their past tenses were pronounced in the right way to fit the metre: 'Till in her blurrèd sight the hills went round . . .' The name Róisín, whom you might well meet in English-speaking parts of the world, has two accents but neither of them are acute. It's the 'fada' from Irish writing, which also employs the 'overdot', a single dot placed over some letters.

Occasionally, a false diacritic crops up. The drink 'maté' is written in Spanish and Portuguese as 'mate' but some marketeers worried that 'having a drink of mate' didn't look right.

By the way, the 'ø' and 'å' used in Scandinavian writing are not diacritics. They are not signs 'over' or 'across' a letter, they are each part of a letter. If you want to avoid irritating someone from that part of the world, don't start asking 'Which way does the line go?' or 'Why's the degree sign on the top?' In fact, what we're talking about here is so non-diacritical that they are letters in their own right coming after the 'z' and the 'æ' in Scandinavian alphabets. The correct spelling of 'smörgåsbord' is 'smörgåsbord'.

Diacritics are a way of trying to make the sounding of letters more precise, though the circumflex in French mostly marks an 's' that disappeared. Generally they are consistent across languages, and you could argue that if they make 'sounding' more precise, then they also make reading and understanding more precise too. Given that vowels (and combinations of vowels) in English are not consistent, you could see ways in which signs over or under letters would be very good at guiding us on which sound to make. You could have different squiggles over the different '-ea-'s in 'meat', 'threat' and 'great', and the different '-ie-'s in 'wield', 'lies', 'sienna' and 'easiest'. But then you would have to learn the squiggles. Maybe not such a good plan, then.

Cities like London have become world cities and plenty of people want to continue speaking the language of their family's place of origin. English starts to look positively naked alongside, say, Turkish, Vietnamese, Czech and Welsh shop-signs, public notices and places of worship. By the way, jocular French teachers taught us that the circumflex was a 'tin hat'; in Welsh, it's called a 'bach' which means 'little roof'. No need for a little figurative jest there then.

I can't resist returning to the adlaut with the story of Häagen-Dazs.

The founder of the business was Reuben Mattus who was born in Poland in 1912 to Jewish parents. He arrived with his mother in New York in 1921. They met up with an uncle who was in the Italian lemon-ice business in Brooklyn. By the late 1920s, the family began making ice lollies and chocolate-covered ice-cream bars in the south Bronx under the name Senator Frozen Products. Mattus met Rose Vesel, who had also arrived in New York as a child aged five. In 1934 she got a job as a bookkeeper at the Senator plant, and Reuben and Rose married in 1936.

The business was going OK (see 'O is for OK') but by the 1950s they found that they couldn't compete with the big guys (in Yiddish: the 'gantse machers') of the ice-cream world so Mattus decided to go for quality not quantity. He started up a new ice-cream company with what he thought was a Danish-sounding name, Häagen-Dazs. Why Danish? As a tribute, Mattus thought, to Denmark's treatment of the Jews during the Second World War. On the labels in the early days, there was even an outline map of Denmark. Now comes a problem: the name isn't Danish, there is no umlaut in Danish, and you never come across a 'z' and an 's' together in Danish; 'zs' just doesn't happen. As a matter of fact, Häagen-Dazs doesn't mean anything to anyone anywhere in any language. According to his daughter Doris, Mattus had sat at the kitchen table for hours coming up with all kinds of 'meshugas' (nonsense) until he hit upon a 'meshugas' he liked.

But it's not all sweetness and vanilla scoops. In 1980, Häagen-Dazs sued the ice-cream company, Frusen Glädjé, on the grounds that it was using similar foreign-branding strategies. Can you imagine the scene? Mattus and Rose are at home. On TV comes someone eating Frusen Glädjé. 'Hmm, Frusen Glädjé, I love Frusen Glädjé.' Mattus leaps up out of his chair. 'Look what they're doing there! These Frusen Glädjé people have stolen our umlaut. We did the umlaut. We were first with the umlaut and along come these people thinking they can do the umlaut thing too? No, no, no . . .'

THE STORY OF

• **AS WE'VE SEEN** with 'U', the letter 'V' grew up in order to make 'w' and 'u' sounds. For 'v' to become a letter that had a distinctly different 'value' from 'u', people had to acknowledge that they were making a sound like our modern 'v'. The Romans didn't. The words that begin with 'v' in Latin, like 'Venus', were pronounced with a 'w' – so 'Weenus' not 'Venus'. The speakers of Old English had a 'v' sound as did the Normans who scored a 'victory' and burned a few 'villages'. However, even as late as the early seventeenth century the printers of Shakespeare's plays represented Vs in the middle of words as 'u'. Initial Vs, either as a capital 'V' or as in, say, 'vain', started to appear as 'v' in the 1400s.

In other words, there was what we would think of as chaos: Us and Vs being used interchangeably yet with obscure rules. What was needed was for printers and lexicographers to agree that there were two letters and each should be assigned a different job, rather than both doing the same job – sometimes! By about 1700, this seems to have happened.

v

A smaller 'v' starts to appear in Latin manuscripts in the middle medieval period but of course this represents both the 'u' and 'v' sounds. It's only when there is a separation of duties that the lower-case 'v' settles to represent the 'v' sound.

PRONUNCIATION OF THE LETTER-NAME

This derives from the French 'vé' and neatly rhymes with 'B' and the 'ee' gang.

PRONUNCIATION OF THE LETTER

'V' almost always sounds the same, though 'of' and the 'w' of German loan words poach on its territory with 'Weltanschauung' and 'wanderlust'.

At the ends of words, we like to put an 'e' to finish: 'curve' 'swerve', though the shortened form of the name 'Mervyn' is 'Merv' and the nickname for a 'pervert' is a 'perv'. Doubling appears in joke words like 'bovver' (a representation of the cockney pronunciation of 'bother') and in the verb made from an abbreviation: 'rev, revving, revved'. 'Rev.' also exists as a legit abbreviation for 'Reverend'. A 'bevvy' is slang for 'a drink'.

The usual rule for 'e' verbs applies: 'move, moving, moved'. An 'o' in front of the 'v' can be pronounced as in 'move', 'love' and 'grove'.

We don't much like combining 'v' with other consonants: 'halves', 'swerve' (if you voice your 'r'), 'envy', 'advertise' and 'invert'. Loan names give us 'Vladimir' and Tolstoy's 'Vronsky'.

Sound-play with 'v' can involve speed: 'vroom' and 'va va voom'. 'Vive' meaning 'long live' is a loan word that's usually used jokily; 'vamp' is the sound you hear when you make dampened chords on a guitar. A 'V' sign can mean 'up yours' (or what my children call 'swearing'), or again, on the hand of Winston Churchill and reversed with palm out, 'V for Victory'. When one of my children was learning to speak, she adopted a Germanic (or Indian) pronunciation for 'wee-wee', calling it 'vee-vee'. Of course this was adopted by the rest of the family.

'Lovey-dovey' plays with the '-vy' sound too.

V IS FOR VIKINGS

IN 1898, IN the rural township of Solem, Douglas County, Minnesota, USA, a farmer found a stone slab. The farmer was Olof Ohman, a Swedish-American who had just taken over an 80-acre stretch of land and was clearing it, ready for ploughing. The stone was lying face down and tangled up in the root system of a poplar tree. Ohman's ten-year-old son, Edward, noticed some markings on the stone which Ohman thought were an 'Indian almanac'.

Before I go any further with this story, I should say that pretty nearly everything I've written so far has been disputed. The stone may have been found in August or November, right after lunch or at the end of work in the evening. Olof and Edward may have found the stone on their own; they may have been with two workmen; they may have been with neighbour Nils Flaten.

The stone was taken to the nearby town of Kensington and transcriptions of the carvings were sent to a regional Scandinavian-language newspaper. Soon after it was found, the stone was displayed at a local bank. Within months it had caused a worldwide stir, the reason being that the carvings on the stones were runes, the alphabet used by the Vikings.

The inscription, when translated reads:

8 Götalanders [people from what is now southern Sweden] and 22 Northmen [Norwegians] on an exploration journey from Vinland westward. We had one camp by 2 rocky islets one day's journey north of this stone. We were out fishing one day. When we came home we found 10 men red with blood and dead. AVM save us from evil. We have 10 men by the sea to look after our ships, 14 days journey from this island. Year 1362.

Here seemed to be proof positive that the Vikings had not only made it to the fringes of the North American continent (Vinland), they had ventured hundreds of miles inland. And it was written in the alphabet associated with the ancient peoples of Scandinavia. The stone is on display at the Runestone Museum, located in downtown Alexandria, Minnesota. Near by at Fort Alexandria you can see a forty-foot Viking ship, the *Snorri*, and you can have your picture taken next to the 'country's biggest Viking'. Many local businesses use the 'Kensington Runestone' or the Vikings as part of their branding, and the National Football League's Minnesota Vikings owe their name to the Runestone. The only problem with this scenario is that most academic 'runologists' think it's a hoax.

The runic alphabets are made up of beautiful, angular letters, each of which has a name, referring to an object, and a sound based on the initial letter of that name. If you were reciting, by name of object, one of the oldest forms of the runic alphabet, you would start off by saying: 'fehu, uruz, thurisaz, ansuz, raidof, cen' (meaning, in order: 'money' (or 'cattle'), 'ox', 'giant' (or 'monster'), 'god', 'riding' and 'torch'). If you were reciting it by letter sound, you would say, 'f', 'u', 'th', 'a', 'r', 'k' – and those letters give the name to the oldest runic alphabet, 'Elder Futhark'.

Purely in terms of the history of the Roman alphabet used by people living in Britain, one reason why runes get mentioned is that the earliest manuscripts written in the Anglo-Saxon or Old English version of the Roman alphabet contained two letters derived directly from the runic letters 'thorn' and 'wynn', and two 'ligatures' (letters tied together), 'ash' and 'ethel', which used Roman letters but were the equivalent of runes (see 'D is for Disappeared Letters'). However, these four letters did not get into the Anglo-Saxon version of the Roman alphabet via the Vikings. To get a picture of what happened, I'll attempt a quick rundown of who went where and when.

In spite of many modifications and caveats, the sequence of the settlement of the British Isles just about hangs together: Celts, Romans, Anglo-Saxons, Vikings and Normans. That's how we drew it at school: a map of the British Isles with big arrows pointing towards it from different parts of Europe, each arrow filled with the name of the invaders and the dates they arrived – and, in the case of the Romans, the date they left.

The many complications to this nice map include the following (not in order of importance):

a) the Celts not being one people – they arrived in many waves from different places;
b) the Romans not being all Roman – it was Roman policy to station people as far away from their original home as possible as it cut down on rebellions, but some 'Romans' who came as part of their Empire's settlement may have stayed;
c) the Germanic peoples who arrived, usually called the 'Anglo-Saxons', were, yes, Angles (from Schleswig-Holstein)

and Saxons (from Lower Saxony), but they were also Jutes
(from Jutland), Franks (from the Rhine) and Frisians (from
coastal north Holland);

d) they may well have started arriving *before* the Romans
packed their bags and left in AD 410;

e) some peoples who arrived in England, like the Belgae, may
well be better described as Celto-Germanic;

f) the Scandinavian Vikings did indeed set out from what is
now Iceland, Denmark, Sweden and Norway but they may
well have started arriving while the Anglo-Saxons and their
pals were arriving too;

g) the Normans came from Normandy, speaking a form of
Old French, but as a people they originated from a Viking
settlement;

h) either under duress or willingly, any or all of these peoples,
to a greater or lesser degree, intermarried;

i) any or all of these peoples shared, borrowed and merged
their ways of speaking and writing;

j) as a rough guide we can say that literate pre-Christian
'Anglo-Saxons' used runes. They encountered Latin through
Christianity and thereafter amalgamated a few adapted
runes into the Latin/Roman alphabet.

Two further examples of sharing: the runic inscriptions found
on the Isle of Man show that people with Celtic names and
people with Scandinavian names (Vikings) were intermarrying
from the tenth century onwards. The modern English word
'wicket' probably came from a Norman-French word, which had
originally come from a Norse word. This is not evidence that
cricket was invented by the Vikings.

So, though life and history would be much simpler if it were
more like the maps we drew in my first year at grammar school

in 1957, for archaeologists and linguists, it's much more complex
– and three cheers for that.

The vikings arrived speaking what's known as Old Norse, though
they didn't say, 'We speak Old Norse.'

They ended up occupying what we now call 'the North' of
England plus East Anglia, Pembrokeshire, the Scottish islands
and the Orkneys, the north and east coasts of Scotland, and
the south-east corner of Ireland. It's almost certain they did get
to the North American continent – Kensington Runestone or
not – and it's completely certain that they got to Turkey and
into the Arab-speaking lands of the Middle East.

Anyone who speaks, reads or writes English cannot avoid
talking Viking. Words of Old Norse origin are everywhere. If
you read this list aloud, it's almost a free-verse poem about the
effect the Norse-speaking peoples had on those around them
in Britain:

Anger, bag, bask, birth, blunder,
both, bull, cake,
call, choose, clip,
club, die, dirt, dregs, egg, fellow, flat, fog,
freckle, gap, get, gift, haggle, hit, how,
husband, ill, knife, knot, law, leg, loose,
low, mistake, muck, muggy, odd, outlaw, raise,
ransack, rid, rotten, rugged, run, same, scare,
scarf, score, seat, seem, shape, skid, skill,
skin, skip, skirt, skull, sky, sly, snare,
snub, sprint, stagger, sway, take, their, they,
though, tight, trust, ugly, until, want, weak,
whisk, window, wing,
wrong.

The patterning of the alphabet on a page of English writing would look fundamentally different if the Vikings had decided to give the British Isles a miss. No 'take' or 'get'. No 'their', 'them' or 'they'. No 'window' which holds within it the beautiful meta-phor 'wind-eye'. No 'egg'. No 'sky'. Indeed that 'sk' combination would hardly have reached Britain. Of course, it goes without saying, there were non-Norse ways of saying these things and we have ways of saying them with words of French origin or from many other places which have influenced speakers of English.

This is a risky thing to state, but it seems as if the Scandinavians who arrived in the British Isles were not particularly literate. However, we can be fairly certain that they were storytellers and poets.

Those Vikings who wrote, wrote in runes. Depending on their age, their alphabets are called 'Elder' or 'Younger Futhark'. At the point at which the Germanic peoples (Frisians, Jutes, Saxons, Angles, Franks) first started arriving they wrote in runes too. Their alphabet is called 'Futhorc'. What has survived of this kind of writing is found on clay pots, metal swords, amulets, and brooches, on bone, stone and occasionally on wood where it has been preserved in airless mud. The British Isles represent a site in which a spectrum of different kinds of runic writing meets over a period of some eight hundred years. Beyond saying that, the runic field is clogged with debate and disagreement. The First Law of Thermodynamics concerns heat and energy. According to the runologist D. M. Wilson, the First Law of Runo-Dynamics states that 'for every inscription there shall be as many interpretations as there are scholars working on it.'

Even so, the subject is worth more than a glimpse. It may seem strange, but at the height of the 1960s, with the air full of protest and revolt, civil rights and anti-war demonstrations, I found myself being excited by something utterly distant and different from Martin Luther King, the Tet Offensive and Wenceslas Square. It was the extraordinary tally between, on the one hand, a mystical Old English poem about the Crucifixion, found on a manuscript in a library in Vercelli in northern Italy, and, on the other, a runic inscription on a stone cross in a church in Dumfriesshire in Scotland. The poem is called 'The Dream of the Rood' and a narrator talks of his dream of the Cross; the Cross itself tells the story of the Crucifixion; the narrator reflects on what he has heard. Written in Anglo-Saxon runes on the fragments of the Ruthwell Cross is a text that overlaps with what is written on the manuscript in Italy: 'I raised up a great king, lord of heaven. I dared not bow down. Men reviled us both together. I was drenched in blood.' And it continues.

Quite apart from the power of personification which I have always enjoyed in poetry, I was drawn to the idea of a line between Vercelli and Ruthwell, at a time when travel was so precarious and time-consuming; a trade route of ideas and feelings preserved by chance in these objects tucked away in libraries or in inscriptions in rural places. In fact, in this case, it was the stone that was more at risk than the parchment manuscript, as seventeenth-century Puritans identified the cross as idolatrous and smashed it up.

The Viking runes in the British Isles are often quite simple: 'A good comb Thorfastr made', 'Dolfin wrote these runes on this stone', or 'Ginna and Tóki had this stone laid'. On a font in Cumbria there's a poem:

Richard, he me wrought
and me, to this splendour, brought.

On a cross at Kirk Michael, on the Isle of Man, it says: 'It is better to leave a good foster-son than a bad son.'

A vision of the popular culture of Viking warriors comes from some graffiti they scratched on the walls of a prehistoric stone grave-chamber at Maeshowe in the Orkneys, where they sheltered or held their meetings:

'Úframr Sigurðarsonr cut these runes'
'Ingibjorg the lovely widow'
'It's true what I say, the treasure was moved out of here. The treasure was taken away three days before they broke into the mound.'
'Happy the man who can find the great treasure'
'Thorni f****d. Helgi carved.'

R. I. Page, who died in 2012, was regarded as the world's greatest expert on runes. He wrote about these graffiti, pointing out that one of them was 'an inscription I would like to have cut myself: "The man who wrote these runes knows more about runes than anyone else west of the sea."'

Page divided runologists into two categories: the imaginative and the unimaginative. Unless an interpretation could be proven, he would declare he was an unimaginative runologist and clearly liked it that way. With barely concealed scorn, he stepped round the New Age enthusiasts who have found comfort in the pagan knowledge expressed through runes. Of the Kensington Runestone, he wrote: 'It is a stirring story, with the sort of detail about Norsemen in midwest America that is not recorded anywhere else. Only the unimaginative runologist will fail to be impressed, but I have already declared myself an unimaginative runologist.'

THE STORY OF

● **CHARLEMAGNE'S SCRIBES CREATED** a sign by placing two Us side by side with a space between. It signified a 'w' sound in the late Latin, German and French of that time, i.e. AD 900. It was described as 'two Us'. So when printers adapted it they started off by printing 'VV' – two Vs next to each other. Only later, by about 1700, did they set in lead a new letter 'W' which was of course still called a 'double u'. In French, though, it is known as 'double v'.

There used to be another sign to indicate a 'w' sound, the 'wyn', which you can find in 'D is for Disappeared Letters'.

W

The lower-case 'w' standing for the sound 'w' had to wait till the upper-case 'W' had been fixed.

PRONUNCIATION OF THE LETTER-NAME

As we've seen, this derives from the Carolingian hand-written double letter.

PRONUNCIATION OF THE LETTER

On its own at the beginning of words, it does service in 'witch' and 'wonder'. Most English speakers pronounce 'w' in the same way as they pronounce 'wh' in 'why', 'where', 'what', 'when' and 'whence'. In 'who' and 'whole' the 'h' does its work, reminding us that in Old English the formation for that breathy sound was 'hw', where the 'w' was a 'wynn'.

'W' combines with vowels to make 'raw', 'new' and 'now'.

It combines with 'r' in unpronounced ways: 'wrong', 'wright' and 'write', and again in 'two' and 'answer'. The initial 'w's were once pronounced but unlike some initial 'h's, once pronounced now not, the 'w' hung about.

You can put 's' in front of it to make 'sweet' but only when imitating people who pronounce 'r' as 'w' do we write things like 'fwee', 'bwight'. 'Twice' reminds us that the 'w' in 'two' was once pronounced as it is in 'between' and the neologism 'tweenies'. 'Dweeb' is doing well at the moment too. 'Kwik' was once a word that advertisers liked. Talking of 'once', it's a word that deserves a 'w' on the front to match 'wonder' but we get by without.

Following 'w' we write consonants as in 'newt', 'gawp', 'news', 'Newfoundland' (a bit of a cheat as it was once three separate words), 'trawl', 'hawser', 'town' and 'shawm'.

'Awkward' manages two Ws in place, in front of and following a consonant.

Norman French brought in 'William' from 'Guillaume', the 'warranty' and the 'guarantee', the 'ward' and the 'guard'.

Sound-play with 'w' can involve crying: 'woo-woo-woo'. Owls go 'woo' or 'whoo' or 'tu-whit-tu-woo'. We stop horses by saying, 'Whoa!' which can also be used to show people you don't want them to go on doing what they're doing or saying: 'Whoa, man!' We can do a 'wee' or a 'wee-wee' or a 'widdle'. Something good is a 'whizz'. We're pleased when we say 'wow!' Things that aren't straight are 'wonky'. 'Wee Willie Winkie runs through the town', because he comes from Scotland where 'wee' means 'small'.

If you're a parent you're probably wondering 'Where's Wally?' though in the US it'll be 'Where's Waldo?' If you can't get to the bottom of the matter, your mind is full of the 'whys and wherefores'. Two old chants go: 'Why are we waiting?' and 'We won't, we won't, we won't be buggered about . . .'

W IS FOR WEBSTER

Dictionaries honour alphabets. American dictionaries, like *Webster's Collegiate*, honor alphabets. As a child I thought that the big dictionaries on my parents' shelves were language. They had captured language. All of it. They sorted it into the right order and anything you wanted to know about language was there. I would say now that if words were bricks, dictionaries put them into neat piles but they don't design houses.

The dictionaries I knew best – two huge books, *The Shorter Oxford English Dictionary, A–M* and *N–Z* – had a joke. If these were shorter, what were the longer ones like? Written inside was 'H. Rosen 1950'. My mother was C. Rosen and her absence implies that while the dictionary housed the words, housing a dictionary was a man's job. By the time I came to study these things, the big names in dictionaryland seemed to be men too. To bring full weight to the words in *The Shorter Oxford English Dictionary on Historical Principles*, they are adorned with a bevy of credits:

William Little, M.A., late Fellow of Corpus Christi College, Oxford, H.W. Fowler, M.A. Oxon., J. Coulson, B.A. Leeds, C.T. Onions,

C.B.E., F.B.A., M.A. Lond., Hon. D.Litt.,Oxon., Hon. F.R.S.L., Fellow of Magdalen College; Reader in English Philology in the University of Oxford, Joint Editor of the Oxford English Dictionary.

It all adds up to telling us that words are safe here. And they were. We loved the two volumes of these blue dictionaries, each entry a tiny essay in the history of the word, jam-packed full of abbreviations: a special scholarly code that only people like my father could unpack.

†Bawdstrot. ME. [OF. *baudetrot,* suggesting earlier OF. *baldestrot, baudestrot,* f. *bald, baud* 'bold, gay' (see BAUDE) + ? Teut. *strut/ STRUT.*] A BAWD, male or female – 1483.

Inspired by the mock erudition of the BBC Home Service's wits, Denis Norden and Frank Muir, my brother and I would take the dictionary down and challenge our father to come up with the right meaning for words that we had never heard or seen. More often than we could believe, he was right. How could he possibly know the meaning of 'heterostrophic'?At other times, he went in for convoluted bullshitting, inventing etymologies based on such things as 'little-known Celtic deities', claiming that the dictionary was wrong and that it had missed out the older, 'original' meaning. My friends couldn't believe that such heavy, scholarly books could include:

Fart [phonetic pronunciation], *v.* not in decent use. ME. [Com. Teut. and Indo-Germ. : OE f**feortan:* – OTeut. **fertan:* – OAryan *perd – (Skr. *pard, prd,* Gr. [greek word] etc.).] 1. *intr.* To break wind. 2. *trans.* To send forth as wind from the anus 1632.

Recently, I was curious about that list of names with their awards on the opening page of the *Shorter Oxford*. When the *Shorter* was reviewed in 1934 by Henry Wyld, Wyld explained that this dictionary was an abridgement of *The Oxford English Dictionary*: 'Mr H.W. Fowler – so well known for his various dictionaries' did the abridging of the letters 'U', 'X' , 'Y' and 'Z', and Henry Wyld explained that it was 'Mrs. Coulson who tackled W'. Why did Mrs Coulson get 'W'? Did she bid for it or was she given it?

The full dictionary that Mrs Coulson et al. abridged is one of the most extraordinary books that has ever been written. *The Oxford English Dictionary* (OED) took from 1857 to 1928 to get from concept to public consumption, involving scholars, intellectuals, Joe and Jo Public and, famously, an American from 'Ceylon', William Chester Minor. A 'criminal lunatic', he had served as a surgeon-captain during the American Civil War but had a history of mental illness and was committed to Broadmoor following an incident in which he shot and killed a man in 1872.

People were invited to send in significant examples of words in use, with a full reference of where this usage came from. The number of contributors reached four figures and their suggestions the tens of thousands, each of which was kept in a pigeon-hole. Here's one of Minor's which was accepted for the verb 'set':

set, v., sense 17 a
'a1548 Hall Chron., Hen. IV. (1550) 32b, Duryng whiche sickenes as Auctors write he caused his crowne to be set on the pillowe at his beddes heade.'

The sixteenth and seventeenth centuries were Minor's speciality.

The dictionary took over seventy years to compile because the OED was like no other dictionary had ever been. It claimed to include every word that had ever been used in English since the earliest records around AD 740 – which embraced literature of every kind: standard; obsolete, archaic, technical, dialect and slang, together with information about each word's form, sense, history, pronunciation and etymology.

To do this, each word is shown in the context of a piece of writing taken from its earliest usage. For 'excellence' we get: '"Sir, are you not ignorant of what excellence Laertes is at his weapon." from "Hamlet v ii 143."'

So, this is a dictionary 'based on historical principles', a towering anthology of etymologies and usages. Thousands of neat piles of bricks, ruled over by the alphabet. Because it gives usages of a word over time, it's a dictionary which charts changes in meaning. On its pages, you can follow the shifts in culture, politics, religion, leisure and thinking across hundreds of years. Historians do this through their narratives as they struggle to turn the great mass of information and detail into comprehensible chunks. Dictionaries don't really do narrative. They codify language into words and then shuffle these into alphabetical order, so the matrix for classifying and ordering the detail is already in place before they get down to work. This matrix had been in place since the sixteenth century and was given real shape and form with Samuel Johnson's dictionary.

With the arrival of computers, though, it's possible to impose categories other than the alphabet, like, say, the year of a word's first appearance. We might wonder, say, what words appeared for the first time during the First World War, or during Cromwell's Commonwealth, and the OED's huge database of words can now be shuffled digitally to give you this information in a moment. It wasn't impossible pre-computer, just very laborious. Indeed, any kind of statistical cross-section through the language can now be extracted from the data. The digital revolution has broken the grip of the alphabet over how we classify words and how we investigate change.

If you keep company with dictionaries, though, you find difference. You could have had a dictionary from the nineteenth century that wasn't alphabetical. One book on our shelves at home was called *Der Grosse Duden*, published in 1935 by the Bibliographisches Institut AG in Leipzig. As it is beside me as I am writing this, I see that it's stamped 'The County Secondary School, Clapham'. One of the mysteries about my parents' books was that some of them had acquired stamps like this. You could put up an argument for saying that my parents were book thieves, kleptomaniacs of a sort, but they were also teachers who took their own books into the schools they taught in. My Beatrix Potter books are signed 'C. Rosen' and stamped 'Harvey Road Junior School' because my mother decided that I didn't need them any more, took them to school and then, when she left, retrieved them.

There is no English word for a 'Duden'. It's a Duden. I have an English Duden. It's called *The Oxford-Duden: Pictorial English Dictionary*. It is an un-alphabetical dictionary of over 28,000 illustrations, each one multi-labelled. So there is an illustration of 'Cement Works (Cement Factory)' and there are sixteen labels including '9 clinker cooler' and '14 gypsum crusher'. My parents' Duden has the subtitle 'Bildwörterbuch' – a 'picture-words book'. 'Der Schlafzimmer' ('the bedroom') has forty-two labels where you can find out, say, the words for 'a bolster': '7 die Schlummerrolle (das Nakkenkissen)'. Neither the themed pictures nor the labels are arranged alphabetically. You go to the index for the alphabetic sorting.

The Duden was invented by Konrad Duden, a 'Gymnasium' (secondary-school) teacher from Thuringia in eastern Germany – coincidentally a place my brother and I stayed in 1957 when our parents spent the summer in East Germany. Duden published his first version in 1872 and it grew to be the official spelling dictionary. Being non-alphabetical it provided an alternative route to solving the problem of a person not knowing where to go in a dictionary when he or she didn't know how to spell a word: you start from the topic, find the picture, find the label and, hey, there's your 'Nakkenkissen'. The 1981 *Oxford-Duden* has '11 [wedge-shaped] bolster'. Disconcertingly, this British version of 1981 follows the German model of 1935, by illustrating, for example, 'Man I' with a naked woman – and fifty-four labels – with no accompanying picture of a man. Presumably, parts of the man were unnameable even in 1981. The page for 'Hairstyles and Beards' is more evenly distributed in the British version: 1–25 are men's beards and hairstyles; 27–38 are ladies' hairstyles. Someone looking incredibly like Sigmund Freud in his later years appears in both the German and the English Duden from nearly fifty years later to illustrate 'der Vollbart', 'the full beard'.

To keep up to date, a Duden ended up being explicitly political. The history of Germany between 1872 and today can be traced through the tiny details in the scenes and people illustrated. As a child I loved looking at the line drawings of a house being built, fifteen different kinds of breads or a cross-section of a gasworks but I overlooked the same attention being given to the eighteen different flashes worn by the different grades of Stormtrooper. When Germany was divided after the Second World War, the home of the Duden, Leipzig, found itself in the Communist East, so the West had to have its own Duden and the two Dudens started to diverge. Russian words and endings began to turn up in the East's Duden, particularly when it came to tractors. As ever, these were non-alphabetical in the front, alphabetical at the back.

If this all seems political in a modern way, an earlier political use of the alphabet could be found in another one of my parents' dictionaries. It was a book that carried a name that millions of Americans then and now are familiar with: *Webster's Collegiate*. As a child and a student in north London I didn't know anyone else who had a *Webster's Collegiate* on their shelves. I didn't know anyone who knew what it was.

My father was born in Brockton, Massachusetts. When he was called up to the US Army in 1945, his first posting was to Shrivenham in Oxfordshire. The American Army had created the US Army University, Shrivenham and with my father's degree in English he was reckoned to be qualified to teach there. Along the shelves in our house sat the evidence of this era in his life, grey-paperback or blue-grey-hardback, multi-volume editions of the history and culture of America. One of these was *Webster's Collegiate*. 'Everyone knows about Webster in America,' my father said.

I don't remember any of us opening it very often and I can't find his particular copy of it any more. I thought at the time that it had one particularly flashy feature: each letter of the alphabet had its own labelled finger mark in the right-hand side of the book, a minute alcove, enabling you to put in your finger or thumb and flick open the book where you wanted. Each letter was printed in gold on black. They were like tiny wayside shrines. As a child, I had no idea that this dictionary and Webster himself – whoever he was – are two of the foundation stones of the United States of America.

The children I work with in British schools will quite often write 'color' and 'center'. My view is that we should just accept these as alternatives just as we accept 'realise' and 'realize'. No, I'll revise that: my view is that within fifty years we will. I often sense that when people on this side of the Atlantic talk about American English, they imply that there's something faulty with it, and a spelling like 'maneuver' shows how sloppy they are and how very disregarding of European history it shows them to be. There's an irony here. The man behind it all, Noah Webster Jnr, was one of the most fastidious, pernickety scholars ever to have attempted to lick language into alphabetical order.

He was a republican, a devout Congregationalist, and an abolitionist. He started out life as a farm-boy in a home that had no book other than the Bible, and by the time he died at the age of eighty-five, he was celebrated as one of America's greatest scholars, patriots and heroes.

He began work on his dictionary in 1800 and first presented its 70,000 defined words to a publisher in 1825. The moment is full of ironies. Webster wasn't just 'American', he was someone who devoted most of his life to trying to define what 'America' meant. In his own words, he once 'shouldered a musket' to define America, by fighting the British. The America that he wanted to help create wasn't just another country. At the age of twenty-three in 1781, he wrote to the son of a pastor:

[The] American empire will be the theatre on which the last scene of the stupendous drama of nature shall be exhibited. Here the numerous and complicated parts of the actors shall be brought to a conclusion: here the impenetrable mysteries of the Divine system shall be disclosed to the view of the intelligent creation . . . You and I may have considerable parts to act in this plan, and it is a matter of consequence to furnish the mind with enlarged ideas of men and things, to extend our wishes beyond ourselves, our friends, or our country, and include the whole system in the expanded grasp of benevolence.

So quite modest in ambition, then.

However, when Webster came first to present his American

dictionary it was in the capital city of his old enemy, red-coat England. If you glance at the title page of the book you are reading now, you will see that it's published by John Murray and it was to the John Murray who had published Byron and Jane Austen that Webster took his dictionary. And John Murray turned it down. (It's OK, we all have lapses in judgement. When I read the first Harry Potter book, I said it was fun but wouldn't sell.)

The Oxford dictionaries to one side, there has never been a more popular or more successful family of dictionaries than the Websters. In fact, the US assault on Brit supremacy across the spelling fields of the world didn't start with the manuscript that Webster presented to Murray. The first salvo came in 1783 with Webster's first hit, his *Blue Back Speller* ('The American Spelling book: containing an easy standard of pronunciation being the first part of a grammatical institute of the English language'). Webster wrote: 'A spelling book does more to form the language of a nation than all other books' and if we are in any doubt about how political he thought his job was, he added: 'It is the business of *Americans* to select the wisdom of all nations, as the basis of her constitutions . . . to prevent the introduction of foreign vices and corruptions and check the career of her own . . . to diffuse an uniformity and purity of *language* – to add superiour [sic] dignity to this infant empire and to human nature.'

In Webster's speller, 'zed' became 'zee'. I can feel a clerihew coming on:

Noah Webster Junior
in 1783
began the revolution:
he turned zed into zee.

Thirteen years later, in 1806, he stormed the barricades with the

Compendious Dictionary of the English Language, in which five thousand words are added to the number found in the BEST ENGLISH COMPENDS; The ORTHOGRAPHY is, in some instances, corrected; The PRONUNCIATION marked by an Accent or other suitable Direction; And the DEFINITIONS of many Words amended and improved.

Out went the 'u' in 'favour', the 'k' in 'musick' ('a Norman innovation', he claimed); the 're' in 'theatre' was reversed and the 'ce' in 'defence' became 'se'. He also took the 'e' off 'doctrine' and 'discipline', turned 'tongue' into 'tung', 'women' into 'wimmen' and 'ache' into 'ake'. Despite its later massive success, his ideas were not initially approved. The *Albany Centinel* said it was 'madness to endeavour to establish . . . an American or United States dialect' and Webster, they thought, had the 'disposition to revolutionize and disorganize the English Language'.

My father's edition of *Webster's* must have been the fifth. As a child, I felt that one other feature marked it out as utterly different from the *Shorter*: its occasional small line drawings. There was a joke going round when I was about ten which was to ask people to tell you what a spiral is without moving their hands. Invariably, they end up waving and pointing. I remember looking in the *Webster's* to see what he said a spiral was. I've forgotten what Webster said, but I remember that there was one of those small line drawings to make it clear. Noah Webster Jnr couldn't do it without moving his hands either.

With the OED and *Webster's*, the two countries created what we might call their 'pride of place' dictionaries, places that people go to for an authoritative voice on spelling and meaning. The publishers of the OED insist that it is authoritative only because every entry can be 'attested', i.e. shown to have really existed. The full dictionary doesn't exist in order to tell us the best words, or to exclude the worst words. For some, this isn't good enough. They see language as unruly, disturbing and ambiguous – which in some senses it is – and hope that a dictionary will lay down the law. They want dictionaries to prescribe and proscribe. You could argue that the shorter the dictionary, the more it makes its entries 'official' through its selection of words and their definitions – albeit by implication.

In my lifetime, I've seen two revolutions in the dictionary world. In the 1960s, publishers discovered (or created) a hunger for encoding the whole world into dictionaries. Almost overnight, it seemed that you could buy cheap 'dictionaries' of any branch of science, the arts and knowledge. Over the next twenty years or so I acquired a shelf of them, supplemented by 'Keywords' dictionaries which isolate the fundamental concepts and offer academically reliable definitions. A cynical interpretation of this publishing bubble would say that it's a product of the need for insta-knowledge in lieu of slow study. Quick, we might have said to ourselves, what exactly is this 'post-modernism' everyone is talking about? What exactly is this 'rood screen' that was being mentioned in a radio programme about church architecture? Then with a speedy use of the alphabet, the word could be found, with its hundred-word definition, provided by someone reputable. Even more cynically, I might say that this was yet another blow in the victory of fact over process that has bedevilled our sense of what thought and understanding are.

In this battle, on one side are people trying to find shape and meaning in the world. On the other are those who construct quizzes, TV and radio panel games based on contestants' memory of names, terms, dates, events and the order of sequences – or 'facts' as these are usually called. The person who wins these is the 'brain of Britain' or the 'mastermind' as if being able to investigate, infer, interpret, plan, test, experiment, deduce and speculate is secondary or unimportant. Perhaps the 1960s wave of dictionaries helped create this lopsided view of the capabilities of the human mind, and, in turn, the alphabet was hijacked to assist in the breaking up of knowledge to suit this view.

The second revolution is digital and is represented by Wiktionary and Urban Dictionary. These are online dictionaries founded on a principle never tried before: that anyone can contribute. Wiktionary asks for its examples and definitions to be attested. The Urban Dictionary is not so bothered. This major change in the compilation method of the two dictionaries coincides with a second change: searching does not rely on the user using the alphabet. As it's online, you simply type the word into your search engine, and the computer does the rest by whatever invisible system computers use. (Excuse my ignorance.) We no longer have to flick pages alphabetically. Perhaps, one day, we shall see this moment of the loosening of the grip of the alphabet over the classification of knowledge as a significant turning point.

Back with that matter of the compilation method, I once witnessed an interesting confrontation between old and new school. I was at university with Jonathon Green but we disappeared out of each other's lives for many years until I started to present BBC Radio 4's *Word of Mouth*. On occasions on the programme, we talk about slang and we turn to someone who has compiled more than a handful of dictionaries of slang and jargon, Jonathon Green. Unlike the OED, Jonathon is not in the grip of Oxford's golden rule that a word must be (a) written down, and (b) written down in a significant publication. Jonathon has given himself the freedom to include words that he's heard spoken, that others have heard spoken and which have appeared in insignificant journals. This means that he can collect much more ephemeral and recent words in use.

For one edition of the programme we invited Jonathon to meet one of the editors of the online Urban Dictionary. In a sense it was a meeting between someone who felt that his overview and knowledge of the field should count for something in the compilation of a dictionary, and someone who thought none of this mattered. In the Jonathon Green school of dictionary-compiling, no matter how slangy or vulgar the content of a dictionary might be, it should have 'authority' and this was provided by the known person, Jonathon Green, whose record could be checked out. In a sense, this is the academic principle – every statement can be tested in terms of who is saying it and where. The editor of the Urban Dictionary was working to a completely different principle: he was just making an internationally viewable loading bay.

'But people could make up any old word,' I said, 'and claim that it meant, say, a provocative way of dancing the samba or whatever.' He made clear that he was utterly unfazed by that possibility. For him, a word existed whether it was in usage amongst this or that group of people, or had been invented that afternoon by Harry Harryface. What's more, if it was good and funny then Harry Harryface's word would go into circulation anyway. And isn't that what newspaper columnists, stand-up comedians, novelists . . . and, holy of holies, William Shakespeare have been doing for years?

I felt threatened. I can't speak with any certainty for Jonathon, but I suspect he was too. All the principles on which we found our sense of what is true were being overthrown by this malarkey.

How could you distinguish between what was a 'real' piece of slang and what was just someone's 'neologism'? The point is, the Urban Dictionary editor wasn't interested in that kind of knowledge, and, he indicated, nor were the billions who read and compile the dictionary. They were just interested readers and users, enjoying surfing the underworld of taboo words and words for taboos, looking to see if their favourites were there along with other uses that I for one couldn't name.

It's probably too early to say where all this is leading. It's not knowledge as I know it – signified by the fact that the alphabet is not needed in order to access it.

When I was ten, it occurred to me that I was learning a set of new words. These were 'rude words'. In fact, there were so many of them, I wasn't sure I could remember them all so I started to compile a glossary. I created a very long strip of paper by sellotaping one strip of paper to another, end to end, and then I wrote each word and its definition along the strip. It included some backslang words that my little bunch of friends and I thought that we had made up. Then, I would sit in bed, feeding the strip through my fingers, reciting what I had written. I didn't list where or when I had heard or seen the word. I didn't shuffle the words into alphabetical order. I just added a word as it occurred to me or as I came across it. Its order was the chronology of the act of my writing the words. I invented the Urban Dictionary in 1956.

THE STORY OF

● **ONE AREA OF** ancient Greece had a letter 'ksi', which was indeed an 'X'. That's pretty well the end of the story! The letter took the usual path into our alphabet via the Etruscans, the Romans and medieval Europe.

x

Our lower-case 'x' comes via the handwritten manuscripts of early medieval times, the 'Carolingian minuscule' and the Italian printers of the late fifteenth century.

PRONUNCIATION OF THE LETTER-NAME

It seems as if the Etruscans invented the name 'eks' for 'X'.

PRONUNCIATION OF THE LETTER

In the middle or at the end of words, it can be 'ks' as in 'next' and 'vex', or it can be more like 'kzh' as in 'luxurious' (which, curiously, we pronounce differently when we say 'luxury' where we pronounce the 'x' as something like 'ksh').

Consonants near 'x' give us 'lynx', 'the Bronx', 'excite' and the whole gamut of 'exes' as in 'ex-husband' and 'ex-politician', as well as more integrated 'ex' words as with 'exhale', 'extend' and 'expert'. We have an 'oxbow lake', the town of 'Uxbridge' and a dialect word for 'armpit': 'uxter', 'oxter' or 'axter'.

Words that begin with 'x' are usually of Greek origin and the 'x' does time as a 'z' sound: 'xylo' means 'wood' as in 'xylophone'; the now-obsolete word for one of the first plastics is 'Xylonite', a substance made very near to where I lived for many years.

For writers of alphabet poems, X is a tough slot to fill and these words are saviours along with names like 'Xavier' and 'Xerxes', a king whose name Edward Lear returned to several times.

'X' also serves as a prefix letter – most famously as 'X-ray' – but in countless other ways too, usually meaning 'unknown' or 'mysterious'.

Sound-play with 'x' is a bit limited. You 'get your kicks on Route-66', there's a children's cough medicine called 'Tixylix' and sometimes foxes in stories are 'foxy-woxy'.

In some Caribbean dialects the word 'ask' is pronounced 'ahx'. Some Londoners who are not of Caribbean origin have adopted this pronunciation too. While we're on Caribbean 'x' words, some Caribbeans say, 'me vex' meaning 'I'm angry'.

 MARKS THE SPOT

ENGLISH DOESN'T REALLY need the letter 'X'. At the beginning of words, if it were replaced by a 'Z', the pronunciation would be the same. 'Zerxes' would sound the same as 'Xerxes' and 'zylophone' would sound the same as 'xylophone'. In the middle or end of some words, if it were replaced by 'ks', the pronunciation would be the same: 'boks' and 'luksury' would still work. You could write 'exile' as 'eggzile'. The letter mostly serves as a nod and a wink to those in the know that what is about to follow is Greek in origin. A maggot that is 'xylophagous' will chew up wood.

Where it has become irreplaceable is when it stands on its own: 'x' for a kiss, 'x' for being wrong, 'x' for the unknown in algebra, 'x' to signify multiplication, 'x' marks the spot, 'x' for the vertical axis on a graph, 'x' for 'extra' in 'extra large', as well as in 'X-rated' movies and the 'X' for 'X-ray' and the 'X chromosome'. In the world of entertainment and commercial products, the cluster of meanings and connotations that has grown up around the solitary 'x' is a gift that goes on giving: *X Factor*, *X-Men*, *The X-Files*, *X: The Unknown*, Generation

X, X-Box, Castlemaine XXXX – and thousands more. You could make a good argument for saying that 'X' has won the right to be called a word. Malcolm X agreed: 'For me,' he said, 'my "X" replaced the white slavemaster name of "Little" which some blue-eyed devil named Little had imposed upon my paternal forebears.'

Part of the story of the settlement of the US is told with the letter 'X'. In the seventeenth century, the majority of people who settled in North America came as 'indentured servants' and many of these were illiterates who signed their papers with an 'X'.

The deal was this: to get to America had a price. If you worked for free when you got there, you could pay off the cost of the trip. The typical term for this indenture was four or five years but it could be for as little as one year or as much as seven. Some people went willingly. The Xs on the indenture papers don't tell us which. Some people were kidnapped and, if they were children, their papers would be signed by others. On arrival in America, the servants could be sold.

The *Pennsylvania Gazette* of 17 August 1774 carried this advertisement: 'Just imported, on board the Snow Sally . . . a number of healthy, stout English and Welsh Servants and Redemptioners . . . farmers and labourers, and some lively smart boys, fit for various other employments, whose times are to be disposed of. Enquire of the Captain on board the vessel, off Walnut-street wharf.'

For the strong and the lucky, that 'X' on their indenture papers could mean a few years of hardship followed by freedom, some land and possible prosperity. For others it was a form of slavery which they didn't survive. The system started in the 1620s and continued till 1917. Peter Williamson, one famous survivor of a kidnapping in Aberdeen, lived long enough to return to

Scotland and sue his kidnappers. In December 1763, in the Edinburgh Court of Session, Williamson was awarded £200 damages plus 100 guineas' legal costs against Bailie William Fordyce who was found to have been personally responsible for the kidnapping.

Thousands of 'X's helped build America. Thousands of 'X's perished before they could.

It's easy to see why 'X' was a favoured symbol for the unlettered: two strokes of a pen or pencil seem more precise and definite than a single stroke. Indeed, the point of intersection of the two strokes takes on special significance when plotting graphs – or, much more importantly, when playing Spot the Ball. For the uninitiated, this involved a newspaper printing a photo of some footballers mid-action but with the ball removed. Your job as someone entering the competition was to mark with an 'X' where you thought the ball was. This involved close examination of the expressions on players' faces and the various body shapes of all concerned. This could fill up several hours of homework-avoidance . . .

For Robert Louis Stevenson, another kind of time-wasting game, doodling an imaginary map with his stepson Lloyd, led to 'X marks the spot' and the invention of *Treasure Island*. Together they created the names and events connected with the map, while Stevenson's father came up with the objects that might lie in a sailor's chest alongside such a map.

The doctor opened the seals with great care, and there fell out the map of an island, with latitude and longitude, soundings, names of hills, and bays and inlets, and every particular that would be needed to bring a ship to a safe anchorage upon its shores. It was about nine miles long and five across, shaped, you might say, like a fat dragon standing up, and had two fine land-locked harbours, and a hill in the centre part marked 'The Spy-glass'. There were several additions of a later date; but, above all, three crosses of red ink – two on the north part of the island, one in the south-west, and, beside this last, in the same red ink, and in a small, neat hand, very different from the captain's tottery characters, these words: 'Bulk of treasure here.'

A version of this map can be found in most editions, some looking like a man's face with a drooping moustache, not unlike Stevenson himself.

X is also used in a very different kind of mapping. The usual line-up for chromosomes in humans is that we have twenty-two plus two 'sex chromosomes'. Females are XX, men are XY. There was a time when I could give an account of the ways in which the different kinds of chromosome divide and combine: an extraordinary, wonderful, chemical, geometric ballet that deter-mines our genetic structure. I could draw complex diagrams full of Xs. As it was something I learned for an exam, the details of the saga have faded, but isolated clumps remain.

When it comes to looking at characteristics that sit on the X and Y chromosomes, the scientific accounts are full of hundreds of Xs and Ys. My notebooks were full of these letters lined up against each other as a way of trying to work out who would inherit what. Remember, under usual conditions you inherit an X from your mother and either an X or a Y from your father. If you are XX, you are female. If you are XY you are male.

The graphic representation of the chromosomes as Xs and Ys, though not truthful, helps in one important respect: you can think of an X as having four arms and a Y as having three. So when you line them up next to each other, one of the X's arms

– let's say it's the bottom right arm – doesn't have an equivalent arm on the three-armed Y.

Now let's say that there's a gene that sits on the X's fourth arm. Let's also say that when this X lines up opposite another X, the characteristics that go with that particular gene (this doesn't apply to all genes) on the fourth arm won't show up in the person. It's as if the opposite point on the fourth arm 'stops' it showing. It will do this if the gene we're talking about is 'recessive' and its counterpart on the opposite point doing the stopping is 'dominant'.

Now let's line up the X and the Y. As there's no fourth arm on that Y, there's nothing 'dominant' to 'stop' the gene of the X's fourth arm from producing the characteristics of that gene. Remember: XXs are female; XYs are male. So, what follows from this is that there are certain kinds of genes which a woman (XX) might carry but not show ('recessive'), while the same gene carried by a male (XY) will show in him even though it is 'recessive'. In a purely symbolic way, what I've said is true, but as the chromosomes are not strictly speaking Xs and Ys, it's not true. I like it that the false representations of chromosomes as the letters X and Y help produce a truth.

'X' is also a letter that stands in for other words: 'Christ' and 'cross'. The first recorded usage of 'Xmas' was in 1551. As I was the child of Jewish atheists, the first place I came across Christianity was at school. This was delivered through daily Christian assemblies, weekly hymn practices, weekly Religious Instruction ('RI') or 'Scripture', carol concerts and occasional trips to the local church.

From the age of five, we children all became experts in the pain of crucifixion. I don't think I ever got a handle on why or how the pain that Jesus underwent was for my sake – nor indeed why his all-powerful father (who knew what I was doing at all times) couldn't have stepped in. And his pain wasn't like the pain of TV cowboys like Tex Ritter, Roy Rogers and the Lone Ranger. It was prolonged, detailed, cruel and arbitrary.

This knowledge was deepened and widened by tales of other crucifixions, in particular, the slow painful death of St Andrew. In honour of his leader and messiah, Jesus Christ, Andrew said that he would not be crucified on an upright cross but on an X-shaped one. We were invited to contemplate the comparative pain of these two crucifixions which were represented symbolically on our nation's flag, the Union Jack. One consequence of this is that though I will often pass by the upright Christian cross without thinking back to those days sitting on the school hall floor, or in a row of desks in a classroom, the diagonal 'X' cross on flags nearly always evokes a St Andrew moment.

The cross of St Andrew (the 'saltire') has figured large in Scottish iconography for over a thousand years and has flourished since devolution. The story goes that in AD 832 the Picts and Scots were hopelessly outnumbered by their enemies, the Angles. When their leader Óengus II prayed for victory, he was told it would be granted if St Andrew became their patron saint. On the morning of the battle, the clouds in the sky above took up an 'X' shape, the Picts and Scots won, and St Andrew was made patron saint of Scotland. Incidentally, if you want to keep witches away – in particular to prevent them from coming down the chimney – some people recommend carving the cross of St Andrew on your fireplace surround.

You can also make this use of 'X' with your arms and I'm fairly sure that I've seen a terrified gravedigger keep Dracula at bay (as played by Christopher Lee) with this 'hex sign'. It worked for him. I use the same principle and same arm-crossing movement as an attempt to stop my children from jumping on me but it doesn't seem to work. Perhaps I should revert to the finger-crossing of my childhood and shouting 'fainites' or 'fainies'. This could prevent you from being 'had' and made 'it' in a game of 'he'. Putting your crossed fingers behind your back guaranteed that the statement you were making was not meant. 'I didn't break your toy car, on my honour,' if said with crossed fingers behind your back, meant you were lying through your teeth.

THE STORY OF

● **AS WE MAKE THE** letter 'Y' do several jobs, its full story is quite complicated. The ancient Greek 'Y' shape, inherited from the Phoenicians and Semites, was 'upsilon' and worked its way into our alphabet as our 'U'. Around AD 100 the Romans added 'Y' to their alphabet from the later Greek Athenian alphabet. The Romans called their 'Y' 'Y Graeca', Greek Y, and it started doing the work of a short or longer 'i' sound that we still see today in a word like 'symphony' or 'sympathy'. However, the Romans already had 'I' to do this job, so it seems as if they used 'Y' to denote that a word was of Greek origin. Old English adopted the Romans' 'Y' replacing a rune.

In medieval writing of English, 'i' and 'y' seem inter-changeable, with 'y' often being preferred. Though we have retained that use at the end of words like 'lovely' and 'happy', we have almost entirely lost it from the middle of short words, apart from words like 'tryst', or the self-consciously medieval computer game, 'Myst'. These uses of 'y' are as a vowel.

y

The modern lower-case 'y' comes via the medieval scribes, Charlemagne's scribes and their standardized 'Carolingian minuscule', and then passed into the print conventions of the Italian printers of the late fifteenth century.

PRONUNCIATION OF THE LETTER-NAME
No one really seems to know why 'Y' is pronounced 'why', other than that it is very similar but not the same as 'I'! In French it is called 'i grec', Greek 'i'.

PRONUNCIATION OF THE LETTER

As we've seen, 'Y' does several jobs. At the beginning of words and syllables it's doing the work of providing a sound before a vowel as with 'year', 'you' and 'yard'.

It can be short as in 'sympathetic' or long as in 'my' or 'fly'. At the ends of adverbs (and one or two adjectives) it appears in the suffix '-ly' as in 'happily' and 'quickly'.

'Y' can combine with vowels to make 'day', 'fey' and 'boy'.

'Y' can combine with 'r' and 'e' to make 'lyre', 'pyre' and 'tyre'.

Readers of ancient texts find it in the word 'y-clept' meaning 'named' as in 'y-clept Michael', though one or two Victorian revivalists kept it alive.

We've also developed 'y' as a way of creating adjectives, especially if we want to make them smaller or more familiar or cutesy as in 'cutesy'. We also have 'hair' which becomes 'hairy' or 'skin' which becomes 'skinny' without the connotations of small. But if we turn 'pyjamas' into 'jimmy-jams' we give it the touch of the toddler. It's why our eight-year-old has banned the term.

The 'yo-yo' has had a long and successful life, while 'yo', meaning 'you', 'yes' and 'are you listening?' is having an even more successful one at the moment.

The 'y' suffix can combine with almost any consonant to create sound-play:

'happy-clappy' (a derogatory word for evangelic Christians)
'nitty-gritty'
'silly-billy'
'namby-pamby'
'Busy Lizzie'

'Andy Pandy'
'Yummy Mummy'
'Nicketty-nacketty-noo-noo-noo' (from an old American folk
    song)
'Dirty Gertie from number thirty'

And so on.

IS FOR YELLOW

WHEN I WAS learning to recite the alphabet I used to get muddled around the 'OPQR' region but once I was over that, and could see 'XYZ' in the distance, I was fine. 'XYZ' was always a cinch and I would gabble the letters off in a burst for the finishing line. But then, bit by bit, the letters 'X', 'Y' and 'Z' started to take on a difference from the rest of the alphabet. They got great scores at Scrabble and with 'X' and 'Z' being such rare and foreign ways of beginning words, homely old 'Y' caught a bit of their exoticism.

'Y', like 'X' before it, is not indispensable. In many circumstances you could replace it with 'I' as 'I' does that kind of job, so theoretically you could write 'iear' for 'year'. At the end of words there are several possibilities – and indeed these have been used in the past: 'ee' and 'ie', so it could be 'babee' or 'babie'. A little more tricky to arrange would be the 'ey' and 'ay' diphthongs but we have the split 'a' + 'e' method: 'late' and 'state' for when there's an end consonant. Trickier would be the 'bay'-type words. Well, let's say we could agree on 'bai' and 'sai' for 'bay' and 'say'. That leaves words like 'rye' which we'll write like 'lie' and, look, we've abolished 'y'.

But we like 'y' and we don't want to abolish it. I particularly like the diagonal slash of it in lower case and when I'm print-writing I get a tiny moment of satisfaction if I can get the two tips of the letter lined up horizontally. The upper-case version is like a funnel or a plumbing diagram.

For thousands of years, people have been hunting for Y-shaped branches to use as walking sticks. When he was fifteen, my brother found a perfect Y-branch, took the bark off it, heated a meat skewer to drill holes in it, so that he could fit a length of rubber cord, which he threaded through a piece of leather. It was a devilishly potent catapult which he would use out the back of our flat. Here there was the perfect mixture: an unlimited supply of pebbles on the dirt track and the stacks of empty drinks bottles from the off-licence a few doors down. He burned a coded signature on the shaft of the catapult – a 'T' (square) – and spent many happy hours lining up bottles and firing pebbles at them. The 'Y' must have done good service in the destructive games of many teenage boys in the 1950s. The fact that neither of us slashed ourselves with flying glass was probably just luck.

'Y' has a symbolic role to play through being the initial for any organization for children or teenagers. It stands in for 'young' or 'youth'. In 1935, my parents met in the YCL – the Young Communist League, which we grew to understand was the place where my mother saw my father across a room playing table tennis and knew in an instant that he was the one. Or, as she put it, 'Once I had made up my mind, he didn't have a choice in the matter.' Soon after, they went youth hostelling with the YHA, a habit they passed on to my brother and me. We wore our little green enamel triangular badges, carried our cards, and earned our stamps from the hostels we stayed at. Between us we tramped through fords, crossed moors, climbed mountains and walked coastal paths all over England, Wales, France and Germany.

The word 'youth' sounds odd to me now. I don't think it was a word that I ever used or heard outside of the youth hostelling. I didn't ever think of myself as a youth. Even today, it survives only in some highly specific ways, institutionally like 'youth unemployment' or in Jamaican patois as 'de yout dem'. Yet, that 'Y' of YHA was definitely me and, for a youth hosteller like myself, walking from Ludlow to Aberystwyth or across Dartmoor in the dark at the age of fifteen was a big deal.

In France, it was the way I discovered the eastern end of the Pyrenees. First by meeting a French family in the Youth Hostel in Perpignan and then, while hitch-hiking across Roussillon, meeting a priest from a village in the mountains where the fields were so steep that when they cut the hay, the peasants tied themselves to a stake in the ground, hobbled by a rope. I've stayed friends with the family from the Youth Hostel all my life, sharing our moments of success and tragedy for more than fifty years. I lost contact with the priest. I wasn't entirely comfortable with the fact that he took me on a picnic up in the mountains and stripped naked to sunbathe. He asked me if I was 'choqué' (shocked), I said that I wasn't, but I suspect I was. He said that I would be very interested in Teilhard de Chardin. I wasn't. If I hadn't been a 'Y' with a place in the YHA I might never have encountered these people.

'Y' also turns up in some synesthesia experiments. I had no idea what synesthesia was until someone said it's like when you say, 'Don't look at me in that tone of voice, you taste a funny colour.' It's 'sensory mixing', as when you might think that a colour has a taste, a touch has a smell, or a letter has a colour. 'Y', some people say unsurprisingly, is yellow. However, for no apparent reason, the same 'synesthete' may well think that 'A' is green and 'G' is red. Jamie Ward, author of *The Frog Who Croaked Blue*, is still trying to figure out why some people are like this. No one is quite sure if the subject of language and synesthesia is significant or just interesting. It may be further evidence that Proust was right about the madeleine cakes, and that if Freud had mentioned Proust, he would have been right about Proust. Remembering the nice taste, sight and feel of a little French cake may actually be about why you love your mother, think you love your mother, hate your mother, or all three.

On the other hand, there is the question of language itself. The old rule was that language is made up of signs and these signs are 'arbitrary'. There is nothing emergency-ish about the sound of the word 'emergency'. We have evolved a way of writing down 'emergency' and there isn't anything 'emergency-ish' about that either. In English there is the word 'book'. To a large degree, it overlaps in meaning with the French word 'livre'. The two 'signs' are different; the meaning a lot of the time, though, is the same. Even more 'arbitrary': the French word 'livre' can mean 'pound' so for a French person there are some associations between a book and a pound. This ought to tell us that speaking and writing have evolved separately from the objects and processes that we are trying to describe.

There are obvious exceptions: pictograms have evolved from ways of trying to represent objects and processes on the page. The letters of the roman alphabet are evolved forms of pictograms, though the link is mostly broken. Is it fanciful to think that 'I' has lasted partly because it represents the upright figure of a person? When we use 'X' to represent the word 'cross' this isn't 'arbitrary'. It is in effect a pictogram. Wouldn't it be brilliant if 'Y' stood for 'which' instead of 'why'? You proceed up the shaft of 'Y' until you reach two roads. 'Which' one should you take? But it doesn't mean 'which', so we'll forget that.

Onomatopoeia is non-arbitrary. 'Crash', 'pop', 'slop', 'bang', 'quack', 'screech' and 'bark' are attempts at making sounds with our mouths to represent those sounds in nature. So, though there isn't anything 'shushy' about 'sh' – the letters are arbitrary signs – the sound of the word 'shush' was chosen by its creators to approximate to the perception of the sound of something, i.e. not arbitrary.

But what if, on analysis, it was found that there were specific letters linked to certain clusters of meanings? What if, say, in Ruritanian language the letter 'Y' was connected to a cluster of meanings to do with unpleasantness? So, in this language, the words for 'evil', 'bad', 'unpleasant smell', 'horrible person', 'cheating' and 'bullying' all began with the letter 'Y'? This would be an exception to the arbitrariness of the sign, and would also be a form of synesthesia. The sound of the word would be linked to its meaning. As it happens, while we're on 'Y', this letter in English has, over several centuries, delivered a good stock of words, many of them slang, to do with talking, shouting and animals making a noise: 'yack', 'yatter', 'yammer', 'yell', 'yaffle', 'yap', 'yaw-haw', 'yawl', 'yelp', 'yodel', 'yoop' and 'yowl'.

These are onomatopoeic, we might say. They are attempts to make words sound like the noise being made. One problem with this: the initial sound of 'y' is as irrelevant to those noises as the 'b' and the 'k' in 'bark'. Dogs don't say either. So, might humans have come to connect the seemingly arbitrary sign of 'y' with talking, shouting, making a noise with our mouths? Interestingly, we have several calls along with variant words of assent which begin with 'y' as well: 'yes', 'yeah', 'yo', 'yep', 'yoo-hoo', 'yo-ho', 'yih', 'yuh' and 'yip', which, when we're listening to someone else speak, we might repeat: 'Yeah, yeah, yeah . . .'

Then we have 'you' and all its variants: 'youse', 'y'all', 'ye' and 'yer', which we can use for calling and which often appear in rapid repetition when we're excited or angry.

So, the question here would be whether the use of the sound 'y' and then, following that, the letter 'y' have evolved so that they have some meaning to do with, say, the making of repeated noise. If so, it has profound significance in the evolution of language. Some sounds that our ancestors made were perhaps connected much more closely to the objects and processes of life than the phrase 'the arbitrariness of the sign' permits.

Leaving 'Y' for a moment, we had a contributor to Radio 4's *Word of Mouth* who came in with a statistical count of 'sl-' words. She claimed that there were two clusters of sense around a significant number of words that begin with 'sl': 'slinging' and 'slimy'. You can spend many a happy hour looking in dictionaries and thesauruses testing out the hypothesis that we have created meaning through attachments to specific sounds.

All this may mean that we are going back to prehistoric times, or it may simply mean that the law of analogy has prevailed. This law tells us that when we invent new words and expressions we do it by making them sound like words and expressions that we have used before and found likeable and useful. Let's say that the Old English verb 'yellan' sounded so good to our ancestors' ears, and to all of us who have come since, that whenever we have thought that we needed another word to describe human or animal noise-making, we've called up 'y' from our sound-bank to kick off a new word. So, it's not that our ancestors had a whole bunch of 'y' words but that we've added to the stock bit by bit, finding that each one fits the bill. The end result is the same. We have a nice collection of 'y' words to describe or talk about human and animal noise-making.

Far be it from me to big up my profession, but poets have

known about this stuff for years. It's called alliteration and part of our trade is to recruit words to sound like the feelings or processes we are describing. If I was writing a poem for children about the sea, I might decide that when the sea breaks on a beach it makes a 'sssss' sound, just as the word itself does. I might collect together some 's' words that connect to the sea on a beach and use them in a song-poem: 'see', 'slip', 'sand', 'soft', 'slide' . . . 'See the soft sea slip, see the soft sand slide . . .' Much more subtly, poets have recruited words to indicate unspoken emotions through the repetition of word-sounds. In Thomas Hardy's regretful poem, 'The Voice', many of the consonants, probably more than in a piece of prose about cooking, say, are continuous: 'm', 's', 'n', 'l', 'f', 'v', 'ss', 'th' and the letter 'w' is repeated seemingly deliberately. It begins 'Woman much missed . . .' and has phrases like: 'wan wistlessness' and 'faltering forward'. Can we say that Hardy tried to express his sadness through the long, non-percussive consonants? Is it a sighing and mourning through the sound of the words?

The famous tongue-twister alliterative poetry cycle, *Peter Piper's Practical Principles of Plain and Perfect Pronunciation* from 1813, has a verse for each letter of the alphabet, including the famous:

Peter Piper picked a peck of pickled Peppers:
Did Peter Piper pick a peck of pickled Peppers?
If Peter Piper picked a peck of pickled Peppers,
Where's the peck of pickled Peppers Peter Piper picked?

And my favourite, ideal for double-entendre parties:

Neddy Noodle nipp'd his neighbour's Nutmegs;
Did Neddy Noodle nip his neighbour's Nutmegs?

THE STORY OF

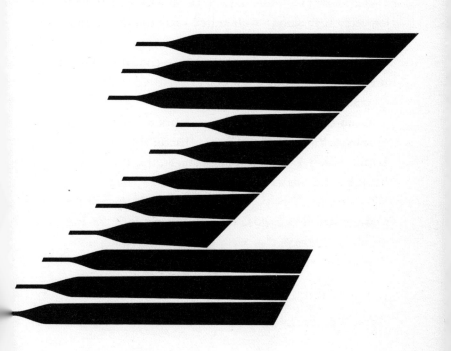

- **THE PHOENICIANS OF** 3,000 years ago had a letter 'zayin', meaning 'axe', with the value of 'z'. It looked like our upper-case 'I' with the top and bottom serifs. The ancient Greeks adopted it as 'zeta' in around 800 BCE. It seems to have slowly evolved into our modern 'z' shape with the sound 'dz'. As with many of the other letters, the Etruscans took it and handed it on to the Romans but then it fell into disuse for a few centuries. In around AD 100, the Romans started to bring in more Greek words and revived 'zeta' to write them. Again, for several centuries it was hardly used – 's' doing the job of both 'soft s' and 'hard s' until the sound of some European languages started to make the 'ts' sound still in use today in a word like 'pizza'. The Norman French arrived with a few Zs in their writing and it's stayed in English ever since but mostly for loan words or coinages that want to evoke something non-British in the look or sound.

z

The lower case 'z' comes from Carolingian minuscule.

PRONUNCIATION OF THE LETTER-NAME

There seem to have been various names for 'z' in and around Shakespeare's time: 'zed', 'izzard', 'ezod' and 'zee' are amongst them. Was 'izzard' originally 'ezz 'ard'? Or did it come from French 'et zède'? However it was, we have 'zed' in British English. In America, there used to be both, but it was regularized as 'zee' by Noah Webster as you can see in 'W is for Webster'.

PRONUNCIATION OF THE LETTER

At the beginning of words, it is the hard 's' sound of 'zebra' and 'zany'. It doubles in 'puzzle', 'drizzle', 'dazzle' and 'jazz' with the same value. It doesn't usually end words with a single 'z' apart from 'quiz', Dickens' pen-name 'Boz' and abbreviations like 'showbiz' and Shakespearean 'coz' (reduced from 'cousin').

In imports from Italy it imitates the Italian 'ts' sound as in 'piazza' and 'pizzicato'.

'Z' can combine with consonants to make words like 'frenzy', 'adze' (a now-extinct carpentry tool) and 'czar', and combines with 'r' to make 'furze', 'Wurzel' (a dialect word for a turnip as well as a character from a children's book).

Some modern popular and slang words have increased the number of Zs in speech and writing: 'zip' (meaning both a 'fastener' and 'nothing'), 'zilch', 'zen', 'zero' (as the verb 'to zero in on' and as a metaphor for 'worthless'), 'zing', 'whizz', 'tizz', 'zizz', 'zhuzh up', 'zit', 'zoom', 'fizz', 'fizzy', 'zed-list', 'zap', 'pizzazz', 'woozy', 'bozo', 'dozy', the comic book 'zzzzz' (also known as 'pushing out the zeds'), the names 'Zach', 'Liz' and 'Lizzie', and a vogue for creating nicknames, like 'Bazza' from 'Barry', 'Dazza' from 'Darren' and 'Tezza' from 'Terry'. The old word 'geezer' lives on too.

The arrival of more Asian names in Britain has provided the language with some Asian 'z' names and nicknames like 'Naz', 'Zeynab', 'Zain' and 'Reza', adding to the Russian or Polish 'Zosha' and 'Zara'. The Old Testament used to provide people with a few Zs in names like 'Zephaniah', now revived with the poet Benjamin Zephaniah. The obligatory US way of writing the suffix

'-ize' is probably upping the rate of Zs in Britain, producing 'liquidize' and 'psychoanalyze' because we can turn any word into a verb that way. Even as I am writing this, I realize that I should 'monetize the economy', 'deodorize the kitchen' and 'valorize the product'. I just hope that this book has been 'editorized'.

IS FOR ZIPCODES

PERHAPS THE MOST universally utilitarian way of using the alphabet has been the invention of postcodes. Our addresses are full of local history: the names of streets and areas are markers of their past. Aldwych means 'old town' in Anglo-Saxon and the street describes a curve around the edge of deserted Roman Londinium; Soho was a hunting cry and the area got its name from when it was a royal park. But many of the same names echo across the map: there are hundreds of Church Roads and High Streets, all describing a particular church or former village. The address scrawled on an envelope coming through your door focuses in on your destination, line by line, like the viewfinder on a camera. But all this history can complicate finding a specific destination.

On 1 July 1963, the word 'zip', which up until then had meant (a) to move along fast, (b) a state of high energy, (c) nothing at all or (d) a mechanical clothes fastener, came to mean in the US (e) the postcode. The term wasn't coined in order to show that postage would now cost zip, nor did it have anything to do with 'Zip-a-Dee-Doo-Dah', the song from the 1946 Disney movie

Song of the South. 'Zip' is an acronym for Zone Improvement Plan and it was chosen in order to suggest that the mail would travel more efficiently, and therefore more quickly, when senders used it.

The basic code at this stage was a two-letter abbreviation of the US state followed by a five-digit number. The person who gets the main credit for inventing this was Robert Aurand Moon from Williamsport, Pennsylvania, who developed the idea in the 1940s while working as a postal inspector in Philadelphia. Moon is the father of the ZIP. When the ZIP came in, in order to coax Americans into using their ZIP codes the postal service used a cartoon character called Mr ZIP. Robert Moon was not Mr ZIP, and neither Mr ZIP nor Robert Aurand Moon invented the zip fastener. However, Robert Aurand Moon earned zip from his invention. Some people earned zip from inventing the zip fastener too.

Original thinker though Mr Moon was, the zipcode was an appropriation of a system that had been invented in Britain almost a century earlier. In 1835, the postal service was patchy, private and under constant surveillance by the censors and political snoopers. When reformer Rowland Hill noticed a young woman unable to afford to redeem the postage (which had to be paid by the receiver, not the sender) on a letter from her fiancé, it apparently inspired him to turn his energies from education and Australia to the post service.

There were no agreed postage rates and all kinds of fiddles and rackets were rife. Hill's first radical suggestion was that all letters should be pre-paid with a universal stamp. Despite a lot of resistance from the House of Lords, the middle classes saw the sense (and profit) in his system and it was approved. The first stamp – the penny black, an elegant rectangle engraved with the outline of young Queen Victoria – appeared in 1840 and was a huge success. It was such a success that Hill came to realize that addresses had to be rationalized and simplified. The person sorting through tonnes of envelopes at top speed didn't have time to read the full address. There were too many words, so what was needed was a straightforward code, like a map reference, that could show the sorting office instantly where the letter should be going.

In 1856 Hill drew a circular area with a radius of 12 miles around London. Using the points on the compass, he divided London up into N, NE, E, SE, S, SW, W and NW. He then divided the central zone into EC and WC. This way of putting addresses on envelopes became fully operational by 1858. A few years later, first NE got the chop with its boroughs being merged into E; then S got split and its parts sent off into SE and SW.

In 1917, the alphabet was called into use again in what must be one of its most puzzling acts of public service. Each district was subdivided into sub-districts. The area served by the head office in each district was given the number 1. Following that, the sub-districts were shuffled into the alphabetical order of their name and numbered accordingly. So, as an example:

SW1	Head district
SW2	Brixton
SW3	Chelsea
SW4	Clapham
SW5	Earls Court
SW6	Fulham
SW7	South Kensington
SW8	South Lambeth
SW9	Stockwell
SW10	West Brompton

For anyone outside of the postal service, this is a fine example of alphabetical order winning out over sense. If you don't know the borders of a given district; or the names of the sub-districts (they don't correspond to all the parish names); or that two of the districts have two head districts so the numbering of sub-districts in these two districts starts at 3; or that several districts have added on sub-districts; and if you don't have an up-to-date map in front of you marked with the postal districts, then the code is of little use to you. The result of this is that people who have lived in London all their lives spend many hours in conversation with loved ones and strangers, looking up from reading an address on a bit of paper in front of them saying things like, 'Where's SW5?' Then everyone in the room has a guess, with most of the guesses not even including places in SW London. Sometimes the alphabet is a false god.

Tip: if someone says to you 'Where's E19?' it's a trick question. There's an E18 and an E20 but no London E19. E20 is the postal district of the BBC Television's *EastEnders*' location, Walford. This is now officially located in a new and real E20: the 'Olympic Park' sub-district. Olympic Park comes after E18 which is Woodford and South Woodford. 'O' comes before 'W' in the alphabet: the postal district rule has been broken.

If you live in, work in or travel through a city and you want to avoid the feeling of being governed by alphabetical zips, postcodes and co-ordinates, you can opt for the 'dérive'. This was devised by Guy Debord and his radical 'Situationist' friends in Paris in the 1960s. It's been taken up as 'psychogeography' by the writers Will Self and Iain Sinclair amongst others. Without getting too overblown about this, it's a way of travelling – usually walking – through the landscapes and cityscapes governed by the guidelines you choose or make.

Not long ago, I came across the fact that during the English Civil War, Londoners who were in support of Parliamentarians threw up a line of defences in a semicircle around London. Clearly, there were sufficient numbers of people who thought that this would help in the event of London being assaulted by Royalist forces. If you so chose, you could decide that this would be your dérive and armed with your plan you could re-create with your feet and mind the map of the Parliamentarians' defences. I've done parts of this semicircular journey and, if nothing else, the result is that a place or site becomes peopled in a new way. The rather dull reservoir banks on the Pentonville Road in Islington, or the graveyard at Shoreditch Church, each surrounded by the roar of traffic, become defence posts where Cromwell or Fairfax clicked their heels.

Alternatively, defiance of zips and postcodes can be more personal and you can – as I have done – pick routes that parents, grandparents or much earlier ancestors have taken across town. Postcodes look like frontiers on maps, while the frontiers in people's lives are usually unmarked. My father talked of crossing a frontier to see my mother when they 'started seeing each other', moving out of the 'safe' area he lived in to the apparently unsafe one where she lived. In my mind's eye this involved an epic trudge with boundaries that were visible in some way.

When I walked it some sixty years after my father had trod that way, it turned out to be not much more than a stroll and of course there were no physical, cultural or mental markers left. I just quietly labelled the cityscape with what I had been told, a personal postcode, if you like.

So here we are at the end of the alphabet. The word 'alphabet' contains something of the same idiom as 'It's as easy as A, B, C,' as it is constructed out of the first two words of the Greek alphabet, 'alpha' and 'beta'. The alphabet is then the 'alphabeta', rather as if we were to call the number system the 'one-two'. Tracing the route back we go to Latin 'alphabetum', back to ancient Greek 'alphabetos', back to Phoenician 'aleph' ('ox') and 'beth' ('house') which were once pictograms. So, incredibly, the word 'alphabet' contains within it the whole history of this particular alphabet or 'ox-house' as we could call it.

But what about the order? Why is 'A' the beginning and 'Z' the end? Or, as the Christmas carol I sang at primary school goes:

Alpha and Omega He!
Let the organ thunder,
While the choir with peals of glee
Doth rend the air asunder.

Why does one letter come 'after' another one? In truth, no one knows. No neat little story there of some ancient high priest claiming that the universe was created in alphabetical order. However, once the human race had developed this order, people started to figure out that it could be used as a means of indexing. Not that everyone has been happy about that. The poet Samuel Taylor Coleridge grumbled, pointing out that encyclopaedias were ordered according to 'an arrangement determined by the accident of initial letters' but the habit has been around since at least the time of the great library of Alexandria.

Step forward Zenodotus, a Greek grammarian and expert on Homer. He came from Ephesus and was the library's first librarian in the late third century BCE. Zenodotus didn't work to the Dewey system; he assigned different rooms to different subjects and then within each room classified the books alphabetically according to the name of each work's author. This is a world first. What's more, the library staff attached a tag to the end of each scroll. This tag contained info on each work's author, the title and subject-matter. This enabled readers to find the scrolls they were looking for – but also, just as importantly, to browse through what was available without having to open each scroll. This too is a world first. For these two breakthroughs in the development of alphabetic 'metadata', I have asked Zenodotus to be the sponsor of this book.

If he can't make it, then I shall approach Marcus Terentius Varro. In the first century BCE, he is known to have written lists of authors and titles in alphabetical order. Varro was appointed by Caesar to oversee the public library of Rome in 47 BCE, but once Caesar had been assassinated, Varro lost his property and his job. With the takeover of Augustus, Varro was able to carry on his studies and writing, including this matter of putting things into alphabetical order. If he was the first to do this, this too was something of a conceptual breakthrough. I quite like the idea of this Varro, a public librarian, in and out of a job as caesars and generals rise and fall, adapting Zenodotus' idea that the names of books and authors could be ordered not by status, wealth, popularity or genre but by the random sequencing of their initial letters.

For all its virtues, alphabetical order has had its drawbacks. Surely it's imposed an arbitrary view of what or who is first, second and third and laid on that a notion that 'A' being first is best, 'B' being second is second-rate and so on. There's something warped about the 'A-list', 'B-movies', or 'Z-list celebrities'. We still have 'A-level' exams – A for Advanced, but subtly indicating they're the highest form of exam in school. When I go online for a plumber, the first one I contact comes first in the alphabetically ordered list. Everyone wonders whether teachers favoured the children who came first in the alphabet. Were they the ones who were more likely to get to ring the bell or take a message to the caretaker? Were the 'X', 'Y', 'Z' kids always last? Or, put another way, did the teacher ever read the register from 'Z' to 'A'? Or from the middle – first forwards and then backwards?

When people change their names, do they tend to change them to names that come earlier in the alphabet? Harry Webb changed his to Cliff Richard, Allen Stewart Konigsberg to Woody Allen, Julia Wells to Julie Andrews, Cassius Clay to Muhammad Ali, Maurice Micklewhite to Michael Caine, Robert Zimmerman to Bob Dylan, while John Wayne and Stevie Wonder demoted themselves.

Though thinking of the world in alphabetical order seems very familiar to us, as recently as the early 1600s the teacher and writer Robert Cawdrey must have thought his readership needed the matter explaining to them. In the introduction to what is the first English-language monolingual dictionary, *Table Alphabeticall*, he wrote: 'Nowe if the word, which thou art desirous to finde, begin with (a) then looke in the beginning of this Table, but if with (v) looke towards the end.' Like Varro, Cawdrey was someone else who got into a bother with authority. As a Puritan, he felt entitled to decide what scriptures he would read in sermons, and even took it upon himself, unauthorized, to conduct a wedding. The Church of Queen Elizabeth didn't take this schismatic behaviour too well and, like Varro, he was out on his ear.

Fifty years ago, the alphabet ruled. So long as the topics, themes, or units consisted of letters, the prime way of ordering was 'A–Z'. Though it still operates as the main methodology for our indexes, its power is being undermined every day. Hyperlinks operate on the system of whole-word recognition. When we use search engines, we don't run our thumbs down any real, virtual or metaphorical alphabet. We write in 'harmonica' and up comes a set of references to harmonicas and – importantly – this set of 'results' isn't ordered in alphabetical order either. It arrives according to the popularity rules of Google Inc. Similarly, we might go online shopping and pull-down menus offer us retrieval options like 'popularity' or 'year of publication' – hardly ever the alphabet. YouTube doesn't order its tunes, lectures, artists, gags and the rest alphabetically and when you are offered alternatives, YouTube has used its own semantic system of finding similar clips. If you write a blog, you are given the chance to add 'labels' in order to aid others to find you. These are single words or phrases which may turn up when people look for subject-matter hanging around on the internet.

Though we are in the midst of what feels like a transition or at least a co-habitation of methods, I feel like sticking my neck out and stating that the secondary use of the alphabet is about to be overthrown. When that's complete, why should the alphabetic order of letters survive? In the initial reading methods being adopted all over the English-speaking world, the order of the alphabet is of little importance; the letters are learned in groups according to the principles of phonics.

In my own life, alphabetical indexes are still massively useful and one in particular: *The A–Z Guide to London*. As I am constantly being sent to different parts of the city, I still use that old-fashioned implement, the book.

It was the brainchild of Phyllis Pearsall, who claimed that she created it by walking the 3,000 miles of the 23,000 streets till it was done. Rain, frost, fog, snow or heatwave were no obstacle for Phyllis. 'I had to get my information by walking,' she wrote. 'I would go down one street, find three more and have no idea where I was.' The story goes that in 1935, tiny Phyllis, aged twenty-nine, earning a living as a portrait painter, was out visiting one of her clients, Lady Veronica Knott, at home in Maida Vale. She was travelling by bus and got off at Warwick Avenue, at the Harrow Road end, but her aristocratic host lived at the other end in Bristol Gardens. (Using your alphabetical A–Z or your non-alphabetic 'Google maps', you'll be able to follow all this.) When she finally arrived at her friend's house, she was soaking wet and when the conversation got going, it turned to the fact that it was so terribly hard finding one's way round London.

Phyllis Pearsall might not have been the first to put together a London street atlas – there were several pre-dating hers – but even so, her achievement was remarkable. She certainly researched, found and mapped the latest roads and estates. She was also the first to put house numbers for streets on a map you could put in your pocket. She was the creator, developer, publisher, wholesaler, salesperson and delivery staff for a phenomenon that has resulted in one of the twentieth century's best-sellers, with at least 60 million sales. The work nearly killed her: flying back from her Dutch printers in 1946, her KLM Dakota plane crashed. However, she ended up living for another fifty years.

Since her death, we've seen the rise of Google maps, satnavs and iPhone maps. These are index-less implements. If you want to search alphabetically, they offer you that as an option, but you can search by name, postcode or by some other half-remembered landmark. The phone you're probably looking at is smaller than the A–Z and covers the whole world. For a moment, I feel like a neolith. I have a *Mini A-Z* in my bag at all times. Then I remember, I haven't opened it in months. I've used print-outs of pages from Google maps – and, to help me find out how to get there, I'm not using the alphabet.

THE OULIPO OLYMPICS

One special group of alphabet heroes are the French writer, Raymond Queneau, and his friends who in 1960 set up 'Oulipo' which stands for 'Ouvroir de Littérature Potentielle' or 'Workshop for Potential Literature'. They wanted to find out how literature works by imposing constraints on what could or could not be written. So, a 'pangram' is the constraint of trying to write a sentence using all the letters of the alphabet. An acrostic is the constraint of trying to write a poem by using the letters of a word as the initial letters of lines of a poem. Oulipo weren't the first to try this but they took it much further than anyone had before. Oulipo procedures produce writing from the source of language's formal structures: its phonetics, alphabet, grammar, literary conventions and the like. The end product is often both surprising and surreal.

Here is a series of twenty games which engage with how letters and the alphabet work. These can all be simplified or made harder depending on the age or experience of the players.

I. ALPHABETICAL AFRICA

In 1974, Walter Abish (who wasn't actually a member of the Oulipo group) published a novel called *Alphabetical Africa* in which each chapter contained only words which began with a single letter of the alphabet. There were fifty-two chapters, so in the first chapter all the words began with 'a', the second with 'b', the third with 'c' until it reached 'z'. Then, the chapters ran in reverse back through the alphabet to 'a'.

As a challenge, try writing a story of fifty-two sentences, each of which follow the same principle and patterns of *Alphabetical Africa*: one sentence, one and the same initial letter for each word. The sentences can be as short or as long as you like. A dictionary by your side will of course be a great help.

2. PANGRAM AND ISOPANGRAM

This rising challenge works like this:

i) Pangram

Write the shortest possible sentence using all the letters of the alphabet. You are permitted to repeat letters. Can you beat, 'A quick, brown fox jumps over the lazy dog'? If not, what's the shortest pangram you can write not using the main words in that sentence?

ii) Isopangram

Write a sentence that is twenty-six letters long in which you use all the letters of the alphabet. In other words, you can use a letter only once. This is probably impossible, so the challenge is to get as near to this ideal as possible.

3. BELLE PRÉSENTE AND BELLE ABSENTE

i) Belle Présente

Write a poem or letter in which the only letters you may use are the ones in the name of the person you are writing to.

ii) Belle Absente
Write a poem or letter in which you may use any letters other than the letters of the name of the person you are writing to.

You can turn either of these into a challenge to a reader to see if he or she can find out who it is the poem or letter is addressed to.

4. N + 7

Take any passage from literature, a proverb or idiom. Locate the noun or nouns in the text you have chosen. Look up the noun or nouns in a dictionary. Find the noun that is seven nouns later in the dictionary. Replace the noun or nouns in your text with the one or ones you have found in the dictionary. This produces such sentences as 'To be or not to be, that is the quibble'.

5. ABC WRITING

You may use only a sequence of words whose initial letters are in alphabetical order. (You can, if you want, not count 'a', 'an', 'the' or prepositions like 'to', 'from' or 'with' as words in the sequence.) You can try this in terms of lines of a poem, a tweet, or lines of dialogue in a sketch or play. To make it harder, one person starts and the next person has to pick up the alphabetic order of words where the first person leaves off, until you reach 'z' and start again from 'a'.

You might begin: 'The Android broke the cup on David's elbow . . .'

6. DELMAS'S METHOD

You produce a phrase or sentence in which several words begin with the same letter. Then you re-write that phrase or sentence replacing that letter with a different single letter. For example: 'Make the meal in a master class'. Replace the 'm' with 't' and you get 'Take the teal in a taster class'.

7. THE EXETER TEXT

Oulipo maître Georges Perec famously wrote a novel in which the only vowel he used was 'e'. He then wrote another in which he banned himself from using 'e'. In 'the Exeter text' you follow the first of these constraints, using only words with the 'e' vowel. The test for this game will be to write the longest passage with this constraint in place in a given length of time, let's say, five minutes. You can of course then try 'the anti-Exeter text', where the 'e' is banned.

8. EYE-RHYME

Here you have to write a limerick or a four-line verse in which the words that would normally rhyme must only *look* as if they would rhyme, but in fact don't. These are words like 'threat' and 'eat', or 'south' and 'youth', or 'was' and 'has' and so on.

9. HOMOCONSONANTISM

Pick a text, e.g. a proverb or famous quotation or newspaper headline. Remove all the vowels. Fill the letters you have left over with any vowels whilst keeping the consonants in the same order and using only those consonants. The result must make some kind of sense!

So, 'Many hands make light work' would give you:

m, n, h, n, d, s, m, k, l, g, h, t, w, r, k

which you could turn into:

'Me? No. He needs my keel. Go, hot, wee Rik!'

10. LEFT-HANDED AND RIGHT-HANDED LIPOGRAM CONVERSATIONS

This is for touch-typists only. The left-handed text can be constructed using only the letters you tap with your left hand. The right-handed text can be constructed using only the letters you tap with your right hand. The challenge is to turn this into a conversation between the two hands.

11. PRISONER'S CONSTRAINT

A prisoner is so short of paper he must maximize his use of it. He decides to not use any letter which extends above or below the smallest letters. This excludes: 'b', 'd', 'f', 'g', 'h', 'j', 'k', 'l', 'p', 'q', 't' and 'y'. He (i.e. you!) now has to write poems or letters to his loved ones, or letters to his fellow criminals with messages about plans to escape or rob a bank.

12. MEMORY-JOGGING ALPHABET

You have forgotten the alphabet, so you need a way of remembering it. So, you create words with each letter which will enable you to remember it. These must include the sound of the letter-name in each word. You can run the letter-names of two or more letters into one word, if you like. You're allowed to cheat. Here's a start:

'Abey, see de effigy?'

If it's too hard to do the whole lot, make up phrases for sequences of any part of the alphabet.

Another layer of this challenge is to come up with a clue for the sequence you've invented and ask someone to guess which part of the alphabet you're talking about. So the clue for the one above might be: 'A biblical figure, known by his nickname, is asked if he can see the statue.'

13. WORD LADDER STORIES

Many quiz and puzzle books invite puzzlers to turn a word like 'head' into 'tail' in as short a possible time by removing one letter at a time, while retaining real words. Lewis Carroll called these doublets.

HEAD
HEAL
TEAL
TELL
TALL
TAIL

So, (1) solve a 'doublet' challenge set by one of these puzzle books and then (2) use these words to make a story or, better still, a short poem. You don't have to tell the story using the words in the same order that they appear in the 'doublet'.

You can turn this into a challenge by inviting the reader of your story to guess the correct sequence of the 'doublet'.

14. PALINDROMES

Some words are the same whichever way you write them: 'pip', or the name 'Hannah'. Some words are mirror images of each other: 'star' and 'rats'. You can also make phrases and sentences which read the same way in reverse. The most successful is perhaps:

'A man, a plan, a canal – Panama.'

The challenge is to make up a palindrome phrase or sentence – short or long – that makes sense.

15. NORDEN AND MUIR

Denis Norden and Frank Muir used to play a game on the Home Service (now BBC Radio 4) in which they took a well-known phrase, saying or proverb and twisted it to mean something else whilst still retaining much of its original sound. 'Yon solitary Highland Lass' became 'One solitary nylon lash'.

Having distorted the original phrase, the trick is to make up the story which leads up to this new phrase being its last line. You can play it by having a book of quotations and proverbs to hand, and one player challenges another with the well-known phrase which the challenged player must then change and invent a story to fit it.

16. SNOWBALL

Your text starts off with a one-letter word and continues by adding one letter at a time:

I
am
the
fool
whose
mother
accuses
generals
viciously . . .

. . . and so on.

17. THE MELTING SNOWBALL

This is the opposite of the snowball – it starts long and ends up with a one-letter word, though you could get away with a one-digit number for this last spot!

18. ANCIENT HEBREW ENGLISH

Ancient Hebrew was written with no vowel letters. Ancient Hebrew English is a procedure which requires you to write notes to one another with no vowels (including 'vowel y' as in 'rhythm' or 'lovely') in order to investigate if we need vowels or not.

19. THE NEW VENTRILOQUIST

When the new ventriloquist starts to speak for his dummy 'Charlie' he tries to say words that include letters that make his lips move, but everyone can see straightaway that he is speaking. He decides to avoid all words with letters that require lip move-ments: 'b', 'f', 'm', 'n', 'p', 'v' and 'w'.

This Oulipo procedure requires two people, one to play the ventriloquist speaking as himself, the other to play the ventriloquist's dummy. The dummy must not say words which include the letters 'b', 'f', 'm', 'n', 'p', 'v' or 'w'. The person playing the ventriloquist can try to trick the dummy into saying these words. Set a time limit, then swap over.

20. ALPHABET ELIMINATION

You write out the alphabet. Then, you take it in turns to (a) remove a letter from the alphabet and (b) spell a word that would have normally used that letter.

This new spelling must be convincing enough to make the word sound more or less the same. Also (c) once a letter has been removed, you can't use it to spell a word.

So, the first player might eliminate 'B' and spell 'thumb' as 'thumm'.

Cross 'B' off the alphabet.

The second player might eliminate 'C' and spell 'ceiling' as 'seeling' . . .

Cross 'C' off the alphabet.

And so on . . .

Last one standing, wins.

ACKNOWLEDGEMENTS

I wouldn't have had the state of mind or outlook on language to write this book if it hadn't been for my parents Harold and Connie Rosen and my brother Brian who were (and in my brother's case, still is) fascinated both by language and the ways in which this fascination can be shared.

I had many teachers both in school and at university who tried again and again to coax me into taking an interest in French, German, Latin, Old, Middle and Modern English, language, literature and literary theory. In particular, I owe a thanks to the people I knew at the time as Mr Brown, Mrs Hill, Mrs Young, Mrs Turnbull, Mr Emmans, Mrs Emmans, Mike Benton, Alan Ward, Ian Donaldson, Dennis Butts and Tony Watkins.

Professionally, I owe it to producer and editor Simon Elmes that I was asked to present BBC Radio 4's programme about language *Word of Mouth*, and a Radio 3 series on the history of European languages, *Lingua Franca*. Amongst the many exceptional contributors I owe a special debt are David Crystal, Jonathon Green, Tony Thorne, John Carey, Bernard O'Donoghue, Oliver Taplin, John Wells and J. C. Smith.

My ears and eyes would not have been as open to popular traditions of literacy if it hadn't been for work, interviews and conversations with Ewan MacColl, A. L. Lloyd and Dick Leith. Aside from my parents, my interest in very young children's literacy, literature and culture has been fostered by encounters with June Factor, Henrietta Dombey, Myra Barrs, Morag Styles, Brian Alderson and Margaret Meek Spencer.

The book includes many references to anonymous children – including my own – who've shown, sung and told me many things to do with language in use, so thanks to all of them.

The origins of the book lie in conversations with its editor Georgina Laycock who has enthusiastically kept up a flow of suggestions and edits. Any errors are mine.

My wife Emma has encouraged, challenged and supported the work while surviving much distracted head-slapping, muttering, swearing, midnight note-making, book-piling, paper-dropping and conversation-interrupting that has accompanied the writing. Love and special thanks to her.

Augarde, Tony, *Wordplay: The Weird and Wonderful World of Words* (Jon Carpenter, 2011)

Bengough, J. W., *The Up-to-date Primer, a first book of lessons for little political economists in words of one syllable with pictures* (first published 1895; facsimile edn Peter Martin, 1975)

Berniere, Vincent and Primois, Mariel (compilers), *Punk Press* (Abrams, 2013)

Brown, Michelle P., *Anglo-Saxon Manuscripts* (The British Library, 1991)

Campbell, George L. and Moseley, Christopher, *The Routledge Handbook of Scripts and Alphabets* (Routledge, 2012)

Chalmers, G. S., *Reading Easy 1800–50: A Study of the Teaching of Reading* (The Broadsheet King, 1976)

Chiaro, Delia, *The Language of Jokes* (Routledge, 1992)

Comenius, John Amos, *Orbis Pictus* (first published 1659; facsimile edn Oxford University Press, 1968)

Crystal, David, *Spell it Out: The Singular Story of English Spelling* (Profile Books, 2012)

David Crystal, *Txtng: The gr8 db8* (Oxford, 2008)

Davison, William, *Halfpenny Chapbooks* (Frank Graham, 1971)

Garfield, Simon, *Just My Type: A Book About Fonts* (Profile, 2011)

Gaur, Albertine, *A History of Writing* (Cross River, 1992)

Hartley, Sarah, *Mrs P's Journey: The Remarkable Story of the*

Woman Who Created the A–Z Map (Simon and Schuster, 2001)

Hilton, Mary, Styles, Morag and Watson, Victor (eds), *Opening the Nursery Door: Reading, Writing and Childhood 1600– 1900* (Routledge, 1997)

The History of Little Goody Two-Shoes (first published 1766; facsimile edn Griffith and Farran, 1881)

Immel, Andrea and Alderson, Brian, *Tommy Thumb's Pretty Song-Book: The First Collection of English Nursery Rhymes: A Facsimile Edition with a History and Annotations* (Cotsen Occasional Press, 2013)

Jean, Georges, *Writing: The Story of Alphabets and Scripts* (Thames and Hudson, 1992)

Johnson, Paul, *Runic Inscriptions in Great Britain* (Wooden Books, 1999)

Kendall, Joshua, *The Forgotten Founding Father: Noah Webster's Obsession and the Creation of an American Culture* (Berkeley, 2010)

Lommen, Mathieu (ed.), *The Book of Books: 500 Years of Graphic Innovation* (Thames and Hudson, 2012)

Loxley, Simon, *Type: The Secret History of Letters* (I. B. Tauris, 2004)

Man, John, *Alpha Beta: How Our Alphabet Shaped the Modern World* (Headline, 2000)

Mathews, Harry and Brotchie, Alastair (eds), *Oulipo Compendium* (Atlas Press, 2005)

Mavor, William, *The English Spelling-Book, accompanied by a progressive series of easy and familiar lessons intended as an introduction to the English language* (Longman, 1822)

Michael, Ian, *The Teaching of English: From the Sixteenth Century to 1870* (Cambridge University Press, 1987)

Neuberg, Victor E., *Popular Education in Eighteenth Century*

England (The Woburn Press, 1971)

Okrent, Arika, *In the Land of Invented Languages* (Spiegel and Grau, 2009)

The Oxford-Duden: Pictorial English Dictionary (Oxford University Press, 1981)

Page, R. I., *Runes* (British Museum, 1987)

Parkinson, Richard, *The Rosetta Stone* (British Museum, 2005)

Peter Piper's Practical Principles of Plain and Perfect Pronunciation (first published 1836; facsimile Huntington Library 1980)

Pitman, Ben, *Sir Isaac Pitman: His Life and Labors* (first published 1902; General Books, Print on Demand)

Robinson, Andrew, *Lost Languages: The Enigma of the World's Undeciphered Scripts* (Thames and Hudson, 2009)

Sacks, David, *The Alphabet* (Hutchinson, 2003)

Sassoon, Rosemary, *Marion Richardson: Her Life and Her Contribution to Handwriting* (Intellect, 2011)

Singh, Simon, *The Code Book: The Secret History of Codes and Code-Breaking* (Fourth Estate, 1999)

Tuer, Andrew W., *History of the Horn Book* (first published 1897; Arno Press, 1979)

Ward, Jamie, *The Frog Who Croaked Blue: Synesthesia and the Mixing of Senses* (Routledge, 2008)

INDEX

Abdülmecid, Sultan, 302
Abish, Walter: *Alphabetical Africa*, 403
abjad, 14
accents: cedilla, 43, 329; umlaut, 327–32; circumflex, 329–30; tilde, 329
acronyms, 96, 118, 188–90, 199, 302, 321, 392
acrostics, 190, 197–9, 403
Action on Smoking and Health, 189
'adlaut', 328–32
Adventures of the Galaxy Rangers, The (TV series), 118
African: peoples, 168, 224; languages, 205
Agüera y Arcas, Blaise, 84–5
Albany Centinel (periodical), 358
Alberti, Leon Battista, 55
Aldermaston, 299
Aldwych, 391
Alexander I, Tsar, 305
Alexandria (Minnesota), 338
Alexandria: great library, 396
Alfred, King, 10
Algonquian family, 169
Ali, Muhammad, 398
Allen, Woody, 398
alliteration, 36, 205, 213, 272–4, 278, 385
alpha: 2–3, 91, 113–14, 182, 396; 'alpha-bravo' lingo, 315
alphabet: square, 55; activities, 171; rhymes, 207; poems, 212; games, 403; elimination, 411
alphabetic cipher, 53, 57–9
alphabetic principle, 32–6, 77, 212
Alphabetical Africa, 403–4
alphabetical order, 255–6, 352, 356, 362, 393–9, 405

alphabets: Americanist Phonetic, 303; Arabic, 89; Athenian, 376; consonantal, 14; Deseret, 247; digital, 171; English, 5, 18–19, 142, 168; evolution of, 12, 17; fictional, 168; Futhark, 339, 342; Futhorc, 342; Goblin, 168; Greek, 115; Hebrew, 15; Icelandic, 19; International Phonetic (IPA), 303; Initial Teaching (ITA), 247; Ionian, 18; Korean, 164; Latin, 20, 130, 192, 340, 346, 396; memory-jogging, 407; New English, 168; Old English, 19, 70, 76, 142; Phoenician, 2, 13–17, 113; phonetic, 111, 231–2, 247, 315; Pitman, 235; Roman, 18–20, 72, 137, 303, 340, 382; Romic, 247; Shavian, 247; Tolkien, 168; Viking, 19, 71, 338–9
America, United States of, 57, 65, 94, 114, 127, 162–3, 169, 171, 177, 180, 184, 199, 219, 246, 316, 319, 337, 357, 368, 389, 391–2
American: Civil War, 55, 351; Army, 88, 355; National Education Association, 245; Philological Society, 245; spelling, 245, 357; Spelling Reform Association, 245; English, 246, 355
Americanist Phonetic Alphabet, 303
Andrews, Julie, 200, 398
Andyoqenya, 168
Angles, the, 19, 339, 342, 372
Anglo-Saxon language, 19, 67–9, 339–40, 391; *see also* Old English
Antony, Mark, 238
Apollinaire, Guillaume, 89, 279
Apple computers, 264
Arabic: language, 10, 14, 116, 253, 276, 295; manuscripts, 10; alphabet, 89

419

Archaea: city of, 91
Aristophanes, 140–2
Arrius, 132–3
art deco, 223
Arts and Crafts movement, 98, 143
Asia, 85
assonance, 36, 213, 272–4, 278
Athenian alphabet, 376
Athens, 140, 237
Auden, W. H., 184
Augustus, Emperor, 397
Aurebesh, 168
Austen, Jane, 357
Austin, Eric, 299
Australia, 232, 247, 392
A–Z Guide to London, 399
AZERTY keyboard, 258; *see also* type-
    writer

Babington, Anthony, 48–50
Bacall, Lauren, 313
Bath Spa University: Pitman Archive,
    234
BBC: Schools Radio, 262; Radio 4, 320,
    360, 409; Home Service, 350;
    Television, 394
Beacon Readers, 37–8, 103
Beatles, the, 67
Belgae, 340
Belle Absente, 404–5
Belle Présente, 404
Beowulf (poem), 67–76
Berlin, 317
Bernstein, Leonard, 313
beta, 22–3, 113, 396
Bible: 27, 84–7, 144, 169, 292, 356;
    Gutenberg, 86; Wycliffe, 279–80;
    King James, 292
Bibliographisches Institut AG, 353
'Big Brother', 322
Bildwörterbuch (picture-words book),
    353
bilingualism, 248
Blake, William, 67
Bletchley Park: codebreakers, 45–6
Blue Back Speller, 357
Bonaparte, Napoleon, 297, 303
Boston, 196, 224–5, 319

Boy's Own Paper, 46, 298,
brachygraphy, 237
Bradford: Commonwealth Collection,
    300
Bradley, Charles, 196
Braille, Louis, 303–6
Bridges, Margaret, 98–100
Bridges, Robert, 98, 279
Bright, Timothie, 239; *Characterie*, 240
Bristol Gardens, 400
British Empire, 98, 161
British English, 140, 177–8, 195, 388
British Isles, 339, 342–3
British Museum, 9–13, 67
Broadmoor Hospital, 351
Brockton, Massachusetts, 355
Brontë, Emily 329
Bronx, 331, 364
Brooklyn, 331
Brooksville, 314
Buren, Martin Van, 224
Burma: language spoken in, 169
Bush, George W., 184
Byron, Lord, 357

cabal, 189
Caesar, Julius, 42, 53, 132, 181, 238, 397
Caine, Michael, 398
'Calligrammes', 89
Calliope, 197
Cameron, David, 320
Campaign for Nuclear Disarmament,
    300
Canterbury Tales, The, 74, 87
capital letters, 69, 83–7, 143, 146
Captain Midnight (radio show), 57–8
Carnegie, Andrew, 246
Carolingian minuscule (lettering), 2, 69,
    87, 108, 160, 176, 204, 252, 268, 310,
    364, 376, 388
Carpathia, SS, 314
Carroll, Lewis: 89, 141, 209, 408; *Alice's
    Adventures in Wonderland*, 89, 209
Carthage, 13, 297
Catholics, 49, 124, 189; *see also* Roman:
    Catholicism
Catullus, Gaius Valerius, 131–3, 276
Cawdrey, Robert, 398

Caxton, William, 87, 290
cedilla, 43, 329; *see also* accents
Celto-Germanic peoples, 339–40
Césaire, Aimé, 168
Champollion, Jean-François, 10–12, 116–17
Chappe, Claude, 297–8
Characterie, 240
Chardin, Teilhard de, 381
Charlemagne: 2, 68, 180–1; scribes of, 108, 136, 150, 160, 176, 192, 204, 252, 268, 284, 310, 346, 376
Charles II, King, 189
Charles VII, King, 86
Chartley Hall, 48
Chaucer, Geoffrey: 73–4, 87, 109, 116; *Canterbury Tales, The*, 74, 87
Cherokee nation, 167
chi, 114
Chicago Tribune, 246
Child, Lauren, 147
China, 164, 169, 239
Chinese language, 12, 164, 205, 253, 276
'chi-ro' symbol, 91
Choctaw nation, 223
'Choson'gul', 164
Christian missionaries, 169
Christianity: 69, 74, 91, 168–70, 188, 340, 371; Irish form, 69
chromosomes, 367–71
Church, the, 74, 276, 299, 393
Churchill, Winston, 335
Cicero, 132, 237–8
ciphers, 45–62, 183; *see also* codes
circumflex, 329–30; *see also* accents
Cirth of Daeron, 168
Clay, Cassius, 398
Clio, 197
code: secret, 47, 49–56, 183, 187, 303; *see also* cipher; Ecriture Nocturne; encryption
Code-O-Graph, 57
code-breaking, 45, 51–3, 172; *see also* Bletchley Park; Enigma machine
Coleridge, Samuel Taylor, 396
Collins, Benjamin, 26
Commonwealth: Cromwell's, 352

Commonwealth Collection, Bradford, 300
communication: long-distance, 301
Communist East, 354
Communist Party, 99, 186
computer: laptop, 236, 264, 265
computer-programming languages, 171
concrete poetry, 89–90, 279
consonants: sounds, 23, 43, 65, 96, 109, 162, 178, 193, 205, 229; silent, 112, 244; consistent, 151; Korean, 166; sympathetic, 204; non-percussive, 385
consonant-vowel formations, 81, 137
consonantal alphabet, 14
Constantine, Emperor, 91
Cook, Captain James, 168
Cooke, William, 301–2
Coulson, J., 349–51
Coupvray, 304
Cree language, 169
Cromwell, Oliver, 352, 359
crossword puzzles: 45–6; *Boy's Own*, 46; *Daily Telegraph*, 45; *Sunday Observer*, 46; cryptic, 47
Crucifixion, the, 343, 371–2
Cruikshank, George, 145
Crusades, 223
Crystal, David, 243–4
cummings, e. e., 83, 87–8, 279
cuneiform script, 13
Czech language, 294, 330

da Spira brothers, 290
Daguerre, Louis, 301
Daily Telegraph crossword puzzle, 45; *see also* Bletchley Park: codebreakers
Danish language, 294
Dartmoor, 381
Dato, Leonardo, 55
David Copperfield, 242
Davis, Miles, 279
Debord, Guy, 394
Delmas's method, 405–6
delta, 49, 64, 113–14, 316
Denmark, 331, 340
Densmore, James, 256–8
Derby, Earl of, 209
Deseret alphabet, 247

Dewey system, 396

Dhi Fonètik Tîcerz' Asóciécon (FTA), 302

diacritics, 233, 303, 329–30; *see also* accents,

Dickens, Charles: 242, 247, 261, 389; *David Copperfield*, 242

dictaphones, 236

dictionaries: Oxford, 142, 303, 350–2, 357; Samuel Johnson's, 142, 352; Nursery Rhymes, 207; Walker's, 233; national, 243; American, 349; *Shorter Oxford*, 349; *Webster's Collegiate*, 349, 355–8; *Oxford English* (OED), 351–2, 358–60; *Der Grosse Duden*, 353; spelling, 354; online, 360; Urban, 360–2; Wiktionary, 360; monolingual, 398

dieresis, 219, 327–9

digital alphabet, 171

Dionysius: Festival of, 140

disappeared letters, 19, 67, 70–2, 311, 339, 346

D'ni, 168

Dodgson, Charles Lutwidge *see* Carroll, Lewis

Donne, John, 205

Doolittle, Hilda, 184

Douglas County, Minnesota, 337

Dr Seuss, 39

Drake, Sir Francis, 240

'Dream of the Rood' (poem), 343

Duchamp, Marcel, 146, 154; *Mona Lisa*, 146, 154

Duden, Konrad, 353–4

Dudley Writing Cards, 98

Dutch language, 110, 294

Dyche, Thomas, 291

Dylan, Bob, 398

Eachard, John, 207

Early Versions (radio series), 67

East Germany, 353

EastEnders (TV show), 394

Ecole des Hautes Etudes, 303

Ecriture Nocturne (Night Writing), 303; *see also* cipher; code; encryption

Edinburgh Court of Session, 369

Egypt, 10, 91, 237

Egyptian hieroglyphs, 9–10, 22, 130, 160, 192, 204, 218, 252, 268

Egyptians: ancient, 11–13, 276

Eisenhower, Dwight D., 184

electromagnetism, 114, 301

elisions, 319

Elizabeth I, Queen, 48–9, 240, 398

Ellis, A. J., 234

Emil and the Detectives, 8; film, 171

Enigma machine, 45, 58–9, 172; *see also* Bletchley Park: codebreakers

Eminem (Marshall Bruce Mather III), 184–5, 194

encryption, 47–52; *see also* cipher; code; Ecriture Nocturne

Encylopaedia Britannica, 292

English Civil War, 169, 240–2, 395

English Monosyllabary, 28

English: Old, 19, 67, 70–7, 81, 109, 137, 142, 245, 274–5, 278–9, 334, 339, 343, 346, 376, 384

English speakers, 23, 131, 162, 167, 178, 205, 214, 234, 325, 328, 329, 346, 399

English spelling: debate about, 243

English Spelling Reform Association, 245

Ephesus, 396

epsilon, 113

Erato, 197

'Estuary' speakers, 129

eta, 114

eth, 19, 76, 339

ethel, 19, 77, 339

Etruscans, 3, 18, 23, 42, 80, 94, 108, 130, 161, 204, 252, 268, 284, 310, 324, 364, 388

etymology, 124, 223, 319, 352

Euripides, 275

Euterpe, 197

Exeter text, 406

eye-rhyme, 406

Facebook, 104, 147; *see also* social media websites

Fair of St Ovid, 304

Fanelli, Sara, 147

Festival of Dionysius, 140

fictional languages, 168
First World War, 88, 143, 222, 302, 315, 352
Flaten, Nils, 337
Follick, Dr Mont, 247
Fordyce, Bailie William, 369
Forster, Georg, 110
Fowler, H. W., 349, 351
France: adopts AZERTY keyboard, 258
Frankfurt am Main, 58
Franklin, Benjamin, 184, 247
Franks, the, 19, 340–2
Fraser script, 169
French language: 42–3, 74, 116, 181, 229, 268, 279, 330, 382; Norman French, 3, 7, 19, 23, 64, 73–4, 80, 137, 218, 268, 310, 340, 347, 388; Modern French, 42, 253, 268
French Revolution, 144, 297
Freud, Sigmund, 354, 382
Frisians, the, 19, 340–2
Frusen Glädjé, 331–2
Futhark (Viking alphabet), 339, 342; see also runes
Futhorc (Germanic alphabet), 342; see also runes
Futura (typeface), 103, 290–1

G: 'insular' or 'Irish', 76–7
Gaelic, 238, 245
Gale, Leonard, 301
gamma, 113
Gardiner, Alan, 12
Garfield, Simon, 291
Gauss, Carl, 301
Gawain and the Green Knight, 88
German dictionary: Duden, 353–4
Germanic: peoples, 7, 339, 342; alphabet (Futhorc), 342
Germany: East, 353; division of, 354; history, 354
Gifford, Gilbert, 48–9
Giss, George see Guess, George
Glover, Sarah, 200–1
Goblin Alphabet, 168
Gondolinic Runes, 168
Götalander people, 338
gothic lettering, 291, 328

Government Printing Office, 246
graffiti, 146–8, 188, 344
grammar, 35, 60–1, 68, 74, 248, 266, 295, 403
graphemes, 32, 196
Great Vowel Shift, 3, 23, 42, 64, 80, 108, 151, 228, 311
Greek: language, 9, 22, 91, 118, 279; culture, 18; letters, 49, 91, 108, 117–19, 140, 167, 303; alphabet, 115; prefixes, 237, 245
Greeks, ancient, 2, 17–18, 22, 42, 64, 80, 89, 94, 111–16, 136, 160, 176, 192, 204, 218, 228, 237, 252, 275, 284, 310, 324, 376, 388
Green, Jonathon, 360–1
Grimm, Brothers, 112, 328
Grosse Duden, Der, 353
Guess, George, 167
Gutenberg, Johannes: 83–6, 105, 290–2; Bible, 86

Häagen-Dazs, 327, 330–2
Hadrian, Emperor, 239
Hadrian's Wall, 94, 239
Hale, William Gardner, 132
Hammer-Purgstall, Joseph von, 10
Handbook of Simplified Spelling, 246
handwriting: standard, 69
'Hangul', 164–6
Hardy, Thomas, 385
Harris, Robert, 237
Harrow Road, 400
Harvey, P. J., 184
Harvey Road Junior School, 353
hashtag, 293
Hastings, Battle of, 74
Haüy, Valentin, 304–5
Hawaiian language, 168
Heaney, Seamus, 279
Hebrew: ancient, 13–15, 410; vowels, 14–15; alphabet, 15; language, 22, 27, 182, 253, 279; names, 218
Hegley, John, 273
Henry VIII, King, 197
Herbert, George, 89
Hercules, 275
Hess, Rudolf, 291

hieroglyphs, 9–10, 22, 117, 130, 160, 192, 204, 218, 252, 268
Hill, Rowland, 128, 392–3
Holland, 340
Holtom, Gerald, 299–300
Holy Roman Empire, 181
Home Service, 261, 409; *see also* BBC
Homer: 275–6, 396; *The Iliad*, 275; *The Odyssey*, 275–6
homoconsonantism, 406
homonyms, 46
Hooke, Robert, 297
Hopkins, Gerard Manley, 278–9; 'The Windhover', 279
Horace, 276
Howell, James, 245
Hughes, Ted, 279
Hugo, Victor, 285
Hungarian language, 294
Hussein, Saddam, 287
Huxley, Aldous, 114

ibn Wahshiyah: 10–12; *Kitab Shawq al-Mustaham*, 10
'ibn Wahshiyah–Champollion' principle of decoding, 12
Icelandic alphabet, 19
idioms, 46, 395, 405
Iliad, The, 275; *see also* Homer
illuminated manuscripts, 83, 144, 182
indefinite article, 3
India: Lisu spoken in, 169
Indian: speakers, 65; pronunciation, 335
Initial Teaching Alphabet (ITA), 247
inscriptions: Roman, 160, 228, 252, 284, 324
Institute for Blind Youth, 304
'insular G' ('Irish G'), 76–7
interculturalism, 225
International Air Transport Association, 316
International Convention for the Amendment of English Orthography, 245
International Phonetic Alphabet (IPA), 168, 302
International Radiotelegraphic Convention, 317

internet, 47, 50–1, 56, 147, 170, 250, 300, 319–21, 399
Interspel, 247
Ionian: alphabet, 18; philosophers, 197–9
iota, 113–14, 136, 188
Ipswich, 240
Iraq, 11–13, 163, 171
Ireland: 69, 124, 233, 341; Northern, 124
Irish: speech, 23; 'Irish G', 76; language, 77; spelling, 96; names, 219; Old, 275; verse, 276; writing, 290, 329
Isis (student magazine), 262
Isle of Man: runic inscriptions found, 340–3
Ismay, Bruce, 314
isopangram, 404
Italy: Etruscan, 18; Roman, 137; northern, 343

Jackson, Charles Thomas, 301
Jae-Sang, Park ('Psy'), 163
Jagger, Mick, 58
jargon, 321, 360; *see also* slang
Jeffers, Oliver, 147
Jefferson, Thomas, 241
Jenson, Nicolas, 86
Jesus Christ, 110, 114, 182, 188, 231–2, 371–2
Jews: treatment in Denmark, 331
Johns, Ted, 127
Johnson, Samuel, 142, 150, 247, 352
jokes, 32, 95, 140, 153, 157, 174, 183–4, 214, 294, 320–1, 335, 349, 358
Judaic texts, 189
Julius Caesar, 42–3, 53–6, 61, 132, 181, 238, 397
Jutes, the, 19, 340–2

Kabbalah, 189
Kante, Solomana, 167–8
kappa, 114, 160
Kelly, Obadiah, 223
Kenosha Telegraph, 256
Kensington runestone, 338, 341, 344
Kiernan, Kevin, 68
King, Martin Luther, 343
King James Bible, 292
Klingon, 168

Knott, Lady Veronica, 400
Kodak, 234
Korea: 163–6, 294; language, 163–6, 294; alphabet, 164–5
Kpo the Leopard, 229

L'Association Phonétique Internationale (API), 302
Lafayette, Marquis de, 301
lambda, 114, 118, 176
language: evolution of, 23, 384; fictional, 168
Language in the National Curriculum Project (LINC), 187
laptop computer, 236, 264, 265
Latin: language, 13–20, 27, 74, 77, 80, 85, 102, 108–9, 124, 130–2, 137, 144, 150, 180–2, 192, 200, 233, 238, 244–5, 252, 268, 279, 284, 295–6, 302, 334, 340, 346, 396; manuscripts, 252, 268, 284, 334; alphabet, 340, 396
Lawrence, D. H., 277
Lear, Edward, 208–10, 365
Lebanon, 13
Lee, Christopher, 372
Leeu, Gheraert, 86
Leipzig, 353–4
Lethe, River, 197
Letraset, 103–5, 145, 262
lettering: Carolingian minuscule, 2, 69–70, 77, 108, 150, 160, 176, 204, 252, 268, 310, 346, 364, 376; serif, 2, 22, 42, 64, 80, 103, 108, 136, 144, 160, 176, 192, 228, 264, 284, 310, 388; Gothic, 27, 71, 219, 279, 291–2, 328; non-Roman, 73; graffiti, 147; Roman 'minuscule', 290
letters: disappeared, 19, 67, 70–7, 186, 262, 311, 330, 339, 346; inverted, 303
Lewis, C. S., 184
lexicographers, 110, 161, 193, 334
Lilburne, John, 242
Lindgren, Harry, 247
Lisu language, 169
Little, William, 349, 368
Londinium, 391
London: accent, 5; vowels, 5, 112, 325; cipher school in, 49; old schools in,

90; School Board for (SBL), 90; speakers, 129; Zoo, 208; *A–Z Guide to*, 399–401; street atlas, 400–1
Londoners, 95, 129, 233, 365, 395
Lords, House of, 185, 247, 392
Louis XVI, 304
Lower Saxony, 340
lysergic acid diethylamide (LSD), 180

McCaffary, John, 256
Maeshowe, Orkneys, 344; *see also* Vikings
Maida Vale, 400
Mainz, 84–6
Manding languages, 167
Mann, Thomas, 291
manuscripts: Latin, 80, 132, 252, 268, 284, 334; illuminated, 83, 144, 182; ancient, 295
Mao Tse-tung, 186
Marvell, Andrew, 272–3
Marx, Karl, 186
Mary Queen of Scots, 48–50, 239
Masefield, John, 253
Massachusetts, 300, 355
Mattus, Reuben, 330–2
Maxwell, Robert, 262
medieval: period, 18, 118, 132, 136, 177, 182, 237, 284, 334, 364; society, 75; scribes, 94, 218, 376; manuscripts, 228, 296; monks, 238, 295; Europe, 364
Mediterranean, 13
Melpomene, 197
Michael, Kirk, 343
Micklewhite, Maurice *see* Caine, Michael
micro-visual appliances, 321
Middle East, 223, 341
Middle English, 19, 73, 339
mikron, 218
Milton, John, 247
Mind Your Own Business, 262
Mini A-Z of London, 401
Minor, William Chester, 351; *see also* *Oxford English Dictionary*
Mississippi Delta, 277
mnemonics, 15, 70, 190, 193, 197, 201, 211

Mnemosyne, 197
Mona Lisa (painting), 146, 154
monoalphabetic code, 53
Monroe, James, 301
Moon, Robert Aurand, 392
Morgan, Edwin, 90
morphology, 29, 61, 74
Morris, William, 98, 186
Morristown: Speedwell Ironworks, 301
Morse, Samuel Finley Breese, 300
Morse code, 298–302, 317
mu, 114, 118
Muir, Frank, 350, 409
Mulcaster, Richard, 243–4
Munich, 58
Murray, John, 357
Muses, 197
Mussolini, Benito, 291
Myst computer game, 168

N'Ko language, 167
Napoleon I, 297, 303
Nash, Ogden, 273
National Biscuit Company (Nabisco), 189
National Football League, 338
National Institute for the Blind (Paris), 304–5
National Phonographic Society, 235–6
Nazi Party, 186, 291
Needham, Paul, 84–5
New English Alphabet, 168; *see also* Tolkien, J. R. R.
New York City, 314
New York University, 301
New Zealand: shifting vowels, 3, 81
Newton, Isaac, 241
Night Writing, 303–5
Nineveh: library, 13, 253
Nobel Peace Prize, 302
nonsense: 207–15; words, 36, 40; writers, 207–9
Norden, Denis, 350, 409
Norfolk, 187, 240, 300
Norman French, 3, 7, 19, 23, 64, 73–4, 80, 137, 218, 268, 310, 340, 347, 388
Normans, the, 3, 42, 124, 136–7, 151, 161, 228, 253, 334, 340

Norse religion, 69
North America: settlers in, 169, 338, 341, 368; continent, 338, 341; *see also* Vinland
Northern Ireland, 124
Northmen, 338; *see also* Vikings
Norwegian language, 151, 294
nu, 113, 204
Nuffield Theatre, Southampton, 262
nursery rhymes, 31

Observer, 47
Odyssey, The, 275–6, 328; *see also* Homer
Óengus II, 372
Ohman, Olof, 337
OK: origins of, 223–4
Old English, 19, 67, 70–7, 81, 109, 137, 142, 245, 274–5, 278–9, 334, 339, 343, 346, 376, 384
Old French, 109–10, 340
Old Germanic, 285
Old Irish, 275
Old Norse, 162, 294, 341
Old Testament, 13, 389
Olivetti typewriter, 261–2; *see also* typewriter
Olympic Games: 1912, 294
Olympic Park, 394
omega, 113–14, 182, 218, 396
omicron, 113
Onions, C. T., 349
onomatopoeia, 60, 162, 383
Opie, Iona and Peter, 207
Orkneys, the, 341, 344
'Oulipo' ('Ouvroir de Littérature Potentielle'), 403–11
Ovid, 276
Owen, Wilfred, 67
Oxford dictionaries, 142, 207, 303, 357
Oxford Dictionary of Nursery Rhymes, 207
Oxford English Dictionary (OED), 351, 358–60
Oxford English Dictionary, Shorter, 349–51
Oxford-Duden, Pictorial English Dictionary, The, 353

Page, R. I., 344
palindromes, 409
pangram, 403–4
Paris, 88, 239, 297, 301, 304–5, 394
Parliament, 137, 240–2, 249, 395
Parthenon, 237
Passy, Paul, 302–3
Pearl Harbor, 314
Pearsall, Phyllis, 399–400
Pennsylvania Gazette, 368
Penny Post, 232–4
Pepys, Samuel, 241
Perec, Georges, 406
Peter Piper's Practical Principles of Plain and Perfect Pronunciation, 385
Phelippes, Thomas, 49–50, 183
Phi Beta Kappa Society, 114
phi, 114
Phoenician alphabet, 2, 13–17, 113, 130, 136, 160, 176, 204, 218, 228, 252, 268, 284, 310, 376, 388, 396
phonemes, 32, 232, 236, 242–3
phonetic: principles, 9–13; alphabet, 111, 168, 231–2, 247, 303, 315; shorthand, 231–4, 242
phonics: 32–6, 40, 129, 196, 205, 229, 399; synthetic, 32, 36, 196; 'Screening Check', 40
Phonographic Festival, 235
phonographic shorthand, 236
Phonography (Pitman), 234–6
pi, 113–14, 228
pictograms, 11, 64, 165–6, 382, 396
Picts, the, 372
Pinner Wood Primary School, 253
Pitman: Sir Isaac, 170, 232, 236; shorthand, 213–50; *Phonography*, 236
Pitman, Jacob, 231; Archive, 234–5; alphabet, 235
Pitman, James, 247; Initial Teaching Alphabet, 247
poetry: convention of starting each line with a capital, 87; e. e. cummings, 87–8, 279; 'concrete', 89–90, 279; Catullus, 132–3; epic, 197; Muses, 197; pulse, 273; rhyme, 273–6; rhythm, 273–8; Old English, 274,

343; troubadour, 276; jazz, 278; workshops, 305; alliterative, 385
Poland, 33
Pollard script, 169
Polybius, 298, 303
Polyhymnia, 168
Polynesian dialects,
Porta, Giovanni, 55
Portugal, 131
postal service, 392–4
postcodes, 391–5, 400; *see also* ZIP codes
post-modernism, 359
Potter, Beatrix, 37, 276, 353
Powell, General Colin, 171
prefixes, 29, 197, 205, 229, 237, 241, 245, 365
Presley, Elvis, 277
Princeton University, 84
printing 'punch matrix' system, 84–5
'Prisoner's constraint', 407
Protestant missionaries: American, 168–9
Protestants, 124, 168, 189, 239
Proust, Marcel, 382
proverbs, 405–9
Psalms, 242, 279
psi, 114
'Psy' (Park Jae-Sang), 163
Ptolemy III, 91
puns, 46
'punch matrix' printing system, 84–5
Punic War, First, 297
Puritanism, 172, 183, 240–1, 343, 398
puzzle books, 408
psychogeography, 394

Qabala, 189, 253
Qenyatic, 168
Queneau, Raymond, 403
Quikscript, 247
quizzes, 199, 359, 389, 408
QWERTY keyboard, 255–66, 271, 293; *see also* typewriter

Ransome, Arthur, 298
Read, Allen Walker, 225, 318
Reading Made Easy (booklet), 30
reading skills, 38

Reed, Lou, 146–8
Reinhardt, Django, 65
Renaissance, 173, 238, 324
Renner, Paul, 290–1
rho, 113, 268
rhymes, 30–1, 36, 136, 151, 271–81, 326, 406; *see also* poetry
Rich, Jeremiah, 242
Richard, Cliff, 398
Richardson, Marion, 97–102
Ritter, Nate, 293
Roman: alphabet, 18–20, 72, 137, 340; Republic, 131; Italy, 137; inscriptions, 160, 228, 252, 284, 324; Empire, Holy, 181; Catholicism, 189
Romans, the, 3, 13–23, 42, 53, 72, 86, 94, 108, 118, 124, 133, 176, 252, 268, 310, 324, 339–40, 364, 376, 388
Rome: Imperial, 204, 228, 268; public library, 397
Romic alphabet, 247
Roosevelt, Franklin D., 184
Roosevelt, Theodore, 246–7
Rosen, Connie (author's mother), 349, 353
Rosen, Harold (author's father), 349
Rosen, Michael: *Mind Your Own Business*, 262
Rosetta Stone, 9–10, 12, 116–17
Ross, Nelson E., 314–15
Rowling, J. K., 184
Royal Academy of Arts, London, 300
Royal Air Force (RAF), 316
Royal Navy, 315
Royal Society, 297
runes: 19, 71, 77, 338–44; inscriptions, 340
Runestone Museum, 338
Runo-Dynamics: First Law of, 342
runologists, 338, 342–4
Russell, George William, 184
Russian language, 125, 129, 161, 205, 294, 354
Ruthwell Cross, 343

Sacy, Silvestre de, 10
St Andrew: cross of, 372
St Bartholomew's Day massacre, 239
St Ovid, Fair of, 304

St Petersburg, 305
Salinger, J. D., 188
saltire, 372
Sandburg, Carl, 277
Sanskrit, 299, 302
São Paolo, 329
Sarati, 168
Saxons, the, 9, 69, 339–42
Saxony, Lower, 340
Scandinavian: 74, 329–30, 337–42; alphabet, 329–30
Scherbius, Arthur, 58, 61
Schleswig-Holstein, 339
Schoeffer, Peter, 84
Scotland, 233, 341–3, 347, 369, 372
Scots: Mary Queen of, 48, 50, 239, 261; language, 90, 178, 224
Scottish islands, 341
scripts: ancient, 12; fictional, 168
Second World War, 45, 143, 300, 317, 331, 354
Sejong, King, 164
Self, Will, 394
semaphore, 296–303
Semites: ancient, 12–13, 160, 204, 218, 284, 376
Semitic: language, 2, 130, 136, 176, 192, 268, 310; writing, 14; inscriptions, 176, 192, 268, 310; sounds, 218
Senghor, Léopold, 168
Seoul, 163
Se-quo-ya *see* Guess, George
serifs, 2, 22, 42, 64, 80, 103, 108, 136, 144, 160, 176, 192, 228, 264, 284, 310, 388
Serre, Charles Barbier de la, 303
Seville, 295
sex chromosomes, 370–1
Shakespeare, William: 5, 48, 183, 194, 219, 240, 243, 261, 276, 286, 292, 334, 361, 388–9; *Twelfth Night*, 183; *Henry V*, 219; *The Tempest*, 292; *Hamlet*, 352
Shavian alphabet, 246–7
Shaw, George Bernard, 141, 246
Shelton, Thomas, 240–1
Sholes, Charles Latham, 256–8
Shoreditch Church, 395
Shorter Oxford English Dictionary, The, 349–51

shorthand: 231–50; phonetic alphabets, 231–5; Pitman's 'New Church', 231; textbook, 232; reformed spelling alphabet, 235; brachygraphy, 237; stenography, 237; used by ancient Greeks, 237; used by medieval monks, 238; used by Charles Dickens, 242; used in court proceedings, 242; Psalms published by Jeremiah Rich, 342
Sicily, 297
sigma, 113, 117–19, 188, 284
sign systems, 9, 78, 286–9, 303, 306
signalling systems, 296–8
signs and symbols: study of, 288
Simplified Spelling Board (SSB), 245–6
Simpson, N. F., 184
Sinai, 12
Sinclair, Iain, 394
Singh, Simon, 55
slang, 70, 85, 96, 173, 179–80, 316, 335, 352, 360–2, 383, 389
Slavic language, 303
Slavonia (Cunard liner), 317
Slovak language, 294
Smith, George, 13
Snorri (Viking ship), 338
Snowden, Edward, 47–52
social media websites: Facebook, 104, 147; Twitter, 104, 147, 293–4; forums, 146; blogs, 147; chatrooms, 293, 319
Socrates, 306
Soho, 391
Solem, 337
'Song of Songs' (biblical), 392
Song of the South (film), 392
SOS, 302, 314, 317
Spain: Arab presence, 276
speech: evolution of, 75
Speedwell Ironworks, Morristown, 301
speedwriting, 237
spelling reform, 73, 81, 177, 236, 243–50
Spelling Reform 1 (SR1), 247
Spot the Ball competition, 369
Ssiquoya see Guess, George
Star Trek, 118, 168
Star Wars, 168

stenographic characters, 242
Stenographic Sound Hand (Pitman), 234
stenography, 237, 242
Stevenson, Robert Louis, 277, 369–70
Strategic Arms Limitation Talks (SALT), 189
Stratford-upon-Avon, 240
Suetonius, 53
suffixes, 29, 219, 241, 285, 294, 377, 389
Sumerians, Ancient, 11–13, 77
Sunday School, 209
Swift, Jonathan, 318
Sydney, 231–2
syllabiary, 77
symbols: used to represent syllables, 11, 77, 167; Phoenician, 17; visual, 32; as phonemes, 236; systems of, 288
sympathetic consonants, 204
synonyms, 46
syntax, 61

Ta Hwa Miao people, 169
Table Alphabeticall (monolingual dictionary), 398
tachygraphy, 237, 240
tau, 114, 310
teaching aids, 98
Tengwar of Feanor, 168
Tengwar of Rumil, 168
Tennyson, Alfred, Lord, 247
Terpsichore, 197
text: left-handed, 407; right-handed, 407
Thailand: Lisu spoken in, 169
Thalia, 197
Thermodynamics: First Law of, 342
theta, 48, 114, 118, 188
Third Reich, 291
Thomas, David, 98
Thomas, Dylan, 279
thorn (disappeared letter), 8, 19, 71, 76, 95, 311, 339
Thorpe, Jim, 294
Tibeto-Burman language, 169
tilde, 329; see also accents
Times, The, 127, 146
Tiro, Marcus Tullius, 237–9; see also Cicero
Tironian notes, 237–8

Titanic, RMS, 314
Tolkien, J. R. R., 168
Tolstoy, Leo, 335
Tommy Thumb's Pretty Song Book, 31
tongue-twisters, 214, 385
Toxic Club (TV programme), 180
Trafalgar, Battle of, 298
Trajan's Column, 2
Treasure Island, 369
trigraphs, 109
Tristram Shandy, 262
Trithemius, Johannes, 55
Trowbridge, 231–2
Tschichold, Jan, 291
Tudor England, 49
Tunis, 13
Turkey, 140, 341
Turkish, 116, 330
Twain, Mark, 188
Twitter, 104, 147, 293–4; *see also* social media websites
typefaces: 8, 22, 67, 102–3, 108, 146–8, 176, 262, 290–3, 296; psychology of, 102–3; Garamond, 108; medieval French, 108; Futura, 290
typewriters: QWERTY keyboard, 255–7, 261–6, 271, 293; keyboard layout, 257; AZERTY keyboard, 258; Olivetti, 261–2

umlaut, 327–8, 331; *see also* accents
Uncial handwriting, 69–70, 290
Unifon, 247
Union Jack, 372
upsilon, 113–14, 188, 324, 376
Uralic, 303
Urania, 197
Urban Dictionary, 360–2
US Army, 88, 355
US Congress, 246

Vail, Alfred, 301
Valmaric, 168
Varro, Marcus Terentius, 397–8
Vatican, 55, 132
Venetian printers, 292
Venice, 86, 290–1

Vercelli, 343
vernacular speech, 144
Vesel, Rose, 331
Victoria, Queen 392
Victorian era, 143, 209, 278
video conferencing, 170
Vienna, Siege of, 297
Vietnamese language, 330
Vigenère, Blaise de, 55
Viking alphabet, 19, 71, 338–9
Vikings, the 71–8, 337–42
Vindolanda, 239
Vinland, 338
Virgil, 276
voice recognition, 7, 170
Voltaire, 116, 276
vowels: Great Vowel Shift, 3, 23, 42, 64, 80, 108, 151, 228, 311; shifting, 3, 81, 324; London, 5, 112, 325; alphabets without, 14; Hebrew, 14; sounds, 15–17, 81, 95, 111–13, 130, 165, 177, 193, 241, 269, 274, 325; short, 65; English, 81; long, 82; separating, 327; *see also* dieresis
Voynich manuscript, 172–4

Wahshiyah, Ahmad Bakr ibn, 10–12
Wales, 178, 381
Walford, 394
Walker's Critical Pronouncing Dictionary and Expositor of the English Language, 233
Walsingham, Sir Francis, 49–50, 239
Ward, Jamie, 382
Wayne, John, 398
Webb, Harry *see* Richard, Cliff
Webster, Noah, Jr, 247, 349–62, 388
Webster's Collegiate (dictionary), 349, 355
Wells, H. G., 184, 247
Wells, Julia *see* Andrews, Julie
Welsh language, 73, 178, 330, 368
Wenceslas Square, 343
West Africa, 167, 224
West African peoples, 224
West Side Story (musical), 313
Western Europe, 20, 238
Western languages, 238

Wheatstone, Charles, 301–2
Wikoff, Viola, 314
Wiktionary (online dictionary), 360
Williams, William Carlos, 277
Williamson, Peter, 368–9
Williamsport, Pennsylvania, 392
Willis, John, 241
Wilshaw, Francis, 298
Wilson, Colin, 88
Wilson, D. M., 342; First Rule of Runo-
    Dynamics, 342
Wiltshire, 232, 236
Wisconsin Assembly, 256
Wonder, Stevie, 398
Woodford, 394
Woolworth, F. W. & Co. Ltd, 296
word ladder stories, 408
Word of Mouth (BBC radio
    programme), 320, 360, 384
Writing Scholar's Companion, 244
Wycliffe Bible, 279–80
Wyld, Henry, 351
Wynn, 19, 71–2, 339

X chromosome, 367, 370
xi, 113
XX chromosome, 370–1
XY chromosome, 370–1

Y chromosome, 370
Yale University, 300
Yiddish: 161, 205, 276, 285, 331; comedy,
    276
yogh, 19, 73–7, 339
Yorkshire, 5, 240, 325
Young, Thomas, 10, 116
Young Communist League (YCL), 380
Younger Futhark, 342
Youth Hostels Association (YHA), 380–1
YouTube, 163, 171, 196, 399
Yunnan province, 169

Zenodotus, 396–7
Zephaniah, Benjamin, 389
zeta, 108, 113, 388
Zimmerman, Robert *see* Dylan, Bob
ZIP codes, 392; *see also* postcodes